Individual Freedom in Language Teaching

D1190848

But the whole story of words is full of mystery, and the attempt to reduce the process of words to a science has always seemed to me ridiculous enough ... human speech is naturally not a set of a few official languages, but a mass of innumerable dialects, all melting one into the other.

Watch carefully, and you will note that in the area covered by the great official languages, most people are bilingual. They can speak the official language, but they usually speak among themselves a dialect of their own ...

Hilaire Belloc, *The Cruise of the Nona* (1928: 14)

Individual Freedom in Language Teaching:
Helping Learners to Develop a Dialect of their Own

Christopher Brumfit

OXFORD
UNIVERSITY PRESS

OXFORD
UNIVERSITY PRESS

Great Clarendon Street, Oxford OX2 6DP

Oxford University Press is a department of the University
of Oxford. It furthers the University's objective of excellence
in research, scholarship, and education by publishing
worldwide in

Oxford New York

Athens Auckland Bangkok Bogotá Buenos Aires
Calcutta Cape Town Chennai Dar es Salaam Delhi
Florence Hong Kong Istanbul Karachi Kuala Lumpur
Madrid Melbourne Mexico City Mumbai Nairobi Paris
São Paulo Shanghai Singapore Taipei Tokyo Toronto Warsaw

with associated companies in Berlin Ibadan

Oxford and *Oxford English* are registered trade marks of
Oxford University Press in the UK and in certain other countries

ISBN 0 19 442174 0

Printed in Hong Kong

For F, R, and S

Contents

List of figures

Preface

Two of my research students, both practising teachers, are partly responsible for the shape and form of this book. They both remarked on the consistency of my ideas over the years, and I felt slightly hurt, as if I had been accused of failing to learn from experience.

But when I read papers I had written over the past 20 years, and when I examined the theses written by my students, I realized that there is a pretty consistent view of language in the world struggling to emerge. Articulating this in full theoretical detail is a task which will require substantial leisure and some years of further work. But in the meantime, the chapters of this book attempt to show how these ideas can affect the practice of language teaching (broadly conceived to include work on literature and culture also) in many different settings.

First, though, it may be helpful to summarize the key beliefs underlying the arguments in this book. Most are defended in detail in the following pages, and all underlie the recommendations for improvement of practice that are offered. Each chapter may be regarded as an attempt to address a particular setting, and a particular educational problem, in the light of the following set of beliefs (chapters which argue these points in detail are indicated):

- the rules of language use, and much of the language system, are inherently fluid and negotiable, but the teaching of languages has to act as if they are stable and unnegotiable in order to offer a supportive base for learners (Chapters 1 and 6)
- because of this paradox, language teaching risks becoming repressive by relying too heavily on generalizations that are no more than artefacts of language study in the past, and thus preventing language being used creatively to express individual and group difference (Chapters 2 and 4)
- because experience (of language and the world) is in constant flux, scholars, teachers, and learners have to cope with the complex and confusing data they receive through their senses; they do this by simplifying, generalizing, and by deriving principles, and all of these involve distortion of experience, though that distortion can be done in a more or less principled way (Chapter 3)
- because of the risk of distortion, all principles, generalizations, and examples derived from experience need to be thought about and discussed with fellow human beings; through such discussion we can reduce the risk of exploitation

by anticipating ill effects and error by minimizing confusion or idiosyncratic interpretation (Chapters 12 and 13)
- because such discussion creates cultural groupings and sub-groupings with shared beliefs and shared points of reference, language is an especially dangerous object of study, for each item studied is an example of 'language' and also of 'culture' in that it instantiates ideas or objects which develop a cultural load independent of the language they are expressed by (Chapters 6, 8, and 9)
- because the same referents can have different significances in different cultural systems, culture can be independent of language barriers and language can never be the same as culture, but every linguistic group has the capacity to incorporate many cultures (Chapters 9, 10, and 11)
- because language is both shared by different groups, to enable us to communicate, and individual, to enable us to think, create, and imagine, language use potentially threatens group solidarity and challenges personal identity, so it is always risky and value laden (Chapters 5 and 8)
- because its use is risky and value laden, language teaching and learning are bound up with ethical and social concerns that need to be openly discussed if they are not to become secret and repressive (Chapters 7, 9, and 11)
- because these complexities need open discussion, any consideration of language in education is partial unless it is prepared to call upon a range of associated disciplines to clarify the object of study: a responsible 'linguistics of education' cannot avoid psychological, sociological, ethical, economic, historical, political as well as pedagogical considerations (Chapters 12, 13, and 14).

The chapters of this book show an attempt to address a variety of settings and practices with these beliefs as a background.

Thus you could say that I examine the science of the study of language teaching within the art of language making. Like most people with an academic background, I believe we should try to understand our field of study as clearly as possible, through examination of empirical evidence and through clear and logical thinking. But like most experienced teachers and language users, I am all too aware that language use and language development reflect human creativity, reveal human identity, and contribute to human aspirations far beyond what can be revealed by the idealizations and generalizations that scientific procedures unavoidably impose. Anyone concerned with language is concerned with human behaviour. Anyone concerned with human behaviour must rejoice and celebrate, empathize and criticize, deplore and oppose, just as much as investigate—for human beings are creative for both good and evil; they identify with communal aspirations which are both constructive and destructive, and they use the power which language gives to dominate as well as to liberate. Amid this welter of conflicting motives and confusing values, language teachers must live—contributing their small offering to world peace and understanding, or (wittingly or unwittingly) to exploitation and suffering.

In the chapters that follow I have drawn upon a view of language which starts from the variety of uses users impose on it, but recognizes that we are partly made by our linguistic inheritance. We make language together, but who we are is partly made by language. What we receive we never hand back unchanged. In addressing key aspects of language teaching theory and practice, I have drawn upon the many disciplines that help us to clarify language and literacy practices in the world and processes of learning and teaching in, and out of, the classroom. No serious discussion of practice calls exclusively on a single discipline, but readers will find that in different chapters I tend to concentrate on philosophy (Chapters 3, 7, 14), psychology (Chapter 2), curriculum theory (Chapters 5, 9), assessment (Chapter 8), ideology (Chapter 9), political theory (Chapter 11), history (Chapter 10), while sociolinguistic and applied linguistic principles underlie most chapters. At the same time, while a few chapters (1, 3, 12, 13, 14) offer general bases for any kind of language work in education, most link for practical exemplification to particular settings or particular types of teaching. Thus second language classrooms are the prime focus of Chapters 2, 4, 5, 9, 10, and 11; mother tongue classrooms in the UK are significant in Chapters 1 and 6; higher education is concentrated on in Chapter 5, literature teaching in Chapters 7 and 8, cultural studies in Chapter 9, and teaching outside the rich industrial countries (from an African perspective) in Chapter 10.

In short, each chapter is an essay trying to integrate understandings from whatever disciplines are relevant, with specific illustration from policy and practice in a particular area of language in education. Where the argument depends on reference to scholarly literature I have provided it, but on occasions I have preferred to outline widely agreed basic issues as clearly as I can as a background to my argument, and I have not referred such uncontentious summaries to standard textbooks.

Overall this book reflects an attempt to develop bases for an educational linguistics; I am currently working on a fuller theoretical development of these ideas. But I hope that as it stands, this book offers a persuasive perspective on the ways in which we use language to educate.

CJB
Centre for Language in Education
University of Southampton

Acknowledgements

The debt I owe to past and present students and colleagues is immeasurable, both for their willingness to argue and force me to clarify, and for their persistently motivating insistence on the central role of language in the education process. I cannot name everyone from whom I have borrowed (and no doubt distorted) ideas, but people who have made specific contributions to the thinking underlying this book include Professors Michael Benton, Jill Bourne, Debbie Cameron, Ronald Carter, Guy Cook, Alan Davies, Eric Hawkins, Keith Johnson, Gunther Kress, Neil Mercer, and Robin Usher, together with George Blue, Dr Michael Grenfell, John Mountford, Elissa Mugarza, Dr Florence Myles, Dr Alison Piper, Dr Ben Rampton, Euan Reid, Alison Sealey, Michael Swan, Catherine Walter, and two anonymous readers. I have long-standing debts in thinking to Dr Dick Allwright, Alan Maley, Earl Stevick, and the late Professor David Stern. Rita Corbidge and Hazel Paul have provided strong secretarial support over the years. Above all, I have benefited from the support of Professor Henry Widdowson (who always believed a project such as this was possible and who has offered many helpful comments, though I have stubbornly failed to act on some of them). My wife, Professor Rosamond Mitchell, has provided expert knowledge, professional collaboration, and personal support, all of which I have persistently exploited. To her, and to my sons Simon and Francis I owe also many personal debts—not least that they allowed a summer holiday to be devoted to writing the first draft of this.

Material in this book has had early versions in presentations to AILA, The British Council (in Belfast, Brussels, Colombo, Ibadan, London, Madras, and Paris), BAAL, BALEAP, BERA, Cambridge University Summer Institute, IATEFL, Korean Applied Linguistics Association, London University Institute of Education, The Open University, South African Applied Linguistics Association, and Vancouver TESOL, and draws upon work which has been funded by the ESRC, University of Southampton, Yapp Educational Trust, BAAL, and my own department. Earlier versions of some of the chapters have appeared in Southampton *Centre for Language in Educational Working Papers*, *AILA Review*, *ELT Documents*, *Franco–British Studies*, *Review of ELT*, and *British Studies in Applied Linguistics*, and in edited volumes published by Oxford University Press, RELC, CILT, Macmillan, Multilingual Matters and Routledge. But overall this is an entirely new work with every chapter either newly written or substantially reworked.

As always, I am solely responsible for errors and omissions, and will welcome correction.

The author and publisher are grateful to the following for permission to reproduce extracts from copyright material:

Edward Arnold for *Learning How to Mean* by M.A.K. Halliday.

Cambridge University Press for *Genre Analysis* by J.M. Swales, 1990.

Cambridge University Press for extract from S. Daniel 'Poems and a Defence of Rime' (1599) in *Images of English* by R.W. Bailey, 1992.

Cambridge University Press for *Introducing Applied Linguistics* by S.P. Corder, 1973.

Cambridge University Press for *Cambridge Encyclopedia of Language* by D. Crystal.

A.M. Heath for *George Orwell: Collected Letters and Journalism*. By permission of Bill Hamilton as the Literary Executor of the Estate of the late Sonia Brownell Orwell, Martin Secker & Warburg Ltd.

Little, Brown & Company for *The Tidy House* by Carolyn Steedman, published by Virago Press.

John Murray (Publishers) Ltd. for *Beyond Euphrates* by Freya Stark, published by John Murray.

Oxford University Press for 'Applied Linguistics: its meaning, its use' by Mackey in *Applied Linguistics* Vol 1.

Oxford University Press for 'Models and Fictions' by H.G. Widdowson in *Applied Linguistics* Vol 1.

Oxford University Press for 'Article 27 of International Covenant on Civil and Political Rights' & 'DocE. CN. 4/Sub.2/1988.25' from *Linguistic Imperialism* by Robert Phillipson © R.H.L. Phillipson, 1992.

Oxford University Press for 'Teacher Professionalism & Research' by Christopher Brumfit, from *Principle and Practice in Applied Linguistics*, edited by Guy Cook and Barbara Seidlhofer © Oxford University Press, 1995.

Oxford University Press for *Fundamental Concepts of Language Teaching* by H.H. Stern © H.H. Stern, 1983.

Oxford University Press for *Principle and Practice in Applied Linguistics* edited by Guy Cook and Barbara Seidlhofer © Oxford University Press, 1995.

Pearson Education for *Planning Language, Planning Inequality* by J.W. Tollefson, reprinted by permission of Pearson Education Limited © Longman Group Ltd. ·

Pearson Education for *Longman Dictionary of Language Teaching and Applied Linguistics* by J.C. Richards, J. Platt, and H. Platt, reprinted by permission of Pearson Education Limited © Longman Group Ltd.

Peters, Fraser & Dunlop for *The Cruise of the Nona* by Hilaire Belloc. Reprinted by permission of PFD.

The Belknap Press of Harvard University Press for *A Theory of Justice* by John Rawls, Cambridge, Mass. Copyright © 1971 by the President and fellows of Harvard College.

The Estate of Sir Karl Popper for *Knowledge and the Mind-Body Problem* and *The Myth of the Framework* by Karl Popper.

The Times Literary Supplement for review by Mary Midgley of *Secrets* by Sissella Bok, *TLS* April 1984, 563.

H.G. Widdowson for *Learning Purpose and Language Use* published by Oxford University Press, 1983.

H.G. Widdowson for *Explorations in Applied Linguistics* published by Oxford University Press.

PART ONE

Language and education

1 Language, linguistics, and education

Introduction

Language is central to education; linguistics is the discipline devoted to the study of language. But the study of language within the educational process takes us far beyond linguistics alone, as the discipline is currently conceived. This book outlines some of the ways in which language interacts with human behaviour, and the ways in which that interaction affects education. The purpose of this book is (1) to describe a field of human enquiry which has only fairly recently been studied in any detail, and (2) to exemplify an approach to educational linguistics which reflects the many disciplines beyond linguistics that must inform our attempts to understand language in social use. Inevitably, therefore, I shall be drawing upon knowledge from recent research and simultaneously describing a current research programme—the process of trying to understand language in education. In this chapter most of my specific examples relate to British education, but the British educational context is shared by many other countries, and as later chapters show, I hope, the principles described below are relevant to most education systems.

We are only just beginning to assimilate recent developments in linguistic understanding to the varying practices of different groups of human beings, and language within the educational process is still a relatively unformed field of study. Indeed, when I was appointed to the Chair of Education at Southampton, in 1984, it was the first appointment of a linguist to such a chair in Britain. Others had been appointed to chairs concerned with the direct teaching of particular languages, but this was the first time that a chair had been set up to relate to the general field of language and linguistics in education. When I gave my inaugural lecture, delivered primarily to a non-specialist audience, I entitled it *Is language education? or Is education language?* Of course, neither 'language' nor 'education' is as limited as this formulation implies—but there is still a sense in which, at the beginning of the twenty-first century, education is conceived of as the accumulation by individuals of discourses relating to different areas of activity, communicating with groups of people with shared interests: in science, in sport, in culture, in technologies. And there is a further sense in which language can be seen as a never-ending process of repertoire extension (and repertoire reduction), in which the learning process cannot be separated from our constantly changing linguistic knowledge and linguistic practice. Understanding how these processes interact is exciting and challenging; but it is also immensely demanding, for if our aim is to understand human beings using language, we are addressing at once the most complex and the most creative aspects of human behaviour. We need to be not just rigorous scientists if we are to comprehend language as fully as possible; we need to be poets and mystics as well.

Academic studies and educational practice

'Language' and 'Education' share two disadvantages that many other areas of study avoid: they are both too familiar. We all use language, and many of us have strong views about it; we have all been educated, and we all have strong views about that. Expertise confronts experience, and experts have a difficult task defending their own expertise against others' perceived experience.

Yet language is full of puzzles that experience alone cannot solve, and one of the greatest of these is the exact relationship between speech, writing, and the whole educational process. For a start, language operates on many levels and with many functions simultaneously, so that the relationship is always complex. Consider as an example a highly formalized educational event, such as the inaugural lecture referred to above. The structure of an inaugural lecture (at which customarily new professors deliver a public introduction to their field to an audience of colleagues, students, and outsiders) seems to be a carefully erected memorial to the relationship between education and language. What, after all, could be more of a memorial to language than a lecture: a text of dead words written to be spoken as if living? And what could be more of a memorial to education than a ritual recitation by an elderly person in formal dress intoned to a silent gathering of fellow mourners? Typically, the inauguration of a new professor is celebrated in a rite of words; typically too for education, some would cynically say, they are words that cannot be interrupted or debated. Yet no one who has experienced education in any form will doubt the major role that language plays in the practice of educational institutions. The desirability of this can be disputed, but we must concede the fact.

The inaugural lecture is partly a means of communication, to a very diverse audience, but it is also a formal rite, a symbolic event in academic life, and perhaps in the social life of the community outside the university. It is a means of communicating knowledge, but it is a means also of establishing solidarity, across academic departments, between the university and the outside world, between staff and students. It may even be a means of challenging ideas, by asking questions rather than providing answers, by asking the audience to rethink long-standing assumptions—and it may also be a demonstration of particular procedures, or particular ways of thinking. It is not just a physical event and a mental event, but an emotional one, and even sometimes a spiritual event. But it can only demonstrate these qualities because of the medium of language: however technical the content, however good the visuals, however spirited the delivery, it is crucially a linguistic event.

And linguistic events constantly surprise us. Here is an example which is outside the major preoccupations of linguistics. None the less, Figure 1.1 shows a text that starkly illustrates some of our problems.

This is a written text, but its message is puzzling and opaque. It is a genuine piece of evidence, the notes of one of my previous MA students (on the role of language in teacher education, as it happens) for her essay answer to an examination question (quoted with her permission). But what kind of language is this itself? How does a student arrive at such an independent and idiosyncratic piece of literacy? What is the relationship between this and the normal language (and the normal education) she has received? Discussion with the student revealed that she associates the images she has sketched with concepts to be used in the essay, but the associations are unique to herself, depending on contingent events in her own personal history. Yet this private 'language' illustrates one aspect of normal language which is little discussed: the ways in which the concepts represented in language possess rich associations that are purely personal to individuals. Lurking behind the shared code of 'normal' language lies a second code of personal associations, like those illustrated here, only partially perceived even by the writers or speakers themselves. The uniqueness of our individual experience colours the uniqueness of our individual understanding. Yet the code used to communicate these is shared.

Much has been written on the relationships between language and learning, but this example should remind us that for every generalization we attempt to make in our textbooks and our teaching, there will be thousands of individuals using language for their own purposes, with their own devices and methods, confounding our general and abstract pronouncements with their own precise and concrete instances. As in any exploration centred on human beings, the fact of our individual self-consciousness destabilizes the response and confuses the questioner. Each unexpected example makes us ask whether we have interpreted our own practice accurately or completely, and each time we do that our certainty is undermined. Certainty becomes the enemy of truth.

The risks that are being hinted at here can be more explicitly illustrated by considering the relationship between any descriptive discipline and a social and institutionalized practice such as education. Education is specifically concerned with intervention by one part of society in the lives of others. Such intervention is meant to be positive rather than negative, and safeguards of various kinds are provided to ensure that unsatisfactory intervention is avoided. But the mechanisms for intervening and the mechanisms for safeguarding are themselves part of the process of education, and have to be taken into account when the relationship between research and practice is examined.

As a field of study, 'education' tries to improve the quality of education provision in two related ways. First, the attempt to understand processes of education, in general and in particular, is needed both as part of our need to understand our environment and in order to inform discussion of educational policy. When it works successfully, this activity should lead—though often

Figure 1.1:   MA student's notes (reproduced with permission)

indirectly and after a long time lag—to more sensitive policy making at local and national levels, and to improved methods of teaching particular areas of the curriculum. Second, the attempt to develop appropriate teaching procedures, through experimentation with new materials and techniques and arising out of dissatisfaction with the old ones, leads simultaneously to criticism of current models of learning and teaching and to greater support for the teaching profession in its task within the educational system. Thus development, enquiry, improvement, and critique operate simultaneously and interactively.

This is of course an idealized picture, though it is difficult to see how we can afford to be content with much less. And, indeed, it does seem to be a realizable ideal, as long as researchers, teachers, advisers, materials writers and other practitioners can interchange roles, collaborate, and have effective administrative support for such close relationships. These are practical needs, but they should not obscure the epistemological difficulties also associated with achievement of such integration.

A rich and complex area of human activity such as education cannot be treated as if understanding and explanation suffice to cause desirable change. Indeed, the current state of schooling, at any time in any country, is never the result of careful planning and coherent policy: too many parents, teachers, learners and administrators subvert plans by a mixture of idealism, effort, divergent views about aims, laziness, incompetence and exciting but unpredictable innovation. For the past 20 years Britain has been going through a period of centralization and control, but schools, teachers, and classrooms still differ markedly, not just in quality of learning experience, but in different types of excellence and creativity. We have to note, though, that the complex task of understanding any aspect of education can in principle be separated from the task of implementing change. Understanding does not necessarily require change to follow. What is crucial is the mediation process, by which understanding from a variety of relevant disciplines is integrated to the needs of particular teachers and administrators in particular positions in particular schools, so that creativity can be maintained.

Some recent controversies in language teaching illustrate the problems in integrating research and teaching. There is, for example, a strong research tradition in second language acquisition studies which maintains that learners of foreign languages acquire much of the linguistic system in predictable ways. Studies of learners in different sets of conditions have suggested that generalizations can be made about the order in which certain language forms tend to appear, and such studies have resulted in substantial debate on their implications for linguistic theory and pedagogic practice (Davies, Criper, and Howatt 1984; Mitchell and Myles 1998). But the usefulness of such studies can easily be exaggerated. Observations about the tendencies of learners can give us a general orientation for discussions of teaching; they cannot tell us how to teach specific groups of learners in any detail. This is because we have no way of knowing the relevance of such studies to particular learners until we know the conditions determining who is where on the scale being used: a collective tendency, however well attested, tells us nothing about the potential behaviour of an individual learner. Similarly, advocates of 'telling' pupils in English classes about, for example, the English writing system (Stubbs 1986: 229) or of listing objectives for teaching English (HMI 1984) are oversimplifying the implications of such apparent reliance on a transmission model of learning. Not only is the direct transmission model concerned with only one half of the activity, the teacher's, but even if the transmission model is desired, the teaching profession needs to understand why it is a better model than alternatives. Matching research to human practice is only simple in the minds of tyrants. But that is not because it cannot be done; rather, it is because the complexity and creativity of human behaviour makes 'simple' answers valid only at a high level of generality. Specific behaviour may operate within these generalizations, but a long process of discussion and interpretation, and of trial and error, provides the only means of avoiding mismatches between general statements and particular interventions in individual lives. Because of this, it is probably more honest to talk about the 'implications' of theory and research for practice than the 'applications'. Theory and research have to be digested by teachers, administrators, and policy makers and converted to something which works in their particular institutions, and with the people who teach and study in them. And this applies equally to other areas where language studies impinge on education. But to justify this argument, it will be necessary to summarize current views on the contexts of language use.

Language and its uses

'Language' has always been an object of interest to scholars outside linguistics itself. Literary theorists and literary critics, philosophers, psychologists, socio-logists and anthropologists have all persistently concerned themselves with language. What is remarkable in the last 20 years has been the degree of consensus over the nature of language that has emerged in education from a diverse range of theoretical perspectives initially established in the 1960s and 1970s. While linguistics has in some traditions moved away from language located in the world towards increasingly abstract cognitive models, educational linguists, and others concerned with areas traditionally regarded as applied linguistics, have found themselves turning more towards the other language-interested disciplines. Indeed, it sometimes appears as if serious research into contextualized language activity is prevented from developing by the dominance of linguistic research concerned with idealizations which remove language from any systematic relationship with users or their purposes.

But other traditions within linguistics have fed the movement towards more socially sensitive language awareness. As descriptive linguists have concerned themselves with meaning, and moved into discourse analysis and pragmatics, so their interests have intersected with the concerns of researchers from other disciplines. Attempts deriving from anthropology to analyse speech events in relation to factors such as participant roles, settings, and topics (Hymes 1967) began the systematization of the interplay between language and social environment. At the same time, sociolinguistic studies demonstrated the ways in which syntactic or phonological rules may be observably adjusted according to the status or social position of users (Labov 1972).

These studies were essentially descriptive in intention. Social psychologists, however, provided the beginnings of accounts of the motivation of such systematic changes. Giles (1977) has suggested that there is a clear disposition to converge on the language of interlocutors where there is goodwill, and to diverge where there is antagonism. A number of studies in areas of ethnic or cultural conflict (for example Wales, Belgium, and Canada) showed that negative relations with outsiders cause speakers unconsciously to increase the dialect features of their locality away from the metropolitan mode to the local, while positive relations with outsiders promote a decrease of such localization. Such evidence is compatible with Grice's conversational maxims (Grice 1975) which are based on the view that a prime function of conversation is to facilitate communication as effectively as possible. To this end, features which might cause confusion in communication will be reduced wherever there is a desire for effective communication. At the same time, we should note that such features may be increased where the intention is to obscure rather than to clarify. There is evidence that children perceive language markers very early (Day 1982 demonstrated that by the age of three they have clear in- and out-group perceptions based on the speech of those they hear), and Reid (1978) and Romaine (1984) produced data which indicates that adolescents have very definite ideas about the social significance of different language forms. Thus language behaviour combines perceptions of group membership and identity with judgements about the degree of communication to strive for.

Such studies reinforce our awareness of the sensitivity and variability of language. The range of associations which may be acquired by any specific symbol available to us is immense, and these associations may be private or public. All families have their own private associations, as well as a certain number of vocabulary items peculiar to themselves. These associations may become highly wrought artefacts and spill over into literature and the public domain, as with the juvenile writings of the Brontës, or Isherwood's early fantasies. Equally, they may remain private and intensely local in range (as Figure 1.1 demonstrated). But the potential scope for interaction between the private and the public is infinite. Every utterance has an internal and an external history, and the speaker or writer will only be aware of a small part of either of these. Because the overlap in experience of a particular language item or language event is incomplete for each speaker and listener, misunderstanding, or legitimate alternative interpretation, is constantly possible. And constellations of personal experience build up into ideologies, patterns of belief that underlie whole modes of human activity, binding the behaviour patterns of groups who identify themselves as cultures—physicists or stamp collectors, educationalists or readers of Kafka, Jehovah's Witnesses or structuralists, undertakers or ministry officials or bakers. There is no group too important or too trivial to bond linguistically and form a temporary culture, with its own characteristic linguistic forms and its own (for the moment) shared assumptions.

It is important to emphasize the variety (and the frequent superficiality) of our linguistic and cultural associations, because there is a strong tendency to see both language and culture as relatively solid and unnegotiable, and the relations between them as fixed. Yet education above all other social forces is concerned with establishing the mutability of culture and the languages that reflect and contribute to it. We have to operate within the linguistic system we receive, otherwise we shall not communicate. But we are never its prisoner, and learning to transcend our current language to perceive and contribute to future communicative and conceptual capacities is the self-educational task for each of us. To make sense of this process, we have to try to locate language in some of its rich context.

Language in the classroom

Let me try to illustrate this principle with a simple example. Steedman (1982) devoted a whole book to a remarkable analysis of a collaborative story produced by three eight-year-old primary school girls. The passage quoted in Figure 1.2 is in fact the sole interpolation by a fourth girl into the lengthy, and eventually incomplete story.

Steedman comments about this episode:

> When the girls worked together in writing, they operated by a model of social life that demonstrated to them more cohesion and co-operation between women than it did between men. There were pressures on the boys to act aggressively and to display their conflict with each other, though the girls too were usually told to hit back. When Lisa, who joined the three writers of 'The Tidy House' after several days of diplomatic approaches, wrote a portion of the text, she had the character Jamie tell her nine-year-old son Carl to fight back in the playground. This scene echoed many conversations with all the children throughout the year in which they would patiently explain to me, yet again, that whilst the school's most stringently enforced rule forbade fighting, they had been told by their parents to hit back ... The passage by Lisa mirrored her own, very recent experience. She had had two close friends, Carla and Melissa. They had gone to nursery school together, walked back and forth together, sat together and played in the streets together through five long years. The arrival of Lindie in the spring had destroyed the balance of this old friendship. Admitted back into the fold towards the end of the week, the constraints of the plot that Lisa was faced with and the gender of the child character she had to write about meant that there was no alternative but to write of herself as Carl, the boy.
> (Steedman 1982: 136–7)

The tidy house
that is no more
as kids house,
When Carl was nine
he was in the middle
School, He only had two
Firends. and one day his
too firends ~~break~~ Firends
With him, he did not
have no firends to play
With. Dow the boys Who
Was his firends got boys
and started to fight
him. When Caril went
home he told Jamie but

Jamiem said "Just stick
up for your self"
"but I" "but What" "I cant
because they are bigger
than me" "you can get
Jason on the ground"
"yes I know but your
get the blam When it
is not you" oh shut up"

Figure 1.2: Carolyn Steedman: The Tidy House *1982: 213–14.*
London: Virago

The point is not whether this was in some sense 'the true' account of what motivated the writing; rather it is that some similar account to this had to be true. Writing of this kind is necessarily reflecting a complex of personal and conventional attributes which must be recognized and responded to (but which may not be precisely identified) by any primary teacher, or indeed in another sense by any reader. For the writer, the conventions of school writing, of children's literature, and of parental expectations all converge in this one short episode in addition to the conventions demanded by the existing lengthy text which was already available. This was simultaneously a public and a private act, as imaginative writing often is. But it functions as part of a cumulative educational process: to assign it an exact and isolated role would be like asking the exact role of each blade of grass in a field. Yet few people would wish to deny that the role of such writing in the process of personal development is important.

If we are to make sense of language use in education, then, the interpretation of meaning is at least as important as the recognition of form. Yet the interpretation of meaning will never be an objective activity, for meaning depends not only on the context and the conventions appropriately deployed to match the context, but also on the interpretations of those who read or listen, and the intentions of those who speak. It is widely recognized that together we make our meanings, but less widely accepted that we cannot be fully aware of the meanings that we make. Language users operate rather like action painters drawing their colours from a moving palette, and spraying them back at it: we take our meanings from the language, but by the time we are ready to return them, the language has subtly shifted. None of us speaks the same language twice, any more than we drive exactly the same route twice. Using language is changing language.

Such recognition of language as necessarily in flux, reflecting the movement and life of the minds that use it, enables us to see language activity in the education system as a process of working, not just a product of learning. Developments in second language acquisition research make it difficult to see the learning even of foreign languages as distinct from the process of language use: learning is using and using is learning (see, from different perspectives, Stevick 1976; Krashen 1981; Brumfit 1984). Of course, there are also formal activities associated with the learning—people learn vocabulary lists off by heart more than is commonly acknowledged—but these activities are preliminary to the language learning process itself, for only when the language items are fused into active meaning systems by the process of use, is the language system developing for the learner's own purposes. We may learn the tokens of language formally, but we learn the system by using it through reading or writing, or conversing.

Learning new concepts and developing new capacities are thus frequently realized through the development of new language, and the development of new language must be realized through the development of meaning. Other systems than language may of course perform similar functions, but in literate societies especially, links between education and literacy are so close that language will remain the dominant code for the foreseeable future. Even a world dependent on the Internet cannot replace language with images that are independent of language.

Language policy

So far, we have been concerned mainly with language in the general educational process. Some commentators, indeed, have come close to arguing that the general educational process is essentially a matter of playing the appropriate language games. Hirst, for example, associated the development of concepts with 'the symbols of our common languages' (Hirst 1974: 83) so that education may become the interplay between (1) the appropriate language forms that we are socialized to produce by schooling, and (2) the ideas that emerge from the context which language both creates and responds to.

Whatever position we take, though, language is clearly important enough to require specific consideration. There is not space here to explore all the implications for a policy for language in education, but one major strand may be appropriately described.

Arising out of the awareness, discussed above, of language as variable and adaptable to users' needs, has developed an increasing recognition of Britain as a multidialectal and multilingual society. A variety of forces have contributed to this, ranging from the concerns of those in the inner cities to avoid alienation of minority groups by the pursuit of policies in language work which inadvertently or intentionally reinforce racism, to the increasing sensitivity to language variation in mainstream discussion, and the serious addressing of issues of language (and other) variation that emerges from the movement towards a common curriculum forced by comprehensivization of secondary schools. Thus, it begins to make sense to demand certain minimum language 'rights' for all learners in state education. I have developed this theme in more detail in Chapter 6, and will only refer to it here in summary.

A minimum requirement for all learners would be: (1) development of mother tongue or dialect; (2) development of competence of a range of styles of English for educational, work-based, social and public-life purposes; (3) development of knowledge of the nature of language in a multilingual society, including basic acquaintance with some languages from the total range of those available in education or in the local community; (4) development of a fairly extensive practical competence in at least one language other than their own (Brumfit 1986a, 1995a).

This minimal set of requirements may look initially puzzling and over-ambitious—and indeed it is necessary to accept that each region and each school will have to determine its own priorities, within the scope of its own funding, for the first requirement particularly. None the less, the case for all of these is very strong if linguistic resources are to be adequately exploited and learning adequately developed. Nor are the requirements very far from what is widely advocated elsewhere. The Swann Report on the education of ethnic minority children (DES 1985) expected schools to be as positive as possible towards the first; the second has been advocated by the last six secretaries of state for education, and is accepted by most English teachers as one of their aims; parts of the third were investigated by the Kingman Inquiry into the teaching of English (DES 1988); and the last was incorporated into the British Department of Education and Science documentation on the core curriculum, and into recommendations on foreign languages (DES 1990).

But these initiatives have not been co-ordinated into a package that has overall coherence, and there are major implications for teacher education. Many teachers will find themselves engaged in work with multilingual classes, and an awareness of children's and adults' capacities to cope with language issues is a necessary prerequisite to successful teaching. Consider Figure 1.3.

This dialogue illustrates (in a fairly unsophisticated form) one teacher's attempt to come to grips with what is happening when a native speaker encounters a non-native speaker in school. Even at this level, conscious exploration of this data by the teacher is likely to sensitize her to many of the language processes that we take for granted in both children and adults. The trouble is that it is still rare for work like this to be carried out, and far rarer for any more sophisticated analysis to be developed. Language, as distinct from language teaching, is still explicitly addressed only rarely in teacher education. Even the very recent moves to impose language tests for teachers are not accompanied by funding for any extra time to develop the sophisticated awareness that is necessary.

Child B	Child A	What A is doing
	Have you got your strong shoes?	
I have got on my shoes.	Yes, but your shoes. The shoes that don't let … that don't get your feet wet.	EXPLAINING the meaning of 'strong'. REPHRASING to make a phrase simpler.
My feet not wet.	Do you like to jump in puddles?	FINDING ALTERNATIVE ways of putting over her idea.
Puddles?	Puddles—water on the floor.	EXPLAINING 'puddles'.
No, I get wet. My feet wet.	Your feet get wet? Not wet now? Have you got your … plimsolls?	MATCHING the 'telegraphese' of B— not wet now/ put plimsolls on.
Plimsolls?	If your feet get wet, you put plimsolls on … like in there— in the hall!	
My feet?	If your feet GET wet. Plimsolls on (demonstrating wildly).	STRESSING WORDS. USING GESTURE.
I don't know.	Ask Mrs M.	
Mrs M.? Why?	She's outside—the teacher outside.	
What she say? (laughing)	What WOULD she say (correcting her).	CORRECTING her directly.
She tells the boys not fight.	No, B. She tell the boys not TO fight.	JUDGING how much to correct—one thing

Figure 1.3: Overheard in a playground: A conversation between child A and child B. Hilary Hester: 'Learning from children learning', in Christopher Brumfit, Rod Ellis, and Josie Levine (eds). English as a Second Language in the United Kingdom, *1985: 56. Oxford: Pergamon Press*

Language in teacher education

For teachers of ESOL (English for Speakers of Other Languages) language has always been a significant element in professional preparation. But for teaching language in Britain the situation has, until very recently, been quite different. The great expansion of teacher education in the 1960s was accompanied by a certain amount of claim staking by particular disciplines for a 'foundation' role in the training of teachers (Tibble 1966; Hirst 1983). Psychology, sociology, history and philosophy all established themselves in strong positions. It remains an arguable point whether education benefited from the fact that linguistics emerged as a fashionable subject just after the partition of the field. Perhaps language studies benefited, for there is widespread dissatisfaction with the divide between disciplines and the practice of teaching (though the problem will be resolved more by giving reasonable time to the high-level training of teachers than by trying to reorganize the inadequate time currently available). Whatever the position, language activity is divided in teacher education across a range of possible courses, none of which has language as a prime focus and none of which is obliged to deal with language at all. Nor, indeed, can we say that teachers typically receive high-level training in language work. A survey I conducted for the National Congress on Languages in Education, which involved sending a detailed questionnaire to nearly 150 institutions concerned with teacher education in the UK, including all state training institutions, revealed for the universities that replied the returns found in Figure 1.4 (Brumfit 1988). It is clear from these that we could not by any means guarantee that all teachers would have any explicit awareness of the nature of the language that is so important in their classrooms. Nor did surveys of the knowledge of language of undergraduates or teachers in training suggest that these figures conceal widespread understanding rather than ignorance (Bloor 1986).

So much for the position in secondary university teacher training in the 1980s, where, if anywhere, the most academically sophisticated teachers should have been found. In the 1990s, government pressure has enforced a variety of unsophisticated linguistic activities on teachers in training, but there has been no effective consultation of linguists or educational experts prior to publication and enforcement on the profession (see Brumfit 1999 for a brief account of the marginalization of experts in this field).

But there is another perhaps slightly more contentious dimension to this story, for in Britain language has customarily been the concern of English teachers. Curiously, English teachers have not automatically (until these recent government initiatives) had any direct training in understanding of language at all. Some degree courses do include some work on language; many do not include anything on contemporary linguistics, sociolinguistics, or psycholinguistics, to mention only three areas of direct relevance to the classroom. Nor, indeed does 'linguistics' have a good name with English teachers (though to what extent that reflects an out-of-date model of what linguistics, and especially applied

ALL STUDENTS

University	1	2	3	4	5	6	7	8	9	10	11	12	13	14	15	16
Compulsory course/hours	–	–	–	4–10	4–10	6	10	–	3	2	15	3½	20+	–	20+	–
Optional course/hours	20	–	10–20	–	–	–	–	–	–	–	–	–	–	10+	–	–
Number of tutors	1	–	5	–	4	2	1		1	1	5	19	5	1	2	–
of which—																
number of full-time language in education	–	–	–	–	–	2	–	–	–	–	1	1	3	–	1	–
number with qualification	–	–	–	–	–	1	–	–	–	–	1	–	2	1	2	–

Figure 1.4: 'Language in education' on university PGCE courses, Christopher Brumfit, (ed.) 1988: Language in Teacher Education, 1988:20 Brighton: National Congress on Languages in Education

linguistics is, to what extent it reflects the failures of undergraduate linguistics courses to convince students of the excitement and relevance of the discipline, and to what extent it is simply fear of a scientific approach, is difficult to determine: probably there are elements of all three). But the fact remains that the prime teachers of 'language' in our schools frequently, perhaps usually, have had no specific knowledge of this field at all.

The difficulty is that this leaves a camouflaged trap. We have qualified 'English' teachers, they are concerned with 'language', therefore we have qualified 'language teachers', is the false syllogism. What we in fact have is an incapacity to provide sensitivity about language as a social instrument, except at an amateur level. I doubt whether this can be said about any other major area of the curriculum. Even one-year, full-time postgraduate courses are few and far between, and of course the weight of the profession lies heavily with those who are understandably committed to the three years of full-time literary or cultural study that has provided them with the academic basis for their English teaching as their undergraduate degree. It is difficult to see how the necessary expertise for basic work in this area can be achieved by less than the equivalent of one year's full-time study at either undergraduate or postgraduate level. And if the study of language (whether it is described as 'language' or as 'linguistics') is to be recognizably the medium we are all aware of in our daily lives, it needs to be based on the broad view of the function of language that I am outlining here.

Yet it is important to see that this is not a conflict between 'arid science and humane creativity', to quote one English teacher in a discussion group I was in at a conference. Language work in education has to recognize the potential impact of literature, the need to write for personal pleasure, and language as a means of personal identity. Anyway, of course, 'humane creativity' can become arid in its own way, as Gorky observed: 'When he was away from a book, its influence remained with him. He saw reality through the dust of centuries and built up a barricade of book-lore to hold off disturbing thoughts' (Maxim Gorky, *The Life of Matvei Kozhemyakin*, 1911).

To experience language without imaginative response is to impoverish it, but so too is to experience language without intellectual rigour. Language is in fact the cheapest scientific data available to schools, and pupils, in my experience, invariably enjoy thinking about it, as a socially significant system and as an abstract system alike, if the teacher is committed, knowledgeable, and enthusiastic.

I have tried to argue, then, that language is intimately bound up with the process of education, at all levels, and that teachers and administrators need to be sensitive to this and informed about the way language operates in society. I have also argued, in passing, that explicit language responsibilities require a policy for all learners about what they are entitled to expect, and that all teachers require some knowledge of language, and teachers of English, particularly (though of other languages too) require specific work on language if they are not to mislead the public about their own expertise.

But I said at the beginning of this introductory chapter that it was both a report on knowledge and an outline of a programme: what is the programme?

My appointment at Southampton implied a local programme and a contribution to a national programme. In 1999 I have to report that the national contribution has been slight, for complex reasons to do with the ideologies of successive British governments, the attitudes to education (and to language) of the press and civil servants as well as politicians, and no doubt to failures in communication by myself and colleagues (Brumfit 1991, 1999; see also Chapter 6). The contents of this book illustrate that there has been much discussion of issues in educational linguistics, but neither I nor colleagues in similar fields can claim to have had significant effects on policy. Why that is perhaps deserves a book to itself.

More locally, the School of Education in Southampton began to systematize its work on language and communication in the initial training of teachers, though a one-year course two-thirds of which is teaching in schools, with many Teacher Training Agency required content commitments, gives us little time to play with, and as increasing government intervention committed more and more time, the amount available to language for all teachers gradually decreased. We were able to establish a full-time master's field of study in language, and later in applied linguistics also, and we have trained more than 30 doctoral students in language in education since 1989. The Centre for Language in Education, founded in 1986, provided a structure through which we were able to link with colleagues in schools, colleges, and other faculties to consider the whole activity of communication in educational settings, including work in literature, drama, and media studies as well as in language. The centre has shared the problems of other university-based groups concerned with the British education system, but has generally maintained a considerable degree of activity and has acted as a research focus for many scholars and practitioners in the field. If disinterested higher education activity has been hard in an environment of pretend (but actually highly manipulated) markets, none the less we have survived with our activity (and we hope our quality) intact!

The potential research programme, however, could provide much greater activity even than teaching—in spite of funding difficulties substantial programmes have been possible with generous support from the Economic and Social Research Council, from the university, and from local authorities and schools in central southern England. Some major questions (for example about explicit knowledge in language learning and in teachers' understanding: Brumfit, Mitchell, and Hooper 1996; about progression in the learning of foreign languages: Myles, Hooper, and Mitchell 1998; about gender and reading: Moss and Attar 1999; about bilingual learners in mainstream schooling: Bourne 1992; Statham 1994; about multilingual literacies in different settings: Kenner 1996, Kamanda 1999) have been clarified by myself, colleagues, and research students. The last, particularly, have added a wealth of data and interpretation from the UK and overseas to clarify these and other related questions. Much of this evidence is cited later in this book. My debt to colleagues and students, as well as to those working in the same field in other institutions, is immense. One encouraging sign is that there are at least five other professorships in Britain now in this field. The possibility of a substantial leap forward in our understanding, resulting from much greater activity in research and in interpretation, can only be welcomed.

But I would like to conclude this introductory chapter with a warning. However euphoric we wish to be about our understanding of language, we have to be willing to ask what it is for. When all the instrumental arguments have been laid aside, we do have to recognize that there is something fundamental about communication, whether oral or written, which is to do with our deepest impulses and which we must not lose. Language connects us with the cultures of our ancestors and those of our contemporaries. If I ask myself why I teach and research in this field, I find that Olive Schreiner, writing from South Africa over a hundred years ago, expresses it better than anyone else I have read:

> He read one page and turned over to the next; he read down that without changing his posture by an inch; he read the next, and the next, kneeling up all the while with the book in his hand, and his lips parted.
>
> All he read he did not fully understand; the thoughts were new to him; but this was the fellow's startled joy in the book—the thoughts were his, they belonged to him. He had never thought them before, but they were his.
>
> He laughed silently and internally, with the still intensity of triumphant joy.
>
> So, then, all thinking creatures did not send up the one cry 'As thou, dear Lord, has created things in the beginning, so are they now, so ought they to be, so will they be, world without end; and it doesn't concern us that they are. Amen.' There were men to whom not only kopjes and stones were calling out imperatively, what are we, and how came we here? Understand us, and know us, but to whom even the old, old relations between man and man, and the customs of the ages called, and could not be made still and forgotten.
>
> The boy's heavy body quivered with excitement. So he was not alone, not alone.
>
> (Olive Schreiner, *The Story of an African Farm*, Part One, 11, 1883)

Education needs language; language needs education, so that we should not be alone.

2 Understanding and the acquisition of knowledge

Introduction

In this chapter I want to begin to answer the question raised in the first chapter about the relationship between language and the learning process by drawing attention to some of the distinctive features of classroom discourse, and relating these to what is conventionally said about classrooms by linguists and psychologists. I shall relate the concept 'understanding' to processes of language use in education, and in the course of the argument we shall see that the idea that language events take place at a particular moment in time is too limited to account for comprehension processes in typical classrooms. Indeed, a close examination of any particular setting will provide a warning against too ready an acceptance of simple models of the comprehension process.

In normal language use, every act of repetition will be an act of reinterpretation. This chapter is based on a paper, which was based on a lecture presented orally some months before the final written version was prepared. That lecture was based on a written version, different from the published paper. And that version had its own history. Even the smallest discourse element was subject to interpretation throughout the preparatory process. Here, for example, is my original intention, itself arising from a telephone discussion, as I offered it in a letter more than a year before the lecture was given. I wrote:

> (1) Understanding, language, and educational processes
> The relationship between studies in Discourse, Conversational Analysis, and Genre, and educational debates will be explored. Particularly, curriculum discussion on ESP, the role of literature teaching, and teaching through other subjects will be considered in relation to the methodological implications of research into understanding. (1a)

I also wrote 'Please amend as you see fit.' That was in May 1990.

In June 1990, a letter informed me that the title would appear on the programme as

> (2) 'Understanding, language and educational processes' (note the lost comma).

In August 1990 the brochure appeared with the title as amended, and a summary as follows:

– the relationship between studies in discourse, conversational analysis, genre and educational debates and how these relate to research into understanding (2a)

This formulation also appeared in the programme. I had agreed to the final copy (as one does, out of a combination of politeness, laziness, and willing tolerance of minor variation), but there are none the less subtle shifts in meaning which the process of reinterpretation for another purpose had imposed on my original intention. A letter in May 1991, however, referred to my lecture as (3) 'Understanding language and educational processes', without any commas, though the preferred form (2) reappeared in the outline programme.

If I had been pedantic, I could have 'corrected' every comma, but I suspect that this record of minor change is typical rather than untypical and that pedantry would not have been welcome. The letters to myself were from different people and were widely spaced out in time, the changes were not usually substantial, and the general area of discussion remained clear. The extent to which individual participants on the Summer Institute at which I gave the lecture might have interpreted my intentions differently from myself, and in what ways, and with what principles, is the subtext to the pedagogic theme of this chapter.

I should emphasize, also, that the contributors to this correspondence were native speakers of English, not second language learners, and we tolerated this variation without necessarily realizing where meanings were being interpreted differently. If I introspect, I can report that for me commas in a list indicate discrete entities: 'Understanding, language, and educational debates' is unambiguously three elements where 'Understanding, language and educational debates' could be two. And perhaps less contentiously, from later in the text, 'X will be considered in relation to Y' is different from 'how X relates to Y'. 'Particularly'... is an emphasizer, which may or may not simply introduce exemplification of an earlier general category, and 'the methodological implications of research' are different from 'research'.

It will be apparent from this discussion that almost any text, however simple and apparently public, has a history. Native speakers tolerate uncertainty without even noticing it, yet changes do carry the potential for different interpretation, and the extent to which we allow this to matter is negotiable (I could have objected, and tried to change the reformulations; or I could have not minded and ignored them, offering my originally intended paper whether or not it was what was expected; or I could have offered a modified paper, accepting the changes implied by the alterations and assuming them to be principled—or no doubt other options). Finally, we should note that such changes are not necessarily linguistic in origin at all: they may be determined by the need to save space in a brochure, by aesthetically acceptable line length requirements, or by careless typing. Even when writers publicly disagree over what they want printed, it is not always easy to interpret whether meaning is at stake. Many native speakers may object to the comma in 'language, and educational debates' and reject the idea of a significant change in meaning.

Native speakers are constantly forced to decide what is and is not significant in linguistic variation, to interpret motives, and to decide on courses of action. More often than not, these will be courses of inaction, for we are busy people who cannot waste time renegotiating the trivial or the obvious. Our judgements may be correct assessments of intentions, but they may also be quite wrong: perhaps it was tacitly assumed that the changes to my original text would be interpreted by me as a demand for a totally different kind of presentation—I was failing to recognize an intended indirect speech act. Perhaps it was not a house style that was being adopted to enable the texts from different people to appear similar, but a carefully considered criticism of my views on the placement of commas which I was too insensitive to pick up! Because we are all free to respond in different ways, we risk misinterpreting the situation—and only subsequent reactions can enable us to judge whether we have or not.

So much emphasis on such minor changes in text may appear to be labouring the point, but it is necessary to insist that native speakers of English (and presumably of all languages) live their lives choosing whether to take any notice of such changes or whether to ignore them. They live their linguistic lives amid such potential confusion, and they generally cope. But second language learners also have to accommodate this complex linguistic process. Experience with their first languages may help—but so many of the problems we are encountering are not solely linguistic. Cultural understanding may help—but so many problems require understanding of particular individuals. Individual contact is worth-while—but individuals are sometimes acting in response to conventions with which strangers are unfamiliar. How do we draw on research and theoretical discussion to help learners in their encounters with unstable constructs like language and culture?

Let me start by considering 'understanding' within pedagogy.

Understanding in education

A perennial theme in educational discussion is the distinction between education and training, and central to this issue is the concept, 'understanding'. Peters for example, writes '... a person could be a trained ballet dancer ... without being educated. What might be lacking is something to do with knowledge and understanding' (1973: 18).

While a great deal of educational discussion bases itself on decontextualized analysis, or psychological generalization from learning or interactional theories, I want to locate my discussion in this chapter firmly within the area of pedagogy, or teaching methodology. I do this for two reasons: first, because teaching theory in practice realizes itself as a relationship between teachers and learners (which may be close or distant but can be neither abrogated nor abdicated); second, because the systematic analysis of institutionalized practices is a major, and often neglected, testbed for applied linguistic theory. If classroom practices do not relate closely to the principles we advance, we should be looking closely at our principles, and be willing to consider adjusting them.

Where, then, do we find 'understanding' manifesting itself in education practices? Clearly, the sources to look to include written materials, especially textbooks and other teaching aids, widely practised classroom organizational structures intended to facilitate oral interaction, and also implicit practices reflected in syllabus and curriculum models and the models used in teacher education. Perhaps more important than any of these, however, is the practice of classroom teaching itself. Classrooms are constructed communities, with their prime function the creation of conditions for comprehension. Yet it is striking how little they have been studied with that as an explicit concern.

General curriculum theory in the past 20 years has shown an interesting parallelism with practices in language teaching. Douglas Barnes' influential *From Communication to Curriculum*, published in 1976, stresses the role of exploratory talk and of negotiated communication between the knowledge systems brought by teachers and learners, in a very similar argument to that used by Widdowson (for example, 1978) and others in their stress on negotiation of meaning in the language classroom. Learners are expected to create the discourse rules for the particular purposes that they share, within the constraints imposed by the teacher's structuring of classroom activity; language users both 'discover' their own rules, and receive them from the nature of the tasks they perform. Indeed, the idea that the understanding of particular disciplines is essentially a language game was explored by Hirst (1974: 83) and is implicit in much philosophy since Wittgenstein.

But our purpose here is to consider understanding/comprehension in relation to language teaching rather than general pedagogy. I shall take as a starting point an analysis of the key categories that are available to teachers for the conceptualization of language teaching, because such categories reflect craft-knowledge of comprehension choices, operationalized to classroom needs. The discussion below draws on ideas on the relationship between content teaching and language teaching that were developed in Brumfit 1984: 95–6, where a diagram summarizes the pedagogic options available to language teachers (Figure 2.1).

In the practice of teaching, the curriculum is frequently expressed in terms of the product of teaching, and the first group of categories lists the types of product that are available for inclusion. Selection of each of these of course carries implications for the manner in which teaching will be carried out; some of them entail substantial understanding (for example, the 'content' analyses) while others may imply, in part at least, a training, or skill-orientated model (for example phonology). But the combination of elements into a coherent system must entail substantial explicit understanding, if not of the structure of language itself, then certainly of the world-knowledge system, and the context of communication of each major speech event.

This context of communication will include a range of 'process' elements which can also be analysed. Language teaching can have only a limited range of

1 **Analysis of product:**

   a Formal analyses   phonological
      (linguists' categories):   syntactic
                                 morphological
                                 notional (semantico-grammatical)

   b Interactional analyses   situational
      (social psychologists',   functional
      anthropologists' and rhetoricians'   leading to:
      categories):   discoursal, rhetorical, and stylistic

   c Content/topical analyses   (i)   socially directed: cultural
      (technical or general categories): (ii) educationally directed: interdisciplinary
                                  (iii) language directed:
                                       linguistics, literature

2 **Analysis of process:**

   a Communicative abilities as goals: conversation/discussion
                                   comprehension
                                   extended writing
                                   (extended speaking)

   b Orientation of activity: accuracy
                                   fluency

   c Pedagogical mode: individual
                                   private interactional
                                     (pairs or small groups)
                                   public interactional
                                   (whole class/large groups + teacher)

Figure 2.1: Basic categories for the analysis of language teaching

real-world interactional goals, and the most frequent ones are listed under 2a. Because the context is educational, the orientation will be either towards 'accuracy' (where formal judgements of the quality of the language used are liable to be made), or towards 'fluency' (where native-speaker like effectiveness, irrespective of code quality, will be criterial). And finally, there are only three major types of interaction possible within a classroom, each corresponding to a particular communicative macro-structure: individual (personal with a text or one's own thinking/writing), private interaction (with others in a small group), or public (large group) interaction. Within each of these, questions of the role of understanding become important, and the differing relationships between these constitute the range of choices that teachers operate. Some of these will be more capable than others of encouraging open-ended and creative response by learners, as we shall see later.

Now if we move outwards from this pedagogically-centred analysis where do we find current discussion helpful? Let us start on the interface between description and practice. How does interaction link to content or subject-matter in language teaching? One approach has been to develop the concept of 'genre', which connects content to context including mode of interaction.

Swales (1990) summarizes much recent discussion in this area, and also provides an interesting and personal account of his relationship with genre studies from the point of view of a practising teacher of English for Academic Purposes (EAP). It is notable that even a recent reference book like Crystal's *Cambridge Encyclopaedia of Language* (1987: 73–8) limits the term 'genre' to the concept of literary form, tragedy, epic, fiction, etc., explored most rigorously by Fowler (1982). However, the more general use of the term, to refer to particular identifiable types of speech event, has been taken up by a number of writers on educational linguistics, particularly those working under Halliday's influence in Australia (see Painter 1985; Halliday and Hasan 1989).

It is difficult for the outsider to distinguish much analysis of 'genre' from the earlier work on 'register', and both terms risk suffering from imprecision. After reviewing the literature, Swales defines 'genre' as 'a class of communicative events, the members of which share some set of communicative purposes' (1990: 58). 'Register' is thus a way of distinguishing between styles, while 'genre' is a way of distinguishing between language events. Swales continues:

> These purposes are recognised by the expert members of the parent discourse community, and thereby constitute the rationale for the genre. This rationale shapes the schematic structure of the discourse and influences and constrains choice of content and style. Communicative purpose is both a privileged criterion and one that operates to keep the scope of a genre as here conceived narrowly focused on comparable rhetorical action. In addition to purpose, exemplars of a genre exhibit various patterns of similarity in terms of structure, style, content and intended audience.
> (Swales 1990: 58)

Swales' work can be seen as an effort to pull the academic tradition of English for Specific Purposes back towards textual analysis, following Widdowson's determined moves (particularly Widdowson 1983) to shift ESP from concerns with style to conceptual and cognitive frameworks. Widdowson sees particular purposes of language use as deriving from the operation of particular modes of thinking rather than as simply a matter of matching style to audience. He suggests that language knowledge is organized at two levels, systemic and schematic, corresponding to linguistic and communicative competence.

> Interpretative procedures are required to draw systemic knowledge into the immediate executive level of schemata and to relate these schemata to actual instances. The ability to realise particular meanings, solve particular problems, by relating them to schematic formulae stored as knowledge, constitutes ... capacity. Capacity ... can be understood as the ability to solve problems and, equivalently, to make meanings by interpreting a particular instance ... as

related to some formula, thereby assimilating the instance into a pre-existing pattern of knowledge.
(Widdowson 1983: 106)

Widdowson thus wants to identify language use with processes of understanding (and it is noticeable that although Piaget is not referred to in his book, terms like 'accommodation' and 'assimilation' from his school of psychology recur), and to tie language for specific purposes to general processes of learning. In this sense, his book is an interesting example of a major theorist of ESP repudiating specificity and subsuming its requirements under the concerns of general education. He thus proposes a sophisticated theoretical basis for the argument that what is distinctive about ESP is the homogeneity of the groups in which learners are taught (i.e. an administrative matter) rather than linguistic or educational principles, that the principles of ESP are the principles of good education, and vice-versa.

We can acknowledge that there is a tension between Swales' concept of 'genre' and Widdowson's desire to impose a neo-Piagetian construct on linguistic differences without accepting that either does justice to the interaction between Swales' pragmatic and Widdowson's mathetic concerns. Educational institutions do not operate in a cultural vacuum, and they both reflect and contribute to their cultures. They reflect these not just in their physical and organizational structures, but also through the disciplinary constructs that are made manifest in the behaviour of teachers and students alike. But precisely because they are made manifest in individual behaviour, the manifestations are modified all the time, accidentally (as in the 'history' of the abstract for my original lecture discussed above), and deliberately, as when individuals decide to modify inherited expectations in the interests of a desired ideological shift.

Second language classrooms raise this problem particularly acutely, for the code is specifically the object of study, so we should consider the problem in that context with some care.

Understanding in second language classrooms

We should note that, in order to make the differences between the learning conditions of first and second languages as clear as possible, this discussion will be based on a stark distinction between first and second language learning which is not always justifiable. However, for most classrooms (where second languages are being learnt in the formal education system) these generalizations seem helpful.

Differences between first and second language learning are of three main kinds.

First, some derive automatically from the fact that second languages are second languages. Learners are already lingual when they approach their second language; they were not when they approached the first. Because we already know language in general through our first language, we can:

1 Draw upon strategies for first language acquisition
2 Draw upon knowledge of probable language systems
3 Draw upon knowledge of how language operates socially, etc.

Second, some derive from the fact that second language learners are older than when they acquired their mother tongues, and thus will be more likely to:

4 Think and talk about learning processes
5 Use conscious memorizing strategies
6 (Perhaps) operate substantially through reading and writing, etc.

Third, some derive inevitably from the social organization of the school. Schools are public places, whereas homes and families are private. Although the effects can be reduced, this difference is in principle unresolvable because it derives from the fact that schooling will always be something that parents and the state have opted for, so learners will be compelled to attend. Thus interaction in school is with people who:

7 Have a professional rather than a personal relationship
8 Are paid to diagnose progress, and notice errors
9 Expect active and efficient participation, discourage opting out, etc.

These elements, and a range of others that are not necessary for establishing the principle, constitute the personal and social settings within which second language understanding occurs. However, they can all be manipulated to varying degrees by teachers and learners alike. Thus pedagogic decisions will determine to what extent explicit attention to first language strategies or forms is called upon, how much reading or memorizing is encouraged, and how punitive the attitude to errors will be. What orientations teachers and learners take to questions such as these will influence the 'culture' of the classroom, just as much as cultural elements in the content or subject matter of the linguistic material provided. Our earlier discussion of categories for analysis of classroom processes provides the key operational terms by which such 'culture' is created and adjusted.

Such arguments may convince us that language teachers habitually operate with non-linguistic as well as linguistic categories, but this could simply be a quirk of pedagogical history. To argue that this is significant for our understanding of 'understanding' requires a more explicit link with theoretical discussion. In the rest of this chapter, I want to provide stronger support for the claim that understanding in educational settings demands a model that is much wider than can be provided by linguistics alone.

The limits of linguistic analysis

It has been claimed throughout this chapter that language use is motivated behaviour. A key question for any linguistic analysis is the relationship between the categories of description provided by the linguist and the categories (if any) that are relevant to the participants in the interaction. While linguists may produce conveniently memorable category systems that have value for packaging descriptions to be read by other linguists, they cannot claim any explanatory value for these until a relationship has been established with the functioning of the human minds that participate in the interaction being described, as Taylor and Cameron point out at the end of a highly critical survey of category systems for conversational analysis:

> Because of the perceived simplicity and systematicity of formalized descriptions, it is a common (but lamentable) tendency to attribute knowledge of the formulae to the actors whose behaviour was at first the object of formal description. Then, it is an equally common practice to make the epistemological leap of assuming that the formulae actually govern the production of the behaviour itself i.e. to equate descriptive formulae with normative rules.
> (Taylor and Cameron 1987: 161)

And, we might add, it is common to believe that teaching the descriptive rules is to teach the means of generating the behaviour itself.

They attribute the weaknesses of many descriptive studies to the presumption that speakers and hearers see their shared conversation in the same way, failing to recognize that individuals have different and competing agendas in their social interactions. These differences manifest themselves over extended periods of contact, and constitute themselves part of the shared experience of colleagues and friends. And there is a sense in which teachers are both colleagues of pupils (at least in the sense that they share much of their working lives in compulsory contact with them), and also friends (in the sense that successful relationships depend on a contact that is more than merely professional consultation). But the numbers of participants involved, and the opportunities for competing and conflicting agendas, are greater in the classroom than in most normal contexts. How teachers and learners achieve mutual understanding is the subject of the next section.

Understanding in the classroom

In an extended study of primary classrooms, Edwards and Mercer (1987) drew on the ethnomethdological tradition to show how 'common knowledge' is constructed through pedagogic interaction. 'Overt messages,' they claim, '... are only a small part of the total communication ... context and continuity are essential considerations in the study of discourse' (1987: 160). Context, as they define it, consists of any elements invoked by any participant, and consequently 'participants' conceptions of each other's mental contexts may be wrong or, more likely, only partially right ... any physical set of circumstances could lend itself to an infinity of possible shared conceptions and relevances' (1987: 161). Thus 'context' connects with one of the key problems in interpretation: recognizing the cultural relationships between what is referred to, as well as the linguistic relationships between elements in the linguistic system. Speech does not consist only of linguistic items, for Swift was right in *Gulliver's Travels*, and all speakers carry not only the language system, but also, like the inhabitants of Lagado, everything to which the language refers, though we do it in our lexicon rather than by carrying the referents themselves. A child's 'box' encompasses that child's 'boxness' and all the relationships entailed by that concept, just as my 'freedom' encompasses characteristics that people of different political persuasions will exclude from theirs. Dostoyevsky's 'Catholic' is not the Pope's, any more than the recent equation of 'democracy' with 'free markets' rather than with—say—'equality of opportunity' is the same concept as the 'democracy' of political discussion 25 years ago. It is not the words that are under dispute, but all the potential associations of the concepts to which the words refer. In so far as concepts are socially constructed, words and meanings will have multi-valenced relationships, and the points of contact will constantly shift over time, across speakers, and according to perceived addressor-addressee conventions within the repertoire of a single speaker. Thus, as ever, it seems easier to demonstrate the impossibility of communication than the possibility. Yet none the less we do communicate.

This paradox is resolvable by recognizing the point where this chapter started. Communication does not consist of identical aims, identically formulated. Identity confuses the issue. Communication occurs as a reflection of individuals' willingness to stay in contact with each other, and some of the mechanisms for doing this can be charted, as Grice indicates.

As Edwards and Mercer show, teachers create a joint context for educational activity. A major means of doing this is to create a common, shared knowledge, relying on an implicit framework which is created in the classroom.

Learners rely on 'educational ground rules' with both social and cognitive functions. These incorporate both social conventions for the presentation of knowledge and also sets of procedures for solving problems. But they tend to remain implicit, and are rarely brought out into the open. Further, some of the knowledge required of learners is routinized and ritualized, while other knowledge, not so constrained in its function, relies on principles for explanation and reflection (Edwards and Mercer 1987: 162). Picking up on traditions deriving from Vygotsky via Mehan (1979) and Bruner (1986), they emphasize a tension between the needs to induct children into 'an established, ready-made culture' and to develop 'creative and autonomous participants in a culture which is not ready-made but continually in the making' (Edwards and Mercer 1987: 164). We have already seen this conflict in our discussion both of ESP and the nature of language. But what is helpful is the insistence of Vygotsky and Bruner on the falseness of the dichotomy, because both culture and education are processes with future orientation, and processes which require a degree of distancing by learners even while the current set of values is being presented. 'Much of the process of education consists of being able to distance oneself in some way from what one knows by being able to reflect on one's own knowledge' (Bruner 1986: 127).

Where would this argument lead us in considering understanding in the second language classroom? It would primarily lead us to ask whether 'context' could be exploited more fully, whether failure to understand was attributable to the inadequacy of the referential framework provided in class. As Edwards and Mercer put it, 'good teaching will be reflexive, sensitive to the possibility of different kinds of understanding' (1987: 167). In second language classrooms the nature of differing understanding for particular cultural and linguistic groups will become crucially important if teachers are to develop the necessary sensitivity to individual needs. Important too will be the relationship between individuals and the different cultural groups to which they attach themselves, or to which they inherit a traditional attachment.

But this argument also has implications for research in applied linguistics, as well as in psychology. The value of experimentation, or of formally structured non-real-world encounters, will be much less than the value of studies of situated discourse, both in and out of school. The development of shared understanding, rather than shared linguistic systems, will become a much more important object of study, and the emphasis will have to be on knowledge as process rather than as a body of static information. This will be particularly important if we are to avoid learners simply engaging in an apparently arbitrary process. Edwards and Mercer's comment on primary classrooms will be instantly recognizable to teachers of foreign languages. They write, 'For many pupils, learning from teachers must appear to be a mysterious and arbitrarily difficult process, the solution to which may be to concentrate on trying to do and say what appears to be expected—a basically "ritual" solution' (1987: 169). In contrast, the effort to relate the individual to the social, seeing the relationship between creative interpretation and social convention as the central content of learning, is compatible with what we know of language learning processes in natural circumstances. But the understanding that is thus being developed arises out of the personal histories of class and teacher, and out of the provisional nature of every group-made text, as well as out of the individual contribution of each learner. The language forms that relate to idealizations by linguists will provide snapshots of speech events only, and snapshots cannot illustrate real-time processes. Because meaning is developed in real time (and because classrooms operate with meaning across time), education forces us to re-examine our concept of context.

3 Simplification and the teacher

Introduction

I concluded the previous chapter with a suggestion that we needed to broaden our view of classroom context. Primarily, we need to recognize that the context is created by intentional, purposeful activity, using the fluid and contingent, world-defining language system in which we are unavoidably immersed. Within that context teachers are the major facilitators and organizers. They use both language and culture as constructs. Most distinctively, they are professionals who simplify and classify, for it is the processes of simplification and classification which enable us to cope with the fluidity and potential chaos of experience.

In this chapter, therefore, I shall argue that simplification is a necessary process for all human beings in coping with the conceptual and experiential chaos that surrounds us, but that it is a potentially dangerous process too, because it risks creating categories that rapidly become too insensitive to cope with changing audiences and changing conceptual needs. Developing a capacity to distinguish between necessary simplification and necessary problematization of accepted categories is an important aim for education. I shall then, in the final section, consider some of the simplifying categories we use in teacher education, and their implications for the practice of teaching.

Simplification

Linguistically and conceptually, like any other attempt to communicate with an audience, this book is an exercise in simplification. From the range of possible approaches I am selecting a limited number which are most appropriate for my argument, ordering them in a way that will enable the reader to make sense of what I have to say as easily as possible, and expressing them in language which will be as accessible as possible to my presumed readership. And I am entitled to assume that anyone else whose work I read will have taken it through a similar process. These activities are built into the co-operative principle (see the discussion of Grice's work in Chapter 1) of endeavouring to work with rather than against a listener or reader, and derive directly from our assumptions about the need to communicate, to persuade, to clarify, and to convert.

If we look at basic manuals for teaching, we find that very similar processes are advised. A popular research-based book on *Classroom Teaching Skills*, for example, includes a classification for 'explanation' which mentions *inter alia* a series of planning strategies:

> Analyse topic into main parts, or 'keys'.
> Establish links between parts.
> Determine rules (if any) involved.
> Specify kind(s) of explanation required.
> Adapt plan according to learner characteristics.
> (Brown and Armstrong 1984: 123)

At least four of these may be related to general discussion of the notion of simplification. The concept of 'main parts' involves a selection and classification of significant elements, a highlighting of sub-components that organizes the stream of experience into socially constructed categories for easier comprehension. The establishment of 'links' similarly attempts to reintegrate the separated elements with a clearly identified set of connecting categories, while the determination of 'rules' is an attempt to impose a helpful pattern on experience. The last two elements are less obviously simplification strategies in their own right, but they shift attention from the topic to the form of presentation. The specification of the kind of explanation is perhaps a meta-activity for the teacher—a classification as a device for adopting a communication strategy. But the adaptation of the plan according to learner characteristics reflects the relationship between choices about the code and the nature of the addressee; what is being identified is a discourse strategy. It is also of course a strategy aimed at a simplified 'learner', for teachers typically address groups, not individuals, and every plan, even for an individualized classroom, presumes one or more generalized 'typical learners'. This is why the issue of the relationship between learners and groups, raised at the end of Chapter 2, is so important.

Although these categories do not derive from a discussion of 'simplification', there is a clear relationship between one of the central activities of teaching and the concept of simplification as described by linguists (see Tickoo 1993, for example). The main purpose of this chapter is to consider the role of simplification as a fundamental communication—or even thinking—strategy, particularly for teaching.

Linguists and simplicity

There are three major ideas underlying the explanation strategies isolated above. First there is the principle of selection, second that of coherence by creating 'links' and 'rules', and third that of adaptation to audience. Examples that may be taken from the history of applied linguistics relate to these quite closely.

To give only one striking example, the structure of artificial languages may reflect each of the first two characteristics, but also deliberately sacrifice the third in the desire to avoid the cultural closeness that some supporters of world peace feel inhibits understanding. Applied and descriptive linguists (whether professionals like Quirk 1982: 37–53, or amateurs like Gowers 1954) who concern themselves with simplification movements, will use selection procedures that depend on a view of internal linguistic coherence with the minimal number of usable elements. They thus willingly sacrifice adaptability to varied audiences in the interests of broader communication. In essence they are bidding for a large-scale homogeneous audience, whether it is an appeal to 'the plain man' (Gowers) or to 'international English-users' (Quirk). The fact that these concepts are a simplification, or a stereotyping based on many different individuals, is precisely what makes some commentators uncertain about their claims (see the debate between Quirk 1990 and Kachru 1991 in *English Today*). Similar points about the value of general but simplified principles have been made with reference to classroom second language development (Ellis 1984: 60–1), or children's L2 acquisition (Fillmore 1979: 211). But simplification procedures, while widely used, have immense importance when there are asymmetrical power relations, as in teaching.

Simplification as a teaching strategy

There is a lexical set that is rarely seen as coherent, but which is of immense importance in teaching. It includes the verbs 'simplify', 'generalize', 'stereotype', and 'caricature'. The first two appear together in the same section of the *Longman Lexicon of Contemporary English* (McArthur 1981, section N63), but 'caricature' there is linked with features like 'mockery', and 'stereotype' does not appear at all. If we summarize relevant *Oxford Advanced Learner's Dictionary* definitions of these (Hornby 1995) in the same order, we see the progression:

1   Simplify: make easy to do or understand
2   Generalize: draw a general conclusion from a particular set of examples
3   Stereotype: fixed idea or image that many people have of a particular type of person … but which is often not true in reality
4   Caricature: a picture, description, or impression of somebody/something that makes them look funny or ridiculous by exaggerating certain characteristics.

Processes of making general statements, of fixing and formalizing, and ultimately of stressing particular features for particular effects are inherent in the simplification process, but they also have inherent risks.

Thus simplification results in a reliance on generalization; generalization can easily degenerate into stereotyping, and insensitive stereotyping rapidly becomes caricature, with associated implications of mockery that are offensive to victims.

The tension for the teacher is between quantity and quality. A key feature of linguistic simplification is reduction in quantity, of sentence length, of vocabulary size, of phonemic range (Ferguson 1977). But this principle cannot be achieved without qualitative decisions being made about the generalizability of particular items. We reduce to the most salient (or functionally generalizable) elements in the discourse; otherwise we lose the overall structure and the discourse becomes incoherent. Thus making a simple statement means acting on generalizations.

Linguistically, these may well become stereotyped, so that the generalized features are adopted regardless of the particular referent (so all Africans were '+ black', and all nurses in British society were '+ female' for many British English speakers pre-1970). When ideologically convenient, such stereotypes become conventional caricatures, so that *Carry On* films can portray nurses as inherently female and sexy, and early twentieth-century children's comics could portray Africans as inherently black and different from the presumed reader. Only after substantial ideological shifts do these caricatures give way to emphasis on either what is shared with the reader (Africans or nurses are people like members of other groups—the readers of the text), or what is distinctive about individual members, or separate sub-groups, of the group being generalized about (some Africans are white or brown; some nurses are male).

This combination of factors is a key point. Generalizations affecting people are made about outgroups; they have a distancing effect. 'The British are Christians' is a simplification because non-Christian Britons feel ignored, but as a generalization from the perspective of Iran or India it has some simplification value because a larger proportion of British people would classify themselves as Christian than would be true in either of those countries. The lifestyle and assumptions of the British are undoubtedly historically Christian rather than Islamic or Hindu. We live by accepting generalizations as simplifications precisely because complexifications are inefficient until we are deeply embedded in the group being generalized about. 'The British are Christians' is not a useful comment in Manchester, but may be in Meshed or Madras.

Thus processes of simplification, whether linguistic, discoursal, or conceptual, involve tacit or explicit judgements about the salience of particular features in relation to the purpose of the discourse, which in turn is responsive to the nature of the audience being addressed. We might go further, and argue that we only establish coherence of viewpoint by creating saliences and debating their appropriateness. The debate about the canon in contemporary literary theory is partly about salience—which are the 'key', 'emblematic', 'resonant' texts for today, which ones encapsulate greatest value for our current world view? Whether your choice is *Ulysses*, *Tristram Shandy*, or *Come Dancing* by Victor Sylvester (a manual on how to ballroom dance), to cite various suggestions from a *Times Literary Supplement* debate in January 1992, depends on a view of which generalizes most usefully to other matters that concern you. (See Chapter 7 for further discussion of this issue.)

What I am arguing, then, is that simplification is a process that enables us to concentrate on what is currently important and to ignore what is currently irrelevant. It prevents clutter in the mind, but risks introducing irrelevant clutter of its own. The reason for this is that generalizations always need to be contextually justified, and when contexts change the justification changes or disappears. Yesterday's generalizations become today's stereotypes and tomorrow's caricatures. Our capacity to process and select concepts becomes dysfunctional, and in extreme cases racist or xenophobic, if it is not accompanied by a capacity to recognize changing contexts, and serious thinking requires a constant internal debate between the demands of quantity and quality.

Implications for practice

I have suggested that the simplification debate, which might at first sight seem to be a technical one for linguists, is bound up with larger issues of comprehension and communication. Teachers of course operate with great power in both these spheres. The centrality of explanation involves them in frequent (and usually implicit) decision-making about salience and generalizability, both conceptually and linguistically. But they are also, as a profession, unusually exposed to cultural variation. Teachers, unusually, operate with many large groups of people in the course of a single working day. Their role is to communicate effectively, and to cause effective communication within these groups—and each group has to be generalized about in planning, in execution of the lesson, in making judgements for assessment purposes, and in dealing with the considerable affective demands that insecure learners make on their teachers. It is little surprise that a process of simplification and routinization is important in general teacher thinking (see Calderhead 1988) or in language teachers' methodological practice (Mitchell and Johnstone 1986).

I would wish to propose that the conceptual tension explored in this chapter is very important for teacher education. The tension between simplification as quantitative reduction (or economy with a smaller lexicon or a limited set of linguistic structures) and simplification as qualitative reduction (or insensitivity to audience by stereotyping) lies behind much trainee teacher failure to meet the expectations of their classes. This formulation may seem a surprising way of looking at the problem, but it should be clear from the argument so far that the quality of conceptualization is dependent on the cultural base from which the reader, listener, or learner is operating. In so far as teachers are necessarily transmitters of culture, awareness of the relationship between the conceptual frameworks of learners and those underlying all generalizations, simplifications, and explanations provided by the teaching process will be crucial. We have to simplify, both in code and in content—otherwise we cannot communicate. But we need to learn to use such processes with skill and sensitivity.

So all simplification betrays somebody; but having no simplification betrays everybody to confused communication. Teachers have to learn to resolve this paradox in their professional practice.

Simplification and categories in teacher education

Let me start this section by referring to a philosophical discussion which exactly identifies the problem I wish to examine. In a *Times Literary Supplement* book review, the philosopher Mary Midgley comments:

> Every large practical problem has its conceptual aspect, which is just what a philosophical training ought to make us able to detect. Because the conceptual system is a continuous whole, this will lead us to the vast questions in the end. But we cannot do effective business with those unless we have approached them by the right path—unless we have picked out the relevant conceptual issues in the first place and have watched out all through the journey for flaws in the system of ideas. The outcome does not depend just on a few abstract concepts ... any more than it depends only on the facts. It involves a whole labyrinth of intermediate ideas by which we group and interpret the facts. And this is where we normally get lost.
> (Midgley 1984: 363)

This section is concerned with the 'labyrinth of intermediate ideas' in discussions of language teaching.

It is a truism as well as a paradox that language controls us as much as we control language. The very process of making a definition, or the explaining of a position, isolates us from other equally valuable and relevant positions or terms. Consider some of the dichotomies usefully explored in various disciplines of relevance to language teachers: 'competence/performance', 'competence/communicative competence', 'acquisition/learning', 'elaborated/restricted', 'accommodation/assimilation', 'illocution/perlocution', and so on. Each of these oppositions was developed as part of an argument aimed at a particular group of workers within a particular field; each of them has been taken over at some point, for better or worse, by language teachers, teacher trainers, and advisers.

The first point I want to make is that such terms cannot be transferred without risk, for they were not intended to solve teaching problems specifically, but problems in their own fields. They also vary, of course, in the extent to which they are based on empirical work or on logical analysis. Krashen (1979), for example, claims that the 'acquisition/learning' distinction as he formulates it is a legitimate extrapolation from research evidence that derives directly from empirical studies. On the other hand Bernstein's 'elaborated/restricted codes' were based on abstract model construction and hypothesizing which was only subsequently (and then only slightly) put to any kind of empirical test (Bernstein 1971). Other major distinctions, such as 'competence/communicative competence', can scarcely be put to any kind of empirical test at all. They represent large-scale formulations whose value will be seen in the extent to which, actually or metaphorically, they are taken up by scholars and used as basic elements in their thinking.

All of these distinctions have value, whether true or false, valid or invalid, in so far as they assist the process of clarifying our ideas, and lead to arguments by which they can be rejected, refined, or accepted for the time being as useful. But the problem within teacher education is that these are not categories which teachers themselves, on the basis of their own professional experience and needs, can easily address directly. Few teachers are able to survey the evidence for acquisition and learning and decide the validity or otherwise of Krashen's arguments; for that they have to rely on his own surveys (Krashen 1981, for example). They have neither the training, the time, nor necessarily the inclination to enter the conceptual worlds of sociological theory, or of philosophical linguistics, or of psychology, in order to understand fully the bases of the arguments which led to categories being established in the ways they have been. Note that writing this is not in any way to denigrate teachers' willingness to think or read or study. We all have the same problem as soon as we move out of our immediate professional spheres. Anyone working in our field soon discovers that the very term 'language' raises quite different expectations to linguists, who have usually thought in terms of rule-governed generative systems, to psychologists, who have been more concerned with the ability to use symbols for the expression of meaning, to sociologists, who are more concerned with the ideological implications of structures of shared meanings. All three of these specifications are simplifications of what has been written in these fields, but the general tendency will be recognized by any observer, I think. Such differences in view surface as soon as we have arguments about (to give only one example) the extent to which chimpanzees have a language faculty.

If we are not careful, the effect of the analysis Midgley calls for will be to downgrade the professional understanding of teachers at the expense of that of theorists, whether linguists, applied linguists, or scholars in other disciplines, for teachers risk being expected to receive categories already validated by others, without being able to evaluate them by procedures which derive directly from the experience of being a teacher. Nor is this a problem which applies only to teaching. It lies at the very heart of applied linguistics, in so far as our discipline claims to be problem-orientated. Every practical problem requires categories relevant to its solution. If language is central to the problem (that is, if it is an applied linguistic problem), the categories referring to language must be directly usable within the problem area. But, if such categories are to be principled, they must be explicitly relatable to appropriate theory. And appropriate theory will be much broader than linguistic theory alone, for the context of real world problems, as we have already seen, is much broader than can be addressed by linguistic theory alone.

For teachers, whose main applied linguistic problem area is language teaching methodology, this means that methodological categories need to be simultaneously capable of being related to current theory, and to be directly interpretable in classroom strategies which can be planned and adjusted by teachers for the benefit of learners. Categories will therefore change, as our understanding of language and the world changes, and also as new generations change their demands on education in general and language education in particular. As in most spheres, the categories taken for granted at particular times may be the greatest barrier to improvement of practice, for they may act as blinkers, closing relevant options, rather than as telescopes, focusing attention on the most important areas to be concentrated on. A good example of the latter category-blockage is the strength of the concept of 'the four skills' in language teaching. I have discussed this in more detail elsewhere (Brumfit 1983, 1984: 69–71; see also Widdowson 1978), and I shall only refer to the issue briefly here.

The conventional set of categories is: 'listening', 'speaking', 'reading', and 'writing'. Built into this is an order of priority, and a view of the separate status of these activities which risks interfering with teachers' ability to consider language as genuine communication. Particularly damaging is the separation of 'listening' and 'speaking', and the implication that 'conversation/argument/ discussion' can be separated into two independent components, or that listening in conversation is the same as listening to extended monologue. In a discussion of skills, Welford notes that 'where the whole task is a closely coordinated activity… the evidence suggests that it is better to tackle the task as a whole', for:

> Any attempt to divide it up tends to destroy the proper coordination of action and subordination of individual actions to the requirements of the whole … and this outweighs any advantage there might be in mastering different portions of the task separately.
> (Welford 1968: 291)

Nevertheless, generations of language teachers have learnt in their training that the most basic categories for describing what they are doing are these separate four. Furthermore, many teacher trainers will testify to writing classes that make no acknowledgement of the structure of written discourse, but are versions of copying, or repetition of structural patterns through the written mode: 'writing' becomes a physical act rather than an organization of discourse.

By concentrating the core of language teaching on the overt acts rather than on the role that those acts play in motivated linguistic behaviour, whether communication, or conceptual self-clarification, or expression, these categories distract teachers from a concern with language acquisition to a concern with pre-acquisition activities which are only a small part of the total process. To be effective, successful language teaching has had to work against, rather than with this categorization.

What categories would provide a stronger base for effective language learning? The following set seems better:

conversation/discussion
comprehension (either speech or writing)
extended writing
extended speech.

Such a set can be defended, though there are still a number of problems, for 'extended writing' does not incorporate all modes of written discourse (for example it excludes email, which may well deserve consideration in some language courses). We can defend the position that planning strategies for extended writing and extended speaking will be similar, but that there are specialized realization skills necessary for both separately which will not be called upon in conversation. But a case can be made for the first three of these categories being more satisfactory as basic categories for general school language teaching than the original four, with 'extended speech' as an optional extra.

Similar points can be made about the ordering implicit in the division of lesson plans into 'presentation stages' and 'practice stages', or writing exercises into 'controlled', 'guided', and 'free'. The ordering in each case has a learning theory built in which conflicts with current views of the nature of acquisition, which is seen as more holistic and tentative than these imply. Textbooks throughout the world (there are so many that it would be invidious to single out particular ones for mention) are written as if every lesson must include new elements for presentation, so that teaching becomes top-heavy with teacher-dominated material, and the opportunities for practice, let alone the much more important naturalistic use of language, are severely restricted. Furthermore, the assumption is that practice will follow from presentation, that the latter cannot be an inductive pulling together of what has already been used and dimly perceived to be systematic, but must be a deductive and controlling mechanism in which the power and knowledge emanates from the teacher and the textbook. The effect of such a strong categorization on thinking teachers is twofold. First, it leads them to identify a conflict with the notion of self-construction of language-systems for communicative purposes (see Chapter 2) so that there is a damaging mismatch between their beliefs about acquisition and the methodological categories that they have to live with. Second, it may lead to inappropriate rejection of the whole idea of presentation and practice, so that any organization of the class at all with clearly structured procedures is opposed because of weaknesses in the categorization system.

The classification of writing activities implies an inappropriate progression, for 'free' activities are rare outside the creative writing class, and the difficulty of working in a guided situation, as when we write a paper for an academic conference, minutes of a meeting, essays for supervisors at university, theses, or reports for newspapers, is in many ways greater than that found in creative writing (though that, too, has its constraints which have to be crafted into the structure). 'Controlled' writing activities, in contrast, are scarcely more than pre-writing activities, since the concern is exclusively with the code at the expense of communication and a motivated organization of discourse. All three types of activity may well still have a valuable place in effective pedagogy, but as a classification system, they imply a false progression towards 'freedom', and a false equality of importance between the three separate types of exercise.

Nor is this kind of problem restricted to hangovers from pre-communicative teaching assumptions. The term 'communicative activity' risks being equally unhelpful for it rarely makes the crucial discrimination between an exercise motivated by the teacher, and one with intrinsic, non-linguistic motivation of the same kind that would apply in mother-tongue language use.

I hope this very brief account makes clear some of the difficulties with conventional categories. This is not, of course, an argument against such categories—without categories we cannot carry on discussion and improve either our thinking or our practice—but it is an argument for an explicit relationship between such category systems and relevant theory. This may sometimes require intermediate categories which enable teachers to make basic classifications which can be theoretically motivated, superordinate to those of direct classroom practice, or of greater generalizability than many of those so far considered.

I have already argued (Brumfit 1984) for the value of the distinction between 'accuracy' and 'fluency' (or language work for pedagogic feedback, and language work for an external, real-life-like purpose). This distinction has both a theoretical dimension and direct practical implications, because the relative proportions of time and activity spent on each of these allows argument about fundamental views on the nature of language acquisition in direct relation to explicit classroom acts.

Another category system which has similar value in the teaching of literature is the distinction between text–text study and text–world study (Brumfit 1981). Other categories with genuine theoretical and practical dimensions include Rivers' 'skill-using/skill-getting' (Rivers 1972) and Widdowson's 'usage/use' (Widdowson 1978). In support of all of these a research literature can be cited, while distinctions in the structuring of the curriculum, teaching materials, or classroom events follow directly from them.

It is not my purpose here, though, simply to list useful categories and assert their value. The major point I want to make is an epistemological one, and relates to the relative statuses of the two activities teaching and applied or educational linguistics. The claim that all language teachers are applied linguists is as vacuous, or imperialist, as the rarer but not unknown claim that all language users are applied linguists. Being a good teacher is never exactly the same thing as producing a body of knowledge about teaching; there are many things we can do well that we cannot fully understand. The accumulated professional wisdom of teachers is a kind of understanding, and so are the accumulated survival techniques of the profession. So too are intelligent conceptual analysis, empirical research, and experimental results. All are valuable, and all are partial. But the intention of applied linguistics is presumably to produce insightful descriptions and explanations of the conditions of language in use in problematic areas. By doing this it contributes to linguistics by validating some concepts, questioning others, and generally providing both a renewal of connection for linguistic theory, and contributions to the problematic area itself by clarifying the underlying pattern of assumptions held by its practitioners. And by doing this, applied linguistics cannot avoid becoming interdisciplinary, for the problems arise out of language in social or psychological practice.

But practitioners in problem areas do not want only to understand, they want to practise effectively, and for this they need their own instrumental criteria for the concepts and categories that they use. The argument that categories should make sense to practising teachers is not primarily an argument about public relations, 'how to get our good ideas accepted' (as criticisms of educational linguistic research often imply: for example, Cheshire 1996), but about validity. Ideas that do not catch on reveal a mismatch between the practices of one set of professionals and another. In principle either could be wrong, for the temptation to do no more than cope administratively is as strong for teachers as the temptation to do no more than cope theoretically is for applied linguists. But the area of mismatch provides a locus for the most interesting practical/theoretical questions, and deserves investigation. Certainly, failures to accept research categories or research findings cannot be lightly dismissed as stubborn and reactionary resistance to change by unenlightened practitioners. Equally, though, examination of the area of mismatch may possibly reveal factors that cause resistance to change, and judgements will need to be made about the justification or otherwise of such resistance.

Underlying the argument of this section is a view of the nature of teaching which should be made explicit, so that it can be criticized and rejected or improved upon. The final part of this chapter will attempt to clarify this view.

Teachers deal with people, just as politicians or town planners do, and unlike, say, doctors and psychiatrists, they deal with people whose crises, if any, are externally imposed rather than resulting from internal disorder. Most other professionals rarely meet clients except at times of crisis when they have defined themselves as needing (for example) medical or legal support. In contrast, the vast majority of people teachers deal with are normal people in normal conditions. The major consequence of this is that experimentation has to be extremely careful, with extremely sensitive feedback mechanism, if it is not to be irresponsible and dangerous. Because we cannot predict our future knowledge, we cannot predict the consequences of our actions, so that methodological reform is more analogous to reform of electoral procedures (proportional representation, for example, rather than a straight victory for the candidate with the most votes) than it is to the application of scientific principles under controlled conditions. Furthermore, the people who spend far and away the most time with learners are teachers—far more time than researchers or advisers or policy makers. People in the first two categories can offer breadth of observation of learners in many situations, to complement the depth of most individual teachers' immersion in one set of local conditions. But the subtle monitoring of change, the recognition that— especially in language teaching—learning and self-consciousness, development and identity go together, the sensitivity to the individual rather than to the group or the stereotype, the inconsistency of observable behaviour that necessarily accompanies responsiveness to personal needs, all this can only come from the teacher. Without such close attention, change in classrooms will remain insensitive and crudely manipulative. Only teachers are in a position to determine whether modes of interaction are to be continued or discontinued, whether change is advantageous or dangerous, whether the class is stagnating or maturing. And all this of course places a great responsibility on teachers. Most teachers are all too aware of this responsibility, and even more aware of the administrative, financial, emotional and personal constraints which prevent them from performing such a demanding task as effectively as they would like to.

But the nature of teaching also places a great responsibility on advisers, educational theoreticians, and applied linguists. We have a responsibility to address, and if possible resolve the conceptual confusions referred to in the quotation with which I started this section, but to do this in terms which make sense of the experience of teachers, as well as the experience of researchers and theoreticians. We have to offer categories which teachers can reject on the basis of teaching experience, without having to become self-taught and inefficient theoreticians or researchers in order to do so. That is, we cannot say in effect, 'These are categories we can vouch for on the basis of the best available research and discussion; take them and implement them as best you can'. We can say instead that there are some sets of categories which (on the basis of our own extensive previous experience of teaching, or of extensive collaboration and consultation with practising teachers) should be considered by teachers because they directly influence classroom planning or improvisation. We have, in other words, in any advisory role to put our conceptual and technical expertise in the service of the different expertise of the people whose work we serve, even when that conflicts with our own hierarchies and academic traditions. For without such a modification there can be no genuine collaboration and our advisory and teacher education communication will be no more than shadow boxing.

I have tried to illustrate some of the difficulties in creating categories which are genuinely practical without being trivial and theoretically valueless. Whether or not the exercise has been done well or badly here, I want to insist in conclusion that it is more important that the service professions for teaching and learning try to create such categories—even if they do it badly—than that they only do the things they can do well already. Without such an effort, allowing theoretical categories to merge with past or present teaching experience, our understanding of teaching and learning will be both partially irrelevant, and irrelevantly partial.

Second language learning

4   Teaching communicative competence

Introduction

I now move to the goals of teaching. The term 'communicative competence' still provides the most widely accepted metaphor in current foreign language teaching theory. The purpose of this chapter is to analyse the major features of this concept, and to relate them to the practice of language teaching.

The use of the term is probably more common in applied linguistics than in any other discipline. Although by the mid-1970s reference to 'communicative language teaching' was becoming widespread, a number of writers nearly a decade earlier referred independently to 'communicative competence' specifically in opposition to Chomsky's formal definition of linguistic competence in terms of language structure. In 1965 he distinguished between competence and performance as follows: 'We thus make a fundamental distinction between competence (the speaker-hearer's knowledge of his language) and performance (the actual use of language in concrete situations)' (Chomsky 1965: 4). The reason for alternative formulations being necessary was primarily the problematic nature of the term 'performance', which Chomsky left largely unspecified. It seemed to include not only lapses in performance which result from tiredness or any other inefficient functioning of human speech capacities, but also other apparently rule-governed language activities such as attainment of acceptable speech (Chomsky 1965: 10–15) and stylistic variation (Chomsky 1965: 27).

In effect Chomsky's way of distinguishing between knowledge and performance enabled linguists to continue to analyse idealized language with some clear principles of idealization to refer to. Some linguists, however, denied the usefulness of the distinction. The British linguist, Halliday, for example, comments that if the distinction is simply meant to convey the difference between what can and cannot be described tidily by a grammarian, then it is unnecessary. If, on the other hand, it is meant to establish a major distinction in principle, elevating psychological knowledge above sociolinguistic responsiveness, it is dangerously misleading (Halliday 1970: 145).

Halliday's subsequent work (for example, 1975, 1978) provides an alternative tradition for communicative language teaching to turn to, but it has been less influential in Europe and North America than that associated with the term 'communicative competence'. This tradition accepts the need for a distinction, but tries to refine the definition of both parts by extending 'competence' to cover all rule systems exploited by language users. Such an argument clearly underlies discussion in Wales and Marshall (1966) and Cooper (1968), and the term 'communicative competence' itself is used by Jakobovits (1970), Habermas (1970), Hymes (1972) and Savignon (1972) among others.

Second language teaching

It is interesting to relate these dates to discussion of second language teaching. Oller presented a paper entitled 'Language communication and second language learning' at the AILA Congress in Cambridge in 1969, Candlin presented one on 'Sociolinguistics and communicative language teaching' to the IATEFL Conference in London in 1971 and Widdowson's influential paper 'The teaching of English as communication' was published in *English Language Teaching* in 1972.

Certainly in language teaching there has been a move away from the idea of language as a static, reified system to be learnt, towards a view of communication as a fluid and negotiable system to be performed. In a widely quoted paper Allwright asked 'Are we teaching *language* (for communication)? or Are we teaching *communication* (via language)?' (Allwright 1977: 2). From such a reorientation, various teaching techniques, packaged teaching methods, sets of teaching materials, and views of the learning process were developed. Even though the resulting teaching was highly varied—more a matter of the abstract principles of an 'approach' than the specific prescriptions of a 'method'—there is considerable agreement among methodologists about the desirable changes in teaching method, and preferred justifications for particular language learning strategies.

A large number of commentators have discussed the principles of communicative language teaching. Particular characteristics that have been isolated include the following:

1 A concern to identify the needs of learners and focus on them
2 An emphasis on conceptual structures and speech acts ('notions' and 'functions') in syllabus organization
3 Tolerance of language variation in the classroom, including mixing target language and mother tongue
4 A concern for individualization and autonomous learning
5 A supportive environment, including a reduction of the teacher's role as sole arbiter of correct language
6 Toleration of errors as an inevitable part of the language acquisition process
7 Presentation of language items in context rather than in isolation
8 A concern to use 'authentic' materials (that is, materials not originally constructed for language teaching purposes at all)
9 Techniques that encourage 'natural' language work, especially in oral activity: group- and pair-work, role-play, information-gap exercises.

None of these features, except perhaps the second item on syllabus organization, is unique to communicative language teaching, but all have received greater emphasis as part of this movement than at other times in the recent past. However, the significant point for the history of language teaching may not be these features in themselves so much as the justifications that have been produced in support of them.

It will at once be apparent that these features concentrate on three major aspects of language. First, there is a concern for the learner's individual language needs (1 and 4); second, an unwillingness to use language without immediate 'face' validity and a concern for realistic contexts (2, 7, 8 and 9); and third, a recognition that language use and language learning produce variable levels of response (3, 5, and 6).

These different aspects interact, of course, but they embody a claim that:

1 Different social situations demand different language use
2 Individuals, since they are likely to encounter different social situations, will have differing needs for the kinds of language they require
3 Giving individuals opportunities to develop their own language system, rather than rigidly reproduce a target model, will help them to acquire a flexible system for future use in unpredictable circumstances.

Communicative competence and language teaching

Let us consider these characteristics in relation to the major elements in communicative competence, as these have been proposed by commentators.

The most explicit general discussion of this concept is that of Hymes (1972). In a paper which was circulated in a number of different versions, he concentrates his definition of communicative competence on four major questions:

> I would suggest, then, that for language and for other forms of communication (culture), four questions arise:
>
> 1 Whether (and to what degree) something is formally possible;
> 2 Whether (and to what degree) something is feasible in virtue of the means of implementation available;
> 3 Whether (and to what degree) something is appropriate (adequate, happy, successful) in relation to a context in which it is used and evaluated;
> 4 Whether (and to what degree) something is in fact done, actually performed, and what its doing entails.
>
> (Hymes 1972: 281)

The first of these relates to formal linguistic competence. The second resolves the problem of the utterance which breaks no grammatical rules but which is too complex to process (for example, to cite Canale and Swain's 1980 example, 'the cheese the rat the cat the dog saw chased ate was green'). The third is concerned with language appropriate to context, and the fourth to the probability of occurrence of a particular utterance.

For language teaching, we could comment that the first coincides more or less with the knowledge-orientated traditional views of language acquisition. Most language teaching has assumed that mastery of the idealized system is a necessary pedagogic goal. The second is to a great extent irrelevant to language teaching; in so far as processing constraints are a given, learners are unlikely to be tempted to do what is physically impossible—nor has there been any suggestion that constraints on feasibility vary from one language to another. The concern for what is appropriate is central to all three of the features of communicative language teaching referred to above. And with the fourth there appears to be some confusion in discussion over what exactly Hymes means. Canale and Swain (1980: 16) claim that this is simply a matter of the relative rarity of the utterance ('God be with you' versus 'Goodbye'). Hymes himself (1972: 286) relates this to several features: the notion of frequency of occurrence, the need to allow for authenticated occurrences that have not been predicted by rules for each of the other three, and (associated presumably with this latter feature) the need to allow for the language to change by having new forms. However, he claims somewhat strangely that 'something may be possible, feasible and appropriate and not occur', which raises the problem of how appropriacy can be evaluated for a non-occurring item. But this is a technical discussion which would be inappropriate to pursue further here. For our argument, it is enough to note that a concern for the unpredictable in language use and language development may be related to this characteristic of communicative competence, and that unpredictability has been made a key feature by some language teaching theorists.

Hymes has been primarily concerned to clarify the role of models in linguistic study. In a more recent commentary on the issue of communicative competence, he states:

> There appear to be three choices for linguistics. One is to consider linguistics to be what in one respect it always has been, the skilled study of the structure and history of particular languages, language families, and language groups. A second choice is to accept the expansion of scope of recent years in terms of the foundations ... which Chomsky has sought to give it. A third choice is to regard the expansion of scope of recent years as requiring foundations deeper than those that Chomsky is prepared to recognize, foundations that include the social sciences and social life. From this third point of view, the expansion of scope would not be a reaching out, as it were, but a reaching down. What one reaches is not a periphery or an implementation but a deeper grounding. (Hymes 1985: 11)

In this discussion, then, the rules of use that are being sought have a role in defining the nature of language. However, in so far as they remain to be formulated, their usefulness to applications like language teaching can only be metaphorical. We may wish to act as if something is true, but the opportunities to test and falsify specific proposals have been too few for us to act with total confidence.

The most extensive paper that has discussed communicative competence from a specifically pedagogic perspective is Canale and Swain's opening article in the first issue of the journal *Applied Linguistics*, in 1980. They survey in greater detail many of the issues touched on in this chapter, and list three areas as a basis for their theoretical framework. These areas are: grammatical competence, sociolinguistic competence, and strategic competence. In a later paper Canale (1983) subdivided sociolinguistic competence into sociolinguistic and discourse competences, and this fourfold formulation has become the preferred basis for subsequent discussion. Grammatical competence relates approximately to Hymes' 'possibility', and sociolinguistic competence to Hymes' 'appropriacy', but the other two are new elements. 'Discourse competence' refers to the ability to construct cohesive and coherent texts in writing or in speech, and 'strategic competence' to strategies for resolving communication difficulties.

It is clear that this breakdown relates much more closely to the features of communicative language teaching listed earlier: all nine of them can be used in support of each of the four elements in Canale and Swain's formulation.

Recent discussion has been more concerned with the implications of these models for testing and measurement (Bachman 1990; McNamara 1996). Bachman (p.87) refers to 'organisational competence', which subdivides into 'grammatical' and 'textual competence', and 'pragmatic competence', which subdivides into 'illocutionary' and 'sociolinguistic competence'. But, as McNamara (p.88) points out, while there are difficulties about achieving Hymes' desire for a model of the ability to use language, the problem will not go away.

The conceptual problem

In fact, there is a major problem with these and all similar formulations for our practices as language teachers. In the rest of this chapter I propose to examine this, and some of the implications it has for us.

The problem is that models of this kind appear static when they are used to specify language teaching goals. This is partly because it is not always clear what purpose they are intended to serve. Are they specifications that will enable us retrospectively to describe what people have done with language—in the past? Or are they actually prescriptions for the future in all but name? Are they the bases for pedagogic devices—instruments to be discarded as soon as the acquisition task has been completed, or are they necessary permanent elements in the equipment of the language-user? Whereas Chomsky's hypothesis is that the human mind, at its current evolutionary stage, is constructed in such a way as to necessitate acquisition of particular grammars appropriate for any natural language, built into the notion of 'communicative competence' is a view of negotiable and socially constructed interaction.

Let me illustrate what I mean by proposing a slight modification to the various formulations so far discussed. There is a sense in which both Hymes, and Canale and Swain, seem to see the language user/learner as a passive victim of the inherited rule systems of the past—there seems to be an almost Whorfian determinism in the discussion of apparently fixed rules waiting to be described. What happens if we suggest that users construct their own responses to rule systems—that probabilities in language are only there because of tacit agreement by language users, including language learners?

If we re-establish linguistic free will:

1 'Possibility' and 'grammatical competence' become sets of conventions to be negotiated according to the capacity of the language to express adequately the needs of the language user. In practice this is unlikely to mean that most users or learners will produce substantial variation from normal usage, but it may mean

(a) that variation in the form of certain types of item will occur fairly frequently: for example, minor syntactic variation (like using *Learning How to Mean* as the title of Halliday's 1975 book, to express a generalization about learning by violating the 'rule' that 'mean' must take a direct object), or new coinages ('Ms' or 's/he');

and (b) that foreign learners may in fact reflect in their use of foreign terms, whether 'interference' or false coinages, ideological or cultural needs that cannot easily be accommodated in current conventional target language (see Brumfit 1978 for an examination of this issue with reference to Chinese and English and Rampton 1995b for a very detailed exploration of second language use as sociolect).

2 'Appropriacy' and 'sociolinguistic competence' will become far more problematic, and much more negotiable. These are the areas of language where there is already wide cultural difference, and where the practice of teaching is most strongly charged with ideology. A language has grammar but it is a culture, not a language, that has conventions of appropriate behaviour, and cultures cross linguistic boundaries. Physicists share many cultural practices across languages to the exclusion of non-physicists who share each individual physicist's languages. Members of religious, political, social, academic or artistic groups will also share cultural practices to the exclusion of their language-sharing brethren, and these practices will be reflected in appropriate local modifications of the language of wider communication. Whose language is the learner to learn? Who says what is polite or rude? Politeness, deference, relevance, emotions, to name only a few of the difficult areas, are all socially constructed concepts. What class, what educational level, what epistemology, what degree of submission or opposition do our statements about language appropriacy impose on learners? The more complex the society, the more likely that there will be many foreign language learners relating to it: the more complex the group the wider the cultural variation. We may, if we wish, oppose variation (and indeed a case can be made for being

parsimonious with tolerance of variety—but that is a moral case, not a linguistic one). What we cannot do is claim that there is an inviolate essence of a language independent of the people who use it. Our defence of a historical and stylistic sense of the nature of any language has to be based on a defence of what it has expressed, and needs to continue to express, not on the linguistic and cultural system in itself.

3 The issue of 'feasibility' will be scarcely changed. There will be many constraints on our capacities to process, recall, and produce language that will have to remain totally outside our control. This area will remain interesting but only marginally relevant to language teaching.

4 'Discourse' and 'strategic competences' will be subject to similar flexibility to that discussed under 2 above. As mentioned in that section, even the nature of relevance is subject to cultural variation, as comparative rhetorical studies have suggested. The kinds of strategic responses that will be required in different circumstances will be dependent on the goodwill, flexibility, and linguistic experience of interlocutors, as well as on general ground rules. It is still an open question to what extent the features referred to in this section and in section 2 really differ massively from culture to culture. Our notion of culture in language teaching often relies on stereotypes, and as we saw in Chapter 3 stereotyping may be dysfunctional. Are there no 'silent' cultures in France, Britain, Germany or the US, or are they restricted (as stereotypes suggest) to Finland or Japan? Is literacy a major language learning determinant for all members of these countries? How homogeneous is any national culture? Is it not possible that the degree of overlap, given goodwill, between any two societies, is greater than the degree of potential incomprehension? (How else can we account for so many successful language learners?)

If the concept of communicative competence is to be applied to language teaching, it must centre on learners, for they are the sole justification for language teaching as a profession. If it centres on learners, it must become a far more dynamic concept than it often appears to be. This is not the place to explore in detail the implications of this for particular societies; indeed, in a sense it would be an impertinence for an outsider to try to do so (for a fuller development of this aspect of the discussion, with a Canadian base, see Ashworth 1985). But the kinds of implications can be listed.

1 Each act of language teaching takes place within a particular social, political, economic, religious and ideological setting. Each act of language teaching is (if the above argument is accepted) an intervention to which learners need to respond. Planning and teacher preparation need to recognize this context, and to ask some of the questions implied by this.

2 Learners are opting for a relationship with some kind of language-using community. What sort is it? What sort is implied by the materials being used? What freedom of choice do the learners have? How rich is the language to which they are exposed?

3 To what extent does the methodology of classroom practice allow learners to be free to use their own language to express themselves as fluently as possible? If it has not proved possible for this to develop to any extent, is it because such a goal is impossible to achieve, or is it because it has not been pursued with great determination? What other means of learning effectively how to vary and develop one's own language can there be, apart from reading, writing, and conversing as naturally, freely, and fluently as one's current language knowledge enables one to?

4 What is the model of the target culture, the original culture, and the learner's position in relation to the target culture, that is presented in written materials provided for language learning?

5 What are the relations between language teachers and the parental and other communities from which their learners come? Who makes the choices about what languages are learnt, who learns them, what is the bias towards oracy and literacy in the programme? And so on.

I do not of course wish to suggest that solutions to these issues can be arrived at easily or without either expertise or careful thought. None the less, they are all areas in which a more learner-centred use of the concept 'communicative competence' would lead us to liaise more closely, analyse more closely, and—perhaps—be more effective and perceptive language teachers. Certainly, if it is to be 'taught', communicative competence has to describe a more dynamic and less passive set of qualities.

5 Language, culture, and English for Academic Purposes

Introduction

The purpose of this chapter is to explore the relationships between language and culture, using overseas learners of English in British higher education as the context for testing out these ideas. They will be used to represent 'other' cultures in order to ground the approach advocated here in a real situation. None the less the principles underlying this approach could be applied similarly to other types of learner.

An immediate problem for British education, when it needs to teach overseas learners, is recognizing the implicit biases of British assumptions about language and language learning. Most people in the world acquire several languages. Although they possess these with varying degrees of competence, most people use several languages in the course of living normal lives, whatever their cultural background. Monolingualism, of the kind that the British educational system tolerated and even encouraged, was to a great extent the product of nineteenth-century nationalism, and the identification of one language with one nation.

Even in Britain, monolingualism may be dying out. The presence in Britain of many speakers of other languages as a result of immigration policies since the Second World War has led to a reconsideration of attitudes towards languages and dialects other than standard English for all groups of language users. Throughout Europe the languages and cultures of minority groups have been seen as important elements in formulating educational policies. Cultural diversity is seen as a legitimate goal for politicians and educationists alike. Thus it is an appropriate time to consider the relationship between culture and language learning. Language can be seen as an agent of major cultural change—a means of freeing repressed groups, or of repressing and marginalizing the small and powerless. As controversies over the role of language study in English teaching and of the role of standard English indicate, language is a major issue in mainstream educational discussion for politicians and journalists; the Swann Report (DES 1985) showed it as a major preoccupation of almost all minority groups in the UK.

Language has simultaneously a public and a private face. On the one hand, it is the most subtle means for our classification of the world, our clarification of our own ideas, our establishment of self-identity. On the other, it is the major means of communication with other people that we possess, and thus has to fit in with the conventions that other people have collectively accepted. It pulls in one direction to the private and individual, and in the other to the public and ritualized.

Both of these aspects of language pose problems for the language learner. Without language, we have great difficulty in thinking about matters that are not immediate to us. Language, and especially written language, enables us to preserve sets of meanings intact while we think about other matters. But sets of meanings may become so rigid that they are entirely conventionalized and prevent, rather than assist thinking. Each learner discovers anew the clichés and set codes of the environment—but at the beginning the clichés are fresh and the stale codes are rich with new possibilities. Each one of us has to fight a battle with the language of our predecessors, to wrench from it the meanings that we want, uncontaminated by the expectations created by the history of the words that we use. Yet we cannot invent our own language, for that would be incomprehensible to others; only by accepting the rules of the past can we play the games of the future. In this paradox lies our problem.

There are two extreme views on culture and language. In one, language is just a tool, or a system of coinage. Coins can buy anything, good or bad, exploitative or liberating, true or false. They are morally neutral. But the metaphor cannot be exact, for language is more like barter; words do mean something, each one is a cultural object, with its own meanings and associations, and no one can escape these entirely.

In the other view, language is inescapably tied up with culture; each word is resonant with the subtle tunes of a family, a tribe, a class, a nation. To change one's language becomes an act of betrayal, a repudiation of one's self, a cultural exile. In this view, language ultimately becomes a form of contemplation, with communication no more than an irritant.

Neither of these views is entirely happy, though both contain some truth. They both fail because neither really conceives of language as a dynamic force. Language changes all the time because human beings are not passive recording machines, they create and develop, and in so doing make new messages and change languages. But the creation and development is through and with the language, the new ideas are tied in with the language itself and no original language user leaves the same language for others to use. Achebe and Soyinka, Koestler and Nabokov, Conrad and Rushdie and Narayan and Jhabvala, all leave us with images and narrative structures, vocabulary items, and linguistic structures, that began as their own and now—inevitably—belong to all of us. Nor is such influence limited to creative writers familiar with other languages. As I have already mentioned in Chapter 4, the linguist Halliday, in calling a book *Learning How to Mean* (Halliday 1975), twisted the syntax of English (for 'mean' was until then a transitive verb) in order to make a point about what young learners do when they acquire language: they do not acquire language, they learn how to mean.

And here of course is the crux of the matter. For we are not talking about language structure so much as the learning of meaning, and meaning is socially constructed. Our meanings come out of our cultures, and we return them, modified or even rejected, to the culture every time we speak.

In the last resort this then becomes an argument about free will. If we believe in linguistic determinism, we receive through our language what we can say, and simply say it. Others do the same with theirs. Communication is difficult to imagine in these circumstances, and argument impossible, for each of these requires adaptation of language to the needs of others. I have yet to meet any people who act as if they are passive recipients of a fixed code. We all have at least the illusion of free will. And if we really are free, then we can if we wish express anything that can be said in language with any language (though the mechanisms we use will vary from language to language). Hence users of American English have been known to argue the most ferocious socialism even in that most unsocialist of contexts, and Russian Christians protested their faith even in the language of Soviet communism.

Language acquisition

Developments in the study of language acquisition are entirely compatible with the view of language and culture that I have just outlined. Language development is seen as a continuous process of human interaction, starting even before the baby is born with responses to sounds in the womb, continuing through non-verbal and verbal interaction with close family members, until language proper begins to develop (Dore 1974). As the child grows up, adults check and expand the language produced to fit it in with the expected meanings of the culture, concentrating more on meaning than on form (Wells 1981). Children themselves frequently expand their language apparently in order to check, by making it explicit, whether the expected implications are justified (Lock 1980), and we are all familiar with children's insistent repetition of questions about meaning and the world: 'What's this?' 'What's this called?' 'Why does it do that?'

The role of language in child development has been well summarized by Halliday:

> Meaning is at the same time both a component of social action and a symbolic representation of the structure of social action. The semiotic structure of the environment—the ongoing social activity, the roles and statuses, the interactional channels—both determines the meanings exchanged and is created by and formed out of them. That is why we understand what is said, and are able to fill out the condensations and unpeel the layers of projection. It is also why the system is permeable, and the process of meaning subject to pressure from the social structure.
> (Halliday 1975: 143)

But to show that there is a close connection between language acquisition and social relations is not enough. We also have to consider some of the links between individuals and their culture. For example, certain cultures may value talk more than others, or storytelling may be seen in one environment as frivolous, or even untruthful, while in another it may be a highly valued skill. Certain personality characteristics may be more highly valued in some cultures than others: extroversion may be more highly valued where storytelling is also valued than in a culture which is heavily weighted towards literacy. It is frequently asserted that characteristics associated with extroversion are valuable in second language learning (Tucker, Hamayan, and Genesee 1976), and there is no doubt that some cultures reward some characteristics relevant to language acquisition more than others. Similarly, people who have negative attitudes to members of other groups are held to have less success as language learners than those who hold positive attitudes (Gardner and Lambert 1972).

Education and culture

We have, then, a situation in which language development is closely associated with cultural expectations and behaviour patterns. What is the role of institutionalized schooling in all this?

Schools and colleges are of course institutions which form part of any culture. Furthermore, like other cultural institutions, they will both reflect and contribute to the culture. But schools come in many shapes and sizes, and in some ways they deflect and distort the process of language acquisition. This is particularly true of second language acquisition. Since this issue sharply raises problems of culture and language, it is worth considering in some detail.

There are a very large number of basic differences between first and second language learning, and (as we saw in Chapter 2) they may be broadly divided into three main groups. If we consider that analysis in a slightly different way, we see that in the first group we can place those which are unavoidable. We cannot learn a second language without having had the benefit of learning a first, and from this several consequences follow. We shall, for example, be able to draw upon our strategies for learning the first language if we wish to, we have the benefit of knowledge of language in general already—we are not learning that along with a particular language, and so on. In addition, it is likely that second language learners will have more intellectualized memorizing strategies available to them, will be able to talk about the process of language learning, and perhaps will be able to use reading and writing in the process of language development. Young children will not have any of these advantages in acquiring their first language. Against these, there will be a second group, a range of disadvantages that derive from the social organization of language learning. Schools usually provide a quite different environment from home, and much second language learning takes place in school. At home, learners are typically encouraged to participate by caring relatives and friends; their mistakes are scarcely noticed in the pleasure of language development, and they spend most of their time exposed to spontaneous speech with a choice about whether to produce language themselves or just to listen. In none of these ways is school the same. Teachers rarely if ever have the tolerance and enthusiasm of caring relatives. They frequently concentrate on pointing out mistakes, and learners receive relatively little language exposure. What they do receive is often unspontaneous and textbook-based, and they may be encouraged (or indeed forced) to produce evidence of learning, by speaking or writing, much of the time.

Many of the problems arising out of the school or college as an institution can be resolved, because they arise out of fashions in teaching methodology which may change. But many of them are inevitable if we have schools at all, and arise out of the differences between the natural environment of home and the public, preparatory, and unnatural environment of school. None the less, the controlled language, the negative attitude to error, and the forcing of productive language use, are all examples of differences between first and second language learning that are created by teaching methodology rather than by maturation of the individual or the unavoidable characteristics of schools as institutions. These constitute the third group.

It would be perfectly possible within the formal school system to have more natural language teaching methodologies than we do have. Of course, in some schools there are important innovations, and the 'communicative movement' in language teaching has done much to close the gap between first language acquisition and second language learning.

But underlying this change (in Britain at least) is an ideological challenge that is frequently ignored. If language and culture are so closely linked, what is the purpose of our language teaching? One answer is to say that we teach language in order to give learners the chance to use particular languages for any purpose they choose. In this sense, the provision of a language is based on a view that effective communication is always preferable to ineffective communication. For this to make sense, it has to be assumed that any language can be used to express the wishes and the needs of any group, and that language teaching is about providing access to necessary media of communication for people's own purposes, whatever they are. Ethically and politically, this view requires no more justification than the claim that it is not good for groups in any country to be unable to talk effectively with each other.

Such a claim may be very radical in its implications, though. To wish for genuine communication between different groups of people is to agree to recognize alternative conceptual frameworks and cultural assumptions, at least in part. To operate with a teaching methodology that offers a language for others to use for their own purposes is quite different from offering to teach how another group's language is used by native speakers. Yet if genuine and effective communication is our aim, it can only be achieved by forcing language to fit the meanings that express differences between different groups. Communication is crucial because of our areas of misunderstanding and difference, not because of our shared comprehension of each other, and it is our ability to communicate difference that needs to be central to our thinking.

However, even if we accept this position, we have not considered language as an instrument of power. Yet that is what it often is. Let us examine this issue more closely.

Language and power

At the beginning of this chapter, I associated the monolingualism of European states with the rise of nineteenth-century nationalism. This was not an accidental conjunction. The history of industrialism has been accompanied by another national and imperial history, of more or less systematic attempts to diminish the linguistic and cultural power of marginalized groups, often for the best of paternalistic motives (see Leith 1983 for an account of this phenomenon in English history).

It would be very naive to imagine that there will ever be a world in which some languages, and some dialects of those languages, do not provide more access to power than other languages or dialects. Nor can we expect that those fortunate enough to be born into families already using powerful language systems will willingly repudiate their birthright out of altruism. Yet a recognition of the power implications of language use can lead us to a more just appraisal of linguistic choices. If communication is a desirable goal, it must not be one way: it takes two to have a misunderstanding. But while issues such as these have increasingly been discussed in debates about English as an Additional Language (EAL) in Britain, or about minority languages in Europe, they have not figured so largely in discussion of English for Academic Purposes. So let us use EAP as a test case for these ideas.

If we believe in the integrity of the language process (and as long as babies acquire the language of primary socialization wherever they are, I feel we have to treat it as essentially the same process wherever human beings occur), some elements of the politicized model I have referred to above must be relevant to any language learning process, however constrained it is. And if we believe in the success of particular procedures, or of particular administrative practices, that success must be measured by criteria that derive from models such as this, as well as from narrower linguistic ones.

EAP in a context of culture and power

How do learners of English for use in universities differ from those who usually figure in discussion of language and power?

First, they are older and more experienced than school learners, both in knowledge of the world, and as language learners.

Second, they are not usually committed to staying in a host country where the target language is being taught.

Third, they are subject to the disciplinary culture which is their prime reason for aspiring to university, and will be unavoidably sensitive to the demands of their teachers and their native-speaking peers in relation to this disciplinary culture.

Each of these factors has implications for power relations.

Older and more experienced learners are being placed in a position of relative inferiority, not just in relation to their discipline, but in relation to the language of that discipline—and simultaneously to the language of social activity, administration, and personal relations. The extent to which this is threatening has been amply documented for many years (UKCOSA 1979; Greenall and Price 1980; Hawkey 1982). Yet their own attitudes to study, and to authority in education, may make it difficult for problematization of their own discipline to take place. And without such problematization, their relationship to their discipline will remain necessarily derivative and passive. The mismatch between their awareness of their own competence, intelligence, and status at home, and their perception of their linguistic confusion and consequently deserved (as they may see it) low status here is a major cause of tension. The conventional 'language and power' answer is to provide learning experiences that allow/ encourage learners to locate themselves within the problematized discipline, and expose the social embeddedness of both the discipline and the student within the Britain-overseas relationship. But such a solution demands an extra investment in a meta-course which may well be perceived as a distraction from the essential task of acquiring the technical competence which is the main justification for being in the university.

Similarly, this potential alienation may be exacerbated by the view that commitment to Britain is only temporary. While some learners may be able to hold their breath and wait, as it were, others will undoubtedly feel the tension between language being divorced from real purposes in all domains except academic work. And this tension will be increased to the extent that teachers (particularly those of mixed native-speaker/non-native-speaker groups) fail to respond to the cultural expectations of overseas students.

But the major issue for advanced learners relates to disciplinary cultures. Achieving success means different things in different disciplines. Writing or reading or participating in a seminar varies from mathematics to English, to social sciences. My personal experience of examining departmental practices as an external assessor makes it apparent that colleagues in different disciplines have clear (though not necessarily clearly articulated) views on what is appropriate student behaviour. The extent to which these expectations are carried over uncritically to groups dealing with students from several disciplines (as in most pre-sessional courses) is an empirical question, but it forces us to raise questions of principle that are very difficult to unravel. For example, advanced work in arts and social sciences often presumes an equality between student and teacher which is more than just a rhetorical or pedagogical device. Judgements may be genuinely open, and the wisdom of the experienced reader or professional may genuinely inform discussion. This is less possible in a technical area where some skills at least have to be acquired through the teaching–learning process. Now, although this polarization is unfair (for arts and humanities too have technical skills to impart, and the judgement element is never absent from high level work in technical areas), the expectation of teachers and peers about the degree of deference to teacher knowledge may differ substantially from field to field.

What, then are the options available to us? The kind of discipline/linguist collaboration reflected in, for example, Dudley-Evans and Henderson (1990) for economics clearly helps at a conceptual level, but in practice there are limitations on what can be done. I have already referred to the difficulties of in-sessional courses in meta-awareness. Pre-sessional activity seems a different matter, however. Most such courses already address themselves to issues of socialization, and include elements of genre study appropriate to particular academic groups. The characterization of culture explored in this chapter suggests, though, that a dimension worth exploring in more detail is the personal location of individual scholars (as scholars in their own home context) in relation to their discipline, set against attempts to locate them in relation to the disciplinary ethos in the UK (Becher 1987). Some of the work on culture and foreign language learning explored by research for schools (for example, Esarte-Sarries and Byram 1989; Roberts *et al.*, 2000) and more global and personal accounts of cultural issues (Harrison 1990) may be suggestive here. These emphasize the need for coherent cultural analysis as an integral part of language learning and language socialization, a point which I develop more fully in Chapter 9 when I discuss British cultural studies. Certainly, the task of locating individuals within the ebb and flow of constantly shifting cultural configurations remains complex, but resolving it is a central need for all teachers.

PART THREE

Language in British education

6 Language in education: coherence or chaos

Introduction

This chapter argues that neither language teaching nor general educational theory has adequately recognized the challenge posed by the view of language outlined in Chapters 1 to 5 which reflects a century of linguistic, psycholinguistic, and sociolinguistic work throughout the world. It also draws upon a body of educational and sociolinguistic research, much of it conducted through the Centre for Language in Education at Southampton University, to show that the range of repertoires exploited by language users is wide-ranging and highly fluid, and suggests further that there is a major agenda of research, development, and theoretical discussion if the implications of current developments are to enrich educational practice as they should.

As we have seen, contemporary linguistics is engaged in a major debate about the nature of language, and contemporary language learning theory is a significant participant in that debate. If we want to provide a robust underpinning for the role of language in the educational process, we must reflect such issues more centrally in our view of education.

Ever since Chomsky burst onto the scene in 1957, the issue of the universality of the language faculty has been central to debate about the nature and role of language. He picked up themes in discussion from the nineteenth century and earlier, but he gave them a contemporary twist which steered them towards computer modelling and the movement which now sees much of linguistics as an offshoot of cognitive science. By emphasizing the allegedly unique characteristics of language in the human mind, he concentrated on a view of language which saw it as species-specific, and almost as the defining species characteristic. Because all normal learners acquire their first languages with great speed and competence, he proposed that the 'language acquisition device' was a unique configuration of elements in the human mind which separated language acquisition in principle from other kinds of learning, and—in later work—related this uniqueness to the way in which the human mind is pre-programmed to identify and use Universal Grammar: the structural principles which underlie every natural language. The study of languages and their structure thus provides an opportunity for unique insights into the structure of the human mind, for human languages are evidence of the shared mentality of the species.

This line of argument rests heavily on a psychological rather than a social view of human linguistic behaviour. It is persuasive to many because it appears to explain many common-sense observations: that all normal human beings learn the languages to which they are initially exposed, that they learn them perfectly (or at least very competently); that they are predisposed to learn human languages, but not a particular human language (there is no gene to enable you to learn Japanese rather than Hausa or Spanish); that all human cultures have complex and fully developed languages of their own.

But, while accepting some aspects of this received wisdom, I would like to start by looking at the sociology of language to produce a different model of language use, and then to relate it to more psychologically sensitive approaches. From the interaction between these two positions, I hope to explore aspects of the educational process which will be significant to any teacher, any learner— and to the administrators and politicians who are their servants!

A social view of language

Let us start with a different set of observations about language.

We cannot define a language. If someone, being honest, says 'I speak French', they are making a statement about themselves, but there is a very large range of possibilities about what the language 'French' consists of. In some circumstances, though I am by no means a fluent French speaker, even I might say that. But the range of vocabulary and syntax, and of appropriate behaviour in real-life situations that I can command will be far smaller than competent, educated English users of French can command. In spite of these differences, we shall probably all be talking about a similar object: the 'French' of educated academic English-speakers, which will overlap substantially with the 'French' of educated metropolitan French speakers. But note that already the qualifications are beginning to pile up: 'educated', 'metropolitan', 'academic', 'native-speaker', 'foreigner'. Soon we shall be defining regional variation more wildly: the 'French' of Brittany, of Marseilles, of Martinique, of Senegal, of Cameroon, or of Nigeria, the southern states of the US, of New Zealand, of Beijing, the nineteenth-century Russian middle class. And social variation: the 'French' of the working class, of peasants, of the city, of the playground. And stylistic variation: the 'French' of diplomacy, of football, of film, of ballet.

Furthermore, these features combine, for as we saw with English-French statements, functional, social, and regional categories overlap, for some functions imply some social groups, and so do some regions. Language use is capable of infinite variation across such categories.

One effect of this is that all boundaries are permeable. If we examine geographical/social borders (Dutch-German; French-Catalan), multilingual communities (Kinyamwezi, Kiswahili, Kiingereza (English) in Tanzania), or social boundaries without geographical overlap ('mid-Atlantic' American/British varieties of English) problems of formal distinction abound. People's affiliations—

that is the languages they claim to be speaking—may be based on aspiration rather than strict linguistic features, or even mutual intelligibility. Spoken 'Dutch' and 'German' on the borders of the Netherlands and Germany reflect political boundaries, not linguistic structure nor intelligibility. Many dialects that speakers would vehemently insist are 'English' are mutually unintelligible, even when written down. And we can test this in our own repertoires, for every person reading this will have some items of 'English' vocabulary in their own personal speech experience which they will know to be unknown to all other probable readers. These may be personal 'family' words, in-group terms from an almost forgotten episode in one's career, very local regional terms, or exotic technical expressions reflecting our secret academic obsessions! The point is that we all have a repertoire which mixes the shared with the personal and largely unshared, and no two speakers of any language have identical repertoires, either across styles, or across languages—for of course in practice we mix languages (whether as beginning learners or as competent users) as much as we mix styles— for joking, because we live in a language-mixing community, to establish academic credibility, for solidarity, or for a variety of other motives. Languages and styles learn to live together (that is, speakers do) with varying degrees of coexistence and conflict. An immensely detailed study of this phenomenon in one broad area, the Pacific region, is Mühlhäusler (1996); Rampton (1995b), documents practices among adolescent bilingual users of English in Britain, while recognition of diversity in literacy practices is reflected in Street (1993). For diversity of English grammars in Britain, see Milroy and Milroy (1993).

Such variation can be studied in any educational setting. A very selective indication of Southampton work will provide references that document our experience in southern Britain. These illustrate the diversity of linguistic/ educational practices in formal education. Statham (1994) reports on the way in which isolated bilingual learners cope with the linguistic demands of schooling; Bourne (1992) documents the tacit marginalization of non-standard learners by teachers in London primary classrooms; Kenner (1996) reports the diverse and cross-linguistic practices of bilingual learners confronted by initial literacy; Grenfell (1995, revised and published as Grenfell 1998) has explored the varied motivations and responses of trainee foreign language teachers; Brumfit, Mitchell, and Hooper (1996) have demonstrated the gaps in belief systems and in practices across English and foreign language teaching, and some of the meta-linguistic categories that learners bring to bear on language; Myles, Hooper, and Mitchell (1998) have examined formation of grammars in foreign language classroom learning; Benton, Teasey, Bell, and Hurst (1988) and a succession of research students have examined learners' varied responses to works of literature; while Moss and Attar (1999) have explored differential reading practices in schools. Similarly, in overseas contexts, Kamanda (1999) has explored the diverse literacy practices of Sierra Leone, Andrews (1999) the metalinguistic understandings of teachers in Hong Kong, and Zotou (1994) the varied beliefs and practices of teachers of language in Greek schools. What links these projects (and many others could be cited to similar effect) is empirical documentation of diverse and individual practices with shared linguistic, social, and pedagogical codes.

Social institutions attempt to control or limit this tendency towards variation. In one direction, pulling towards the 'purity' end of the spectrum, religion, high literature, tradition and the desire to exclude will operate as forces, sometimes through institutions such as churches and mosques, law courts, universities, publishing and the media, and academies. Conversely, against this, secularism as opposed to religion, speech as opposed to literature, progress as opposed to tradition, inclusion as opposed to exclusion, will act as 'impurity' agencies. And creativity and with it the process of education will draw upon both these tendencies, for both creativity and education are dependent on the stability provided by tradition (which enables links with good achievements of the past to be maintained) and the dynamism of change (which both reflects the unavoidable sociolinguistic profile of new generations of thinkers, makers, and learners, and acts as the means of renewal and improvement on the past inheritance).

One effect of this tension is that the distinction between language and dialect becomes eroded, so that it reflects an insider/outsider definition by language users, but has no useful bearing as a distinction on concepts of linguistic repertoire. More significant for education is its erosion of the concept, central to the Chomskyan tradition, of the privileged native speaker. The 'ideal speaker–listener, in a completely homogeneous speech community' (Chomsky 1965: 3) is a metaphor, for there are no homogeneous speech communities, let alone idealized speakers. As soon as we consider language as a social practice, native speakers have no privileged role, other than as a social construct (Rampton 1990; Davies 1991) and the wealth of non-native-speaker literature and scholarship that has enriched writing and speech in English (and no doubt Russian, French, Arabic, Spanish and all other major international languages) becomes comprehensible. Instead, we have language users with ever changing (though not necessarily ever-extending) repertoires.

This recognition of richer diversity leads to an acknowledgement that the processes of interpretation and comprehension require us to respond to many different features of language, and their interaction with world knowledge. It is not only in literature that utterances are multi-functional. An apparently straight-forward imperative such as 'Shut the door, please' may also signal—through intonation, accompanying paralinguistic features such as facial expression or body stance, and prior world knowledge of the hearer (in relation to roles, statuses, etc.)—affection, solidarity, modesty (for example if it is a bathroom door), a desire for privacy, and irritation. All of these may be present at once in the same utterance, and all may contribute to misreadings of intention (that is, alternative interpretations) which may feed in to any response. Such complexity is typical of casual language use, and is only reduced when there is a conscious intention to create message clarity for an agreed purpose. One of the most frequent purposes is development of understanding, establishment of knowledge for future development, in other words, education and science, learning and knowledge formation, research.

Behind this fact is a paradox, for language variation is only occasionally motivated by a need for precision such as education often requires. It is usually motivated by a need for communication, which is central to the process of education but which depends on negotiated levels of acceptable imprecision. Learning language requires initially the promotion of an ability to use it purposefully, which itself requires greater vagueness than is customarily expected by educational tradition.

Precision is a matter of judgement. The appropriate response to the question 'Where do you live?' is only occasionally the full details of your address. Depending on where you are in the world, and your judgement of the purpose of the question, appropriate answers for a Brighton resident may be 'Britain', 'England', 'the south of England', 'south of London', 'Brighton', or a more precise designation. Language use demands the exercise of judgements of this kind all the time, and the repertoire we build up is not an incremental collection of individual items. Rather, it is a constant reworking of categories at all levels, so that we play with phonological variation, as in tongue-twisters ('Peter Piper picked a peck of pickled pepper ...'), with syntactic form ('See no evil, hear no evil, do no evil'), with semantic/syntactic categories ('Work is the curse of the drinking classes'), with social, literary, and historical metaphorical reference ('Her children are the greatest cross she has to bear'; 'a gargantuan feast'; 'a linguistic trade gap'; 'a quisling'), and direct quotation or reference ('slings and arrows'; 'the Venice of the north'). Every element in our cultural experience, however complex, can be drawn into our linguistic repertoire to provide allusions of immense complexity and depth, so that a passing reference to Big Ben, the Treaty of Rome, the Spanish Inquisition, or Hiroshima can carry cultural and social overtones which identify class, educational background, personal attitude, insider- and outsider-ness, and many other features (see Kramsch 1993 for a discussion of these issues in relation to language teaching). The conventions of understanding that enable us to know who might recognize what references, and thus to use them with an appropriate degree of precision, derive from our own rich personal experience of other language users. For example, '375' and '501' are (in 1999) resonant numbers to cricket lovers; '1917' and '1949' in left-wing political history; '4005' and '4007' in the room-booking system for the language group in my department. Each reflects a link that has significance for some sub-group of English speakers. Yet we play with categories such as these all the time. We may use them ironically; we may use them to put down someone who will recognize the special effect without understanding the precise reference; we may require them simply to indicate that we are literate, or insiders to a particular group, without expecting (or even ourselves knowing) the exact reference. Indeed most of our fixed-phrases and allusions are quite unconscious, so that we refer to 'sour grapes', 'kith and kin', 'all the world's a stage', 'tilting at windmills', or 'all is for the best' with no more recognition of allusion than we recognize the origins of the words 'berserk' or 'maniac'.

To insist on language as a form of cultural play is not unusual (see most recently Cook 2000). In the twentieth century, a strong Russian tradition deriving in different ways from Vygotsky (1962) and Bakhtin (for example, 1981; see also Holquist 1990), post-Wittgensteinian philosophy, and a range of recent critiques of conventional linguistic theory from the school associated with Roy Harris (Joseph and Taylor 1990; Harris 1996) have provided a counter-stream to the US post-Sassurean (Saussure 1916) tradition via Sapir (1921), Bloomfield (1933) through— with more continuity than generative grammarians always acknowledge—to Chomsky (1957, 1965). Indeed, Saussure himself may be lined up to support a much more culturally located view of language than the American tradition has highlighted. In education, Vygotskian views have been significant in the work of Bruner (1985) and Mercer (1995), in Britton (1970) and others' discussions of English mother tongue teaching, though only recently in foreign language teaching (surveyed in Mitchell and Myles 1998, Chapter 7; see also their Chapter 8 on second language socialization).

Language and education

But language teaching, and language in schools, have generally moved to one of two extreme positions. On the one hand language has been marginalized in a desire to subsume it under 'literature', or 'creativity', or 'cultural studies'; on the other it has been treated as a set of formal categories for work with foreign or second language learners, or increasingly—with the government frustration and impatience visible in contemporary policy—in the back-up material for the National Literacy Strategy and, by implication, for English teaching in general.

It is striking that when there have been attempts to link language to cultural categories (most notably in the LINC—Language in the National Curriculum— Project, see Carter 1990a), there has been little official support forthcoming. The refusal by the British education minister to allow publication of materials produced by this £21 million project was based on the view that language was too strongly linked with social forces and not taught as a decontextualized code.

Experience in other parts of the world bears out this judgement. The innovative work on genre which Australian educationalists claimed to derive from the work of the linguist Michael Halliday throughout the 1980s resulted in strong debates about the formalization of the procedures (Christie 1989; Martin 1989), but has not resulted in a consensus. Language policy in schools, if it ever gets beyond issues of linguistic choice to pedagogical concerns, tends to polarize into formalists on the one hand and progressives on the other. Yet language is so central to schooling, that we cannot afford to let policy drift. Somehow we need to retrieve a view of language which is compatible with the evidence briefly outlined above, but also capable of being linked directly to language teaching and learning, and the role of language within educational institutions.

Note that this is asking for more than the entitlement issues which have characterized much discussion of language in education policy. These we have addressed elsewhere in our concerns for a language entitlement charter (explored most extensively in Brumfit 1995a, and discussed later in this chapter).

What, then, would the view of language in educational practice look like?

It would have to recognize the following facts about language:

- that everyone learns it whether they have formal education or not
- that everyone learns first the language of their immediate carers, but that this is rapidly augmented by the language of the family, the home, the local community and the school, and that the combination of these constitutes the repertoire of the school-age learner
- that for many learners this repertoire involves a variety of languages, and for all learners a variety of styles/dialects
- that schooling offers also a range of discourse styles associated with the learning of different subjects in the curriculum
- that school also introduces the opportunity of learning foreign or classical languages
- that the strength of the frame associated with particular styles and languages may vary, but in principle boundaries are always permeable and mixed forms are often widespread
- that as linguists cannot distinguish in principle between languages and dialects we cannot make a strong division in principle for education between learning the first language and learning others, either simultaneously or later
- that languages, dialects, and styles are so bound up with identities and reference groups that any new reference group carries significant linguistic implications
- that the link between learning language codes (language teaching) and language use (subject teaching) is secure in non-educational practice but broken by our educational traditions
- that a language policy for learning has to re-establish this link if there is not to be a mismatch between what we know about language acquisition, human learning, and education practice.

The implications of these for an integrated policy in schools require more sustained discussion—but if we accept these as 'facts', current policy and inheritance looks increasingly strange in the light of what we now know about the nature of language and language use.

Thus there is much to do before we can consider language work in formal education to be well-founded as an activity. In addition to analysis of ideas, to be found in a wide range of books by (to give only a few examples) scholars of the stature of Britton, Hawkins, and Widdowson, we need mechanisms for the synthesis, analysis, and evaluation of a wide range of relevant empirical projects, procedures for the re-evaluation and replication of studies to enable us to make robust statements about what is and is not sound knowledge, and a steady flow of well-trained and committed researchers, who genuinely keep abreast with ideas on language teaching, and who desperately want to understand its processes and procedures. Few if any countries provide the infrastructure for such a research base to develop, but language teaching benefits from an international market, and international organizations such as the Association Internationale de Linguistique Appliquée (AILA) have for years provided an infrastructure which the education profession exploits less than it should. Similarly, the British Educational Research Association (BERA) has a far more distinguished record as an agent for the study of educational institutions and policy than for the study of the teaching of particular subjects. The political paradox (from which we are still suffering the backlash) is that for most outsiders (parents, politicians, journalists) 'education' is about teaching particular things ('subjects', 'disciplines'), more than it is about anything else—hence the structure of the National Curriculum, and the targeted initiatives in literacy and numeracy through which the Labour government has expressed its frustration with the profession's presumed lack of dynamism and innovation. A case for systematically establishing links with the organizations that research language is very strong. Fortunately, the Committee for Linguistics in Education (CLIE), jointly sponsored by the British Association for Applied Linguistics (BAAL) and the Linguistics Association of Great Britain (LAGB) already has links with such subject specific bodies as the Association for Language Learning (ALL: modern foreign language teachers), National Association for the Teaching of English (NATE: English mother tongue teachers) and National Association for Language Development across the Curriculum (NALDIC: teachers of English as an additional language), as well as with advisers and bodies like the UK Reading Association (UKRA). A more systematic link between all of these, as well as the major international teachers' bodies such as the International Association of Teachers of English as a Foreign Language (IATEFL) and the American-based Teachers of English to Speakers of Other Languages (TESOL) could only be a worthwhile activity for educational research. Thus there is a need for a broad-based language interest group which could link the activities concerned with literacy, mother tongue, second, foreign, bilingual and classical language development, and the broader concerns with language as a central component in the learning process.

In addition to organizational links and further research, though, we need proposals for the key elements in a coherent language policy for education. I have already outlined these, in Chapter 1 (p.13) but a discussion of the British context, together with a more detailed specification of the arguments for a four-item agenda (or charter), will clarify the concerns of this chapter.

Background to the National Curriculum for England and Wales

In 1988 the Education Reform Act established the most sweeping range of changes seen in British education since it was first established as a major state concern in 1870. Among these changes, for the first time the government laid down a national curriculum for all learners between the ages of five and sixteen in England and Wales (for historical reasons, Scotland and Northern Ireland had similar but independent provision, which resulted in significant differences in detail and sometimes in general approach). Previously, the similarity between syllabuses for external examinations had provided the main constraint on the curriculum.

In principle, the National Curriculum had the power to provide an important impetus towards equal provision for all learners, for it implied an entitlement for all. Dissatisfaction with the quality of British education, first signalled by Prime Minister Callaghan's Ruskin speech of 1976, gradually led to a determination by civil servants and politicians, with the active support of many journalists, to intervene more directly than ever before in the professional activities of teachers and teacher educators. The emphasis shifted from an education system which identified learners who worked hardest or most effectively, to one which offered learners certain specific entitlements. The curriculum became a description of what all learners were entitled to receive, laid down by the authorities who paid out of taxes for the education service. This shift could have been liberating, and perhaps in due course will prove to have been so. But at the time it was introduced at great speed, wholesale, from the top down, without any of the implications being carefully considered. Conservative politicians in the late 1980s were in a hurry; they needed to show their successes before the next election. 'Consultation' was rapid and perfunctory, successive working parties met shorter and shorter deadlines, and there was little time for examination in detail of the strengths and weaknesses of provision in other countries, or of learning theory for particular subject areas. The education service was turned upside down, and—among many other unanticipated results—the national curriculum established a *de facto* language policy in British education by laying down which languages should be centrally available in different regions of the country (see Brumfit 1995a: Chapter 2).

However, as the policy was not created deliberately but on the back of these wider reforms, and as it was not accompanied by substantial discussion of its implications for learning, it contains inconsistencies, and has not been subject to coherent analysis as a package within the government agencies which have to implement it. It arose by accident, in the course of laying down guidelines for the teaching of all subjects, and needs to be reviewed before setting into a stable shape.

The 1988 Education Reform Act was only the beginning of a flurry of legislation on the curriculum, for difficulties in implementing the rushed and ill-thought-through policy led to a succession of revisions. Thus curriculum reform dominated the latter years of the Conservative regime that was led successively by Margaret Thatcher and John Major, even though it was only a small part of the massive reorganization of all aspects of British education.

It is worth noting the decline in this period of government willingness to call upon expertise in language or in education, for curiously the rise of applied linguistics as a discipline coincided with a retreat from expertise by successive governments. The Bullock Report (DES 1975) was probably the last substantial government report (609 pages) to involve a body of linguistic/language education experts (eight out of twenty members of the committee) directly in its writing, and the Thatcher government's suspicion of the 'education establishment' and later of academics in general made willingness to consult increasingly rare. The Swann Report (807 pages) on the education of ethnic minorities (DES 1985) was the last 'heavy' education report produced by government, and Professor Eric Hawkins, the only linguist on the original committee (out of 21 members) had resigned along with the original chair, Mr A Rampton, in a disagreement with government over the interim findings about racism. He was not replaced by a linguist, and the extensive discussion of language issues in the report (the whole of Chapter 7, significant parts of Chapters 10–15, and some reference in all other chapters) reflects the lack of informed background.

But during the late 1980s, the arrival of the National Curriculum was preceded by political unease about the way English teaching was going, and education policy makers flirted briefly with applied linguists, as they groped their way towards a prescriptive national curriculum. In principle, there was a substantial amount of informed work to draw upon. In the late 1970s, BAAL and LAGB had held joint conferences about the role of linguistics in schools, as a result of which CLIE (the Committee for Linguistics in Education) was set up as a joint standing committee which co-opted members from many interested constituencies, including the schools inspectorate, NATE, English and modern language local authority advisers, and others. A series of working papers, and regular slots in LAGB conferences (for BAAL there was more overlap with general activities of the association, and CLIE reported more than it ran special events) established CLIE's presence on the national scene. At the same time, publishers through the 1970s produced significant materials aimed at the English mother tongue market, most notably Edward Arnold with a series of background books for teacher training, and the materials incorporated in the *Language in Use* folder (Doughty, Pearce, and Thornton 1971).

But it was not the people who had been active in any of this work that were drawn into government advice. Nor did they directly draw upon the people (such as David Crystal and John Sinclair) who had been prominent in the 1970s attempts to make linguistics central to the preparation of teachers in British schools. Still less did they draw upon those who were prominent and experienced in teacher education for British teachers of English, whether linguists such as Mary Willes or methodologists with an interest in linguistics such as Harold Rosen. Indeed, after the early enthusiasm for linguistics in the training of teachers, language departments fell victim to the 'last in/first out' principle. One of the best departments, at West Midlands College, closed after 1976 (Willes 1988), and many others reduced their activity to a minimal linguistic requirement.

Yet the quantity of linguistically informed expertise available continued to increase, and individuals with applied linguistics backgrounds became more senior (and therefore in principle potentially more influential). In the late 1970s, even by a generous definition of applied/policy oriented knowledge, not more than seven people in the whole country held chairs in relevant fields; in 1999 there must be at least 25. When, eventually, in 1986 Kenneth Baker, the Secretary of State for Education, appointed two experienced linguists to the Kingman Inquiry, he drew upon those whose language interests were primarily overseas: Professors Gillian Brown and Henry Widdowson (both former members of the Edinburgh Applied Linguistics Department). They shared membership with 13 others: four creative writers, one literary critic, four teachers or trainers (with no significant activity in applied linguistics), two industrialists, one broadcaster and the chair, who was a science-oriented vice-chancellor. The terms of reference of that inquiry were quite technical:

1   To recommend a model of the English language, whether spoken or written, which would: (i) serve as the basis of how teachers are trained to understand how the English language works; (ii) inform professional discussion of all aspects of English teaching.
2   To recommend the principles which should guide teachers on how far and it what ways the model should be made explicit to pupils, to make them conscious of how language is used in a range of contexts.
3   To recommend what, in general terms, pupils need to know about how the English language works and in consequence what they should have been taught, and be expected to understand, on this score, at ages 7, 11, and 16.
(DES 1988: 73)

Compared with Bullock or Swann this report was brief (less than a hundred pages), and contained no references to scholarly literature consulted (though texts for teachers to use in relation to the 'model' were appended). Certainly there was no attempt to look at authoritative models in use in teacher education, or discussed by CLIE, except in so far as these may have been introduced by individuals who lobbied—many of whom of course had opinions but no particular expertise. The final proposal consisted of five rather routine checklists of topics which might have appeared in a conventional undergraduate linguistics course. Widdowson made some cogent criticisms in a minority statement included in the report, but neither these nor the report's findings were taken up by later developments in the English curriculum, and Kingman remains an interesting, but sidelined piece of linguistic advice.

Next, Professor Michael Stubbs, initially a modern linguist by training with a strong research record in classroom interaction, was appointed to the Cox Committee to devise the National Curriculum for English, and following Roald Dahl's resignation, Katharine Perera (with a strong track record in linguistic work for English teaching) was appointed. Seven others without special linguistic experience were also members. Their report was probably the most acceptable English curriculum that could have been achieved with any hope of professional acceptance, and was by no means linguistically naive.

It was only when Professor Ronald Carter was appointed to direct the Language in the National Curriculum (LINC) project that an attempt was made directly to connect linguistic understanding with the normal practices and knowledge bases of English teachers. This project, taking an eclectic, but loosely Hallidayan approach, was linked to a massive programme of short in-service provision for teachers throughout the country. Nevertheless, as we have seen, it eventually fell foul of the responsible minister, who was worried about materials too concerned with social context, and too little with formal (by which he probably meant 'instructional') grammar (Carter 1990a). This was primarily a development project, rather than one concerned with advising on policy, but it did have the effect of establishing that what were quite mainstream views for both linguists and teachers were felt to be highly threatening by politicians and most of the press.

In spite of the demise of LINC, 'grammar' is increasingly visible in the successive stages of national curriculum definition. By the mid 1990s, however, 'experts' had been largely ignored or abandoned. The Cox recommendations proved too 'traditional' for a government bent on reform, and the highly centralized system that had been created by the 1988 Education Reform Act enabled the views, even the whims, of ministers or senior civil servants to be incorporated into policy with little need either for consultation or even planning. 'Consultation' there was in abundance, but increasingly it took place on a short timescale, often across the August or Christmas period when schools and universities were likely to be on vacation, and seemed to be concerned with response to pressure groups rather than searching for expertise.

Consultation and lobbying became identical processes, and—in all professions— complaints were rife about the waste of time in preparing considered responses which would be ignored or at best filed in someone's 'for or against' trays. Only in highly technical areas did the views of experts carry any authority. Across the professions, and especially in the social sciences and humanities, a major authority crisis developed. Researchers were no longer those who knew most about their area of expertise, but those who had certain skills which could be used for someone else's agenda, just as 'market researchers' have no specific interest in, or knowledge of, the product that is the subject of their surveys. The revisions published in 1993 following widespread unease, particularly among English teachers, about the over-heavy prescribed curriculum, relied on no public committee, and introduced a knowledge about language element which appeared to view this as primarily about understanding the grammatical properties of standard English.

And the centralized procedures continued after the 1997 election. Indeed, the new government was all too willing to use its central powers to circumvent gradualism in its desire for speedy reform. The National Literacy Strategy emerged not from the Qualifications and Curriculum Authority (QCA)—the eventual successor of the National Curriculum Council that had produced earlier work—although that continued to operate, but from a working group working directly from the ministry. Yet it has been in effect imposed across the statutory National Curriculum. Interestingly, the National Literacy Strategy expects teachers to understand a much greater technical apparatus than previously, and to pass much of it on to learners. Unfortunately the linguistic conceptual base is ill-digested in the first round of published materials (as most obviously visible in the inconsistent and inaccurate definitions of 'terminology' provided), but that should not obscure the major jump demanded in linguistic expectations of teachers. Whether linguists who have volunteered to 'correct' what has already been published will be any more successful in persuading politicians and civil servants of the authority of what they have to say remains to be seen, though there are encouraging signs of a greater sympathy for expert knowledge in some recent discussions.

The story I have told so far may sound outlandish or biased to those who have not been close to any of this action; indeed, if we report some of these events outside the UK we are greeted with genuine disbelief by linguists and scholars.

One reading of this situation is that scholars are simply failing to get their messages across. But I do not think that the problem was primarily their incapacity to be persuasive, and too many academics have reported similar marginalization to suggest that individuals are really the issue. I think the problem lies partly in the suspicion of anything more than common sense on matters to do with language and with education (on both of which everyone can be a self-styled expert), partly in the atmosphere of the times, when the power was so centralized that few can afford the luxury, which university staff do still retain, to argue back, and partly in the strength of the purity and complaints traditions (Thomas 1991; Milroy and Milroy 1991). People want grammar taught because they think that otherwise the language will become even more impure than it is, compared with what it was in the past. I scarcely need to cite the range of 'authorities', from Prince Charles to the politician Norman Tebbitt, to the novelist P. D. James, who have expressed such views as part of the national debate on language. Academics' views are often too careful and too tentative to be able to compete with the conviction and certainty of lay opinion.

At the same time, we should not underestimate the disenchantment with traditional expectations about language within the education system. There is undoubtedly authority loss in social sciences, and particularly in educationally relevant theory. One explanation of this phenomenon in relation to language is the account of commentators such as Crowley (1989) who traces the establishment of standard English, relates it to aspects of the complaints tradition, and sees it as part of the repression of diversity and the establishment of political hegemony by London and the middle classes. This is a convincing account, but used too simplistically risks being seen as a conspiracy theory in a field where confusion and conflicting agendas are rife (I pick up this theme again in Chapter 11). Such an account is opposed by Honey (1998, for example), who links most mainstream applied linguists with Crowley-like beliefs. Aside from his tendency to imply a tacit applied linguistic conspiracy, though, many of his arguments do need to be explicitly addressed—for they reflect with some sophistication the views of a very large number of people in the country, including many of the politicians and civil servants who wield the power and control the funding. We cannot brush aside the view that standard English may be emancipatory as well as repressive without rendering much of our work, both national and international, incoherent, or hypocritical. This is because the tension between languages and styles of wider communication, on the one hand, and those of the personal and individual, on the other, is built into the concept of education. Education is about changing language (and culture) at least as much as it is about maintaining and supporting them—and it cannot avoid this. So we cannot afford to be too glibly dismissive of Honey's claims about the need for education to support a highly influential sociolect such as standard English.

There is another way of looking at the same question, though. This is to accept that the argument by non-specialists is driven mainly by an unclearly articulated set of non-linguistic concerns about such concepts as 'responsible citizenship', 'heritage', and 'entitlement'. None of these need be ignoble goals, but they can be used to implicate language issues without clear thought. Because linguists have failed themselves to engage adequately with non-linguists' perceptions of the role of language in society—the tendency has been simply to deplore these (see, for example, Aitchison 1997)—they risk being perceived as irrelevant or obstructive.

Towards coherence

But it is possible to produce a principled position which is compatible with national curriculum legislation, and—since the structure of the curriculum is in a state of permanent review and revision—such a position is very important, if revisions are not to be simply the prey of fashion or the latest whim of the civil servants or politicians who have the power. The more centralized the system, the more important well-argued principles become.

In the following section, I shall try to present key principles that could underlie the teaching and learning of language within British education. They are based partly on interpretation of international research on processes of language learning and teaching, and partly on work in Britain. Studies of learners and teachers of English mother tongue, foreign languages, and ethnic minority languages, as well as investigations of teachers in training support the general position outlined below.

1 A policy for language, not policies for languages

Language provision in schools cannot helpfully be broken down into disconnected compartments. Although learners understandably perceive separate language classes as offering separate activities, research into the psychological bases of language acquisition show learners developing an ever-extending linguistic repertoire through interaction with their social environment. Schools can assist and guide this process, and can help it to be more effective than it would be unassisted—but the process continues with or without schools. And foreign languages can be as much a part of this process as the languages spoken in home and school. While major differences undoubtedly exist in the conditions of language learning at different ages, there is never a clear-cut boundary between one type of learning and another. Many people who live in environments where different languages coexist cross linguistic boundaries all the time; after the earliest years, there are no circumstances where explicit and conscious learning may not be combined with implicit and unconscious acquisition. Moving from the intimate language of the home to the more public discourses of the school, or from the improvisation of speech to the more controlled environment of reading and writing, are not permanent shifts where one mode is left behind and another adopted. We move to and fro all the time, in and out of different styles and different dialects and—to varying degrees—across different languages. In contemporary Britain (as the analysis of one evening's viewing on a single television channel makes abundantly clear) stylistic, dialectal, and linguistic variation is an unavoidable fact of our environment, and as language users we all participate in creating that environment. So because language is so central to processes of learning and processes of socialization, and because we live in such a rich and potentially fluid environment, thinking about one part of the language curriculum in isolation from other parts makes very little sense. Drawing the separate parts together is sensible because of the ways we learn languages, because of the ways we use them, and because of the nature of our linguistic environment.

Thus Panjabi speakers mix languages, and cross between Panjabi and English both in school and at home, sometimes speaking Panjabi to grandparents, a mixture to parents, and varying in their choice with brothers and sisters; so too do children of mixed linguistic parentage where (for example) one parent uses French and another English, and so do most advanced learners of foreign languages, whether at university or home, if the conditions favour such mixing of codes.

2 The fact of English

In the UK any coherent language policy for foreign languages must start with the central fact of the British situation—that English is the main language and that, because of the dominance of the US, it is the language of world economic power. The majority of fluent English users in the world are non-native speakers. This is true of no other language, and because this is true, learning foreign languages in UK poses problems for teachers that are not found in more multilingual countries, or in those where the economic pull of English as a foreign language provides strong motivation to learn. A language policy for Britain must recognize the implications of this fact, and at the same time be sensitive to the negative effects it may have. These vary from individual weaknesses such as complacency about the need to learn other languages, to institutional risks such as arrogance about the nature of the English language itself leading to racism and xenophobia in organized attitudes to those who resist the domination of English. But even more important than these, because less obvious and more subtly damaging, is the implicit assumption that monolingualism is the norm, which can imperceptibly shift into an assumption that not just monolingualism but monodialectalism is the norm, especially for 'educated' people. This view is damaging, not just because it causes its adherents to be insensitive to the wide variation of linguistic styles that make up any rich dialect, however educated, but because it is predicated on a restricted view of the role of language in enabling different cultural groups to express themselves in varied ways by both communicating and by refusing to communicate with others. Language conceals as well as reveals, and it is the interplay between these processes that makes linguistic communities active changing and living entities. To start with the current fact of the linguistic hegemony of English is realistic; to rely on it for a curriculum is to misunderstand the nature of language and of communication.

3 Bilingual learners

In addition, any language policy which is to command widespread acceptance by the monolingual majority must simultaneously be responsive to the complexities of the British linguistic context for bilingual learners. A language policy must be just to all learners, and at the same time accept the needs of typical learners. There are, it is appalling to state, no reliable figures on bilingual speakers in Britain, so planning takes place in a relative vacuum—but Alladina and Edwards (1991) report on 32 separate and active speech communities within the UK, and in 1987 the Inner London Education Authority reported 172 languages active in London schools. In the Southampton area alone, more than 70 minority language maintenance classes have been active through the 1990s, and 26 different new languages can be learnt from scratch in adult education classes. Further, these figures disregard those who, while being native English speakers, regularly read, write or speak other languages as part of their work. If the policy is to be an entitlement policy, it cannot helpfully differentiate between English and other languages as the starting point at birth, although of course any curriculum has to distinguish certain end points as more important than others. Recognition of all languages active within Britain is a necessary precondition for starting the process of language learning. But effective use of the language(s) of work, public life, and government, are essential endpoints for participation in democratic processes, so English (and in some areas other languages) are necessary as minimum conditions for adult life.

4 Functions of language

Broadly, language can be said to perform three main roles. It has a pragmatic function as a means of getting things done in the world ('Please shut the door'). It has a learning and conceptualizing function, as a means of understanding the world, of making sense of ideas and evidence ('If we examine T. S. Eliot's work in relation to that of a French poet he greatly admired such as Laforgue, what influences do we find?'). And it has an archive function, as a means of storing understandings from the past ('The rules of chess', 'The works of Shakespeare', etc.). Different languages will provide bases for different kinds of experience. Some (and particularly the major languages of national and international communication, including English) will provide a basis for action in the world, as well as for learning and conceptualizing. Some (and particularly mother tongues in the early years) will be crucial at particular stages as the major means by which learning takes place. Some (particularly classical languages and those with strong literary, religious, and scientific traditions) will have a major role to play in reinforcing understanding of heritage—a result of the archive function. All may have some role to play in relation to each function, but how these roles operate for particular speech communities at particular times will vary.

5 Identity

In addition, language use will be closely bound up with individuals' and groups' identities, and in so far as those are contested because of particular social or political frameworks, language may become a symbol of independence or subservience, and language issues a central issue in debates about power and cultural autonomy. Thus the privileged status of Welsh in British education, compared with—say—Panjabi or Cantonese, is largely a product of assumptions about the political role and social coherence of Wales (see discussion in the introduction to Alladina and Edwards 1991).

6 An equality of provision

Thus, as far as resources permit, and subject to local demands and needs, we should aim to provide what is outlined in the charter below, for all learners.

What, then, do such principles imply for all learners in schools? If we assume that a specification of entitlement is what is required, what could that look like? I have tried to encapsulate a proposal for an agreed agenda in the form of a charter for all language learners. This charter offers an agenda to define what—subject as always to resource limitations—we should be trying to provide as an entitlement (see Brumfit 1986a for the first outline of the charter idea, and Brumfit 1995a for a development of the ideas in relation to National Curriculum provision).

It is the policy of
(insert name of institution or authority)

_____

to enable all learners, to the maximum extent possible within available legislation and resources
(i)   to develop their own mother tongue or dialect to maximum confident and effective use;
(ii)   to develop competence in a range of styles of English for educational, work-based, social and public-life purposes;
(iii) to develop their knowledge of how language operates in a multilingual society (ideally including basic experience of languages other than their own that are significant either in education or the local community);
(iv)   to develop as extensive as possible a practical competence in at least one foreign language.

It is our belief that the development of these four strands in combination will contribute to an effective language curriculum for Britain in the twenty-first century more than emphasis on any one of them separately at the expense of the others.

Signed: _____

Date: _____

Figure 6.1: Language charter

Let us consider the specific example of foreign languages in Britain as a way of glossing the implications of the charter. For them to thrive in schools, they should be systematically linked to provision under the first three of these headings (the fourth of course is a statement of foreign language entitlement). Why?

Very briefly, they should be linked to (i) because there is convincing research evidence that people learn second languages well when they are confident language users, and they develop that initial confidence through their mother tongues. And further, as their repertoire extends, the standard language, the languages of literacy, and eventually foreign languages, have the potential to grow out of that confident language use.

They should be linked to (ii) because English is the dominant language of education and public life, so competence in foreign languages should accept and relate to the competences that are required in English. Further, translation, interpreting, mixed English/foreign language activity, cross-referring to activities taking place in English—all these will help to overcome the distance between English and foreign languages that is so distinctive a feature of UK culture. The link between grammar and descriptive work in English and that required in foreign language learning needs to be made clear, also.

They should be linked to (iii) because unless all learners understand what it is to be part of a multilingual country in a multilingual continent, in a multilingual world, the point of foreign language learning will be lost. And knowledge about language helps effective language learning.

Implications of the language charter for the curriculum

Language is a vehicle for a wide range of activities and, as we have argued above, is closely bound up with personal development, concept formation, and identity. Simultaneously, it is tied in to public and private communication processes. The language curriculum must therefore reflect a range of activities with different purposes.

Drawing upon our discussion of the functions of language, we can define them broadly for the charter as follows, with the operational consequences following:

Function	Operational consequence
developmental and concept-creating	helping learners to become confident users for purposes of their own choosing, to become creative and imaginative, to be willing to think about and reflect on their own language practices
understanding heritage	making sense of past achievement and traditions with language
functional	enabling learners to operate with the conventions demanded by society

Figure 6.2: Functions of the curriculum

Most language work should incorporate aspects of all three of these.

Furthermore, enabling this to happen requires the curriculum to draw upon institutionalized language practices: within language work specifically, literature, drama, and media understanding may be significant elements; within other subject areas, understanding the genres of scientific or historical writing (for example) become important. Implementation of the Language Charter requires integration of all these activities, though the ways in which this will happen will vary at different levels of education, and with different language groupings.

The charter proposal is based on views of social justice. It is entirely compatible with National Curriculum orders, but it provides a coherence and a focus on learners' entitlement which is more specific than offered there.

It could also be translated into any level of education, for it can be adapted to pre-school, community, further, and higher education as well as mainstream schooling and provides a rationale for language teacher education.

Specifying its implications with greater delicacy for particular groups is a task primarily for practitioners. I have outlined some of these implications, for bilingual learners in Mitchell and Brumfit 1997, and for foreign language learners in Brumfit 2000.

The general strands in the charter, as defined below, can apply in any educational system as key agenda items for language in education:

1 Language of personal life
2 Language for education/ public life
3 Language knowledge and awareness
4 More distant cultures: foreign or classical languages

Figure 6.3: General strands of the charter

These categories describe the essential dimensions of language work for any education system.

PART FOUR

Literature and education

7 Literature, power, and 'the canon'

Introduction

So far I have limited exemplification of the view of language I am presenting to specific illustrations drawn from language teaching. But it is also helpful in thinking about other institutionalized language practices, such as literature. In this chapter I consider the relationship between the social construct 'literature', and recent discussions about the curriculum and power. I shall examine the concept of the canon, and follow this with a discussion of the role of literature in the life of committed readers, finally relating this briefly to a consideration of the role of literature in education.

The canon

The *Shorter Oxford Dictionary* defines 'canon' as 'The list of books of the Bible accepted by the Christian Church as genuine and inspired', and it is worth recognizing the theological origin of the term, for it relates directly to discussion of values, and to claims for a more than rational base for the concept, depending on the highest authority. Much of the heat of current discussion (see Bloom 1994, for example) derives from the uneasy status of 'English Literature' as a discipline—a study concerned in the past with history, biography, philosophy, philology and social criticism, but under increasing attack for its dogmatism in advancing values based on taste or on moral commitment. The confidence of the first sentence in Leavis's *The Great Tradition* (1948) is unimaginable nowadays: 'The great English novelists are Jane Austen, Henry James, and Joseph Conrad— to stop for the moment at that comparatively safe point in history' (Leavis 1948: 9). Against this we have to set the counter-claims of Eagleton:

> The so-called 'literary canon', the unquestioned 'great tradition' of the 'national literature' has to be recognized as a construct, fashioned by particular people for particular reasons at a certain time. There is no such thing as a literary work or tradition which is valuable *in itself*, regardless of what anyone might have said or come to say about it. 'Value' is a transitive term: it means whatever is valued by certain people in specific situations, according to particular criteria and in the light of given purposes.
> Eagleton (1983: 10–11)

Thus, it is argued, the concept of a canon incorporates the notion that there are individuals or groups who hold power enough to wish to persuade others that their views of the status of 'important' literary works are correct. From this position it is a small step to the view that because power resides more with whites, or males, or Protestants, or rich people, the canon is an unthinking reflection of the world views of these groups. Yet this apparently easy step raises more questions than it answers. On the one hand, it is difficult in practice to see the advocates of a canon as neatly fitting in to conventional power categories; intellectuals (of whom literary critics are a subset) tend to be marginal rather than central, the most alienated section of totalitarian states, and genuinely powerful groups rarely remain powerful if they divert their attention from the practical task of remaining in power.

More significantly, Eagleton's position implies an emphasis not so much on what human beings share in experience, as on what separates them. His 'particular people' are set against other people, in opposition to us, his presumed readers—he invites us to share his argument, in rejecting the claims of their arguments for literature as a reflection of (at least potential) shared experience.

The problem is that his insistence on the uniqueness of particular viewpoints makes a concept of a communicating culture difficult to maintain. Further, it conflicts with the attested experience of many individual readers. As an illustration (from many possible) consider Freya Stark's account of her discovery of the *Odyssey* while travelling at sea.

> The tourist class in the *Athenia* was a distraction of wailing children and howling winds ... Yet as I lay in my bunk between distasteful meals I read the *Odyssey* for the first time in Butcher and Lang's translation; and the roar and hiss of the waves was a part of its music. I was so transported with delight that I leapt up at intervals to walk about the narrow cabin floor, in an ecstasy that had to be expressed somehow, or choke me. Except Shakespeare, who grew from childhood as part of myself, nearly every classic has come with this same shock of almost intolerable enthusiasm; Virgil, Sophocles, Aeschylus and Dante, Chaucer and Milton and Goethe, Leopardi and Racine, Plato and Pascal and St Augustine, they have appeared, widely scattered through the years, every one like a 'rock in a thirsty land', that makes the world look different in its shadow.
> (Stark 1951: 25)

Clearly, there is little sense in pretending that the notion of a 'canon', along with all other ideas and all theories, is anything but a social construct. But to attack a view that there is a set of pre-ordained 'great' works of literature is too easy. There have been no serious defences of such a position, and there is no point in wasting time on trivial ideas. Rather than fighting straw opponents, critics might find it much more valuable to attempt to locate a discussion of the function of literature in the practices of readers. The rest of this chapter tries to explore ways of recognizing the experience of readers like Freya Stark within an educational and literary tradition which has had to respond to the radical critique. It does this by emphasizing the process of reading and discussing literature, rather than the results of such discussion. We cannot argue, I contend, that because the results will always be argued about, the process of reading highly-valued works ought to be abandoned.

I propose, therefore, to outline a view of literature and its role in society, and from that, to examine what we use literary texts for—for any 'use' of literature in any kind of teaching must presuppose some elements of literary response on the part of the reader.

The nature of 'literature'

The widespread use of the term 'literature' in educational discourse implies recognition of a phenomenon that most people in the western educational tradition accept—an open-ended set of texts (which may be either oral or written in origin). The list is open-ended because it is constantly being added to by a number of processes: new works being written, old works being discovered or rediscovered, and (above all) by old works being reinterpreted.

What distinguishes these texts as literature, is that their function is not primarily transactional. They are available to enrich our imaginative, metaphorical, and symbolic needs, not to provide us with information. They are not necessarily fictional, but the truth or falsehood of the details they impart is irrelevant to the use we make of them as readers. Thus some of these texts are incontrovertibly 'literature' (though of varying merit), because they set out to be fiction and have no pretensions otherwise. Others, however, may acquire the status 'literature' only when their traditional use has expired. Thus we may consider that Burke's political speeches, Gilbert White's *Natural History of Selborne*, or Gibbon's *Decline and Fall of the Roman Empire* all achieve literary status when the main purpose of the reader is to enjoy the reading experience rather than to respond to political debate, learn about Hampshire wild life, or discover the state of our historical knowledge. For these purposes other books may supersede them, but providing there continue to be readers who return to these works for enjoyment they will contribute to the enrichment of our inner lives. On the other hand, novels by Jeffrey Archer, Ian Fleming, Simenon, or Barbara Cartland, cannot be judged except as contributions to literature, for no sophisticated reader could take them primarily to be manuals for understanding political, forensic, or social behaviour.

What then distinguishes these works from accepted 'classics', from Dickens or Tolstoy, Flaubert or Galdós, or of critically admired twentieth-century authors such as Golding, Bellow, Solzhenitsyn, or García Márquez? After all, more people read Archer et al. with pleasure than all eight of the critics' preferred authors put together.

One solution to this major problem for critical theory is to follow Eagleton's argument, and to refuse to accept anything other than a sociological view of literary texts, to deny a distinction between 'literature' and 'reading'. By this argument, the key questions are what groups read what, and what for? Answering this undoubtedly illuminates our understanding of social structures, the roles of education and the interests educational institutions can serve, and the varying purposes that writers and critics have at different times defined for preferred reading texts.

But there is a risk in this enterprise that all knowledge is seen reductively, to be significant merely as an expression of social relations. Freya Stark's response cannot be explained away by locating her in a particular social and economic environment. Nor is it the case that there have simply been uncontested 'preferred' texts at particular times. The history of western literature reflects a constant struggle by writers and commentators to assert the values of particular authors from the past for present use. We have only to consider the role of classical literature in Renaissance debates, of the ballads in the Romantic debates, or of the metaphysicals in early twentieth-century arguments, to see the force of this point. In such debates, to ask the question should Donne, or Gaskell, or Constant, or Hoffman, rate higher (or lower) than previously perceived is not a trivial question, because shared reading is a serious, self-defining means of establishing our agreed values and of reorientating them when we feel adjustments to be necessary. The role of tradition, and which is the relevant tradition at a particular time, the appropriate discourse for a particular period and place, the key beliefs to concentrate on, right and wrong sensibilities, even right and wrong political strategies, will all be measured, in part, by the nature of literary criticism at a given time. Criticism will not simply reflect such debate; it will be a contribution to it.

Consequently, argument about which texts from the past are to be highly valued (and all literary texts are from the past once they have been performed or published), is an argument about what we are and why we behave as we do. It is part of what defines us as human rather than animal, for it is a discussion of how culture (in the anthropological sense) will and should affect present and future culture. In this sense, any 'canon' is in a state of constant redefinition unless it is dead, irrelevant to present debates, and therefore useless. But, of course, in so far as it is capable of usefulness, it is also available for misuse—and critics like Eagleton rightly point out the dangers of such misuse. Where they are wrong is in suggesting that it is possible to avoid a selection from past texts (or indeed from past historical events) for current use. There always will be a 'canon' of some kind as long as people read at all, because that will be no more (and no less) than the collection of tokens of our shared experience that we need in order to establish contact with each other—through discussion and debate—and with our human roots. Thus we select and simplify from the infinite range of potentially relevant texts.

Within this view of literature, contemporary works live alongside works of the past, for their value to us now. For not only is the past another country, but each poem, each story, however contemporary, is another country for each of us too—we reuse everything we experience, and the process of discussing that reuse is an essential part of making contact with each other. It is precisely the isolation and uniqueness of our individual experience that makes necessary our establishment of shared points of contact—and out of these shared points of contact we make our culture. If we cannot do this because we do not believe that any works (or events or memories) are more useful, resonant, or instructive than any others, we have actually lost faith in our capacity to value at all, or to learn from the past. And if we have truly reached that degree of faithlessness in the value of the human condition, where is a role for education, for reading, or for argument? Without inherited traditions to argue about, we have no culture and lose what distinguishes us from animals, our greatest instrument of adaptation and survival.

What differentiates classics from popular works, in this view, is not their status (for that can always be renegotiated, as it is for many early women writers in contemporary criticism), but their capacity for sustained, complex, and sophisticated contribution to our understanding of the human condition.

Clearly, what has been outlined above does not apply uniquely to literature—all other art forms could be subjected to the same discussion. What is being defended is seriousness and a kind of truth—not 'truth' in the sense of establishing new facts, but in a refusal to oversimplify, in a belief in the complexity, subtlety, richness—and indeed uniqueness—of each human experience, expressed through metaphor and the working of human imagination.

And this notion of a kind of truth enables us to return to the values of imaginative writers whose canonical status is more problematic. Whether or not authors are popular or not is irrelevant; there have been popular canonical authors (Bunyan, Dickens, Graham Greene). The argument is about the value for readers of the view of the world put forward by particular authors. To put it at its crudest: someone who believes that people are really more or less as Jeffrey Archer portrays them is (I would be happy to argue) wrong compared with someone who believes them to be more or less as Dostoyevsky portrays them. We may not like or agree with Dostoyevsky's vision, but it does not trivialize; rather, it expands, and makes us think of possibilities that are both important to us, and hitherto unimagined. The depth of the human spirit is reflected in his view of the world where lesser writers concentrate on the surface only. (And a crucial part of the discussion of any novelist may involve attempting to define which end of this spectrum they are nearest, so critics concern themselves with the seriousness/profundity of the world view of—for example—C. P. Snow, Ken Kesey, A. S. Byatt, Julian Barnes, or Roddy Doyle.)

Clearly it would be an error to suggest that literary criticism can be reduced to single-issue discussions of this kind, but the accumulation of such issues defines world views and critical positions. Similar considerations influence discussion of other art forms, and of real-world events.

The teaching of literature can thus be seen as a means of introducing learners to such a serious view of our world, of initiating them in the process of defining themselves through contact with others' experience. How it is best done, what the relationship between 'reading' and 'literature' needs to be for the greatest number of people to be led to literature, exactly what books are most appropriate at what levels—these are questions for teachers to address. But the seriousness of the enterprise should not be doubted. It is only when these reading processes are centrally addressed as processes, and when the debate moves away from content to what we do with literary texts, that genuine literary issues can be addressed. Otherwise any curriculum will remain vulnerable to Eagleton's criticisms.

8   Assessing literary competence

Introduction

Because literature has the intimate relationship with values that I outlined in Chapter 7, it raises special problems in assessment. This chapter tries to isolate major themes in educational discussion of that topic and considers their relevance for teachers of literature. It is particularly useful to do this because the assessment of literature has attracted less attention from commentators than language assessment has. The points made in this chapter apply with modifications to the assessment of language too, but taking literature as my starting point enables me to raise some of the problems with conventional views of assessment within a strongly value-oriented context.

Committed readers believe that literature has an important role in education. We want it to be taught, in some form, so that learners receive benefits that we feel we have received from our reading of literature. But many teachers are wary of testing or assessing literary competence, and for many years they were able to limit assessment to formal, summative examination. Discussions of teaching literature, unlike those of language teaching, often ignored assessment issues. Within the British tradition lay a scepticism about formal testing which showed itself particularly in areas where values, either aesthetic or moral, were considered central, and also something of a sense that 'If you can count it, it is trivial'. But the revolution in attitudes to education of the 1980s and 1990s means that if we want literature to be taught, in most societies, we have to put up with it being tested.

The sceptics are not without worthwhile arguments, but there are also good reasons for testing which need to be taken seriously. Learners want to know how they are progressing, and want some formal feedback as well as our informal comments and encouragement. Parents or employers want to know that learners are receiving effective instruction, and governments and tax payers want to know that teachers are not wasting precious resources by self-indulgence or laziness. In addition, teachers and teacher educators will look for the best available information on successful teaching styles, procedures, and curriculum organization.

These demands pose special problems for a number of subject areas, and particularly for those where success is not easily defined. If you are repairing a car it either goes satisfactorily or it does not; if you are writing legibly, you can judge the result by the success of the reader in deciphering your work. Even though neither of these, even, is as clear cut as might appear at first sight (Who is a suitable decipherer? How far must a car go without being unsatisfactory?), the difficulties of judgement are not as extreme as for those subjects involved in (1) interpreting the world, or (2) responding to taste or style, or (3) assessing sincerity and genuineness. Judgement for the first involves considering different ideologies that operate in different places and times, for the second it involves crucial questions of who determines what is a good response, for the third it involves unavoidably subjective assessment in which personal characteristics of the learner come into play. And 'literature' finds itself firmly in the middle of all these problem areas. A successful reading of a work of literature is an act of interpretation, in a context where taste and style is often highly valued, and where inexperienced learners face an enormous temptation to rely on secondary understanding, parroting the opinions of teachers, textbooks, or critics.

Assessment of matters of judgement is always a complex process, and there are a number of forces in education which work against acknowledging complexity. Particularly where there are external examinations for large numbers of candidates, the procedures used will always aim at administrative convenience, and professionals will have a constant struggle to ensure that what is being measured bears some relationship to what teaching aims at achieving.

Principles of testing

None the less, these are not problems unique to literature. Underlying any discussion of testing literature must be a number of basic principles of testing that are shared by all subject areas in the curriculum. In this section these principles will be briefly surveyed.

In practice, in many countries, the various requirements of accountability referred to above are frequently put together, so that schools and colleges are judged by their students' results in tests that are intended for more limited purposes. Imagine a set of student results from a particular final examination in literature. If we analyse the ways in which such tests may be used, we can see that there is little value in using one test to try to perform too many functions. Often, a set of results from a particular test is used as evidence to assess:

1 Whether the student has learnt all that was required by the syllabus
2 Whether the student has an aptitude for the subject
3 Whether the teacher has taught the syllabus
4 Whether the teacher uses successful methodology
5 Whether the student's attitude to the subject is positive
6 Whether the student should go on to further study in the subject
7 Whether the student will develop further competence in years to come
8 Whether the student is competent/proficient in the subject
9 Where the processes of teaching need improvement
10 Where the students need particular help in the subject
11 Where the students' particular strengths are in the subject.

In practice, though, producing separate tests for all these purposes will be expensive, and will result in students spending all their time being tested. So judgements on all these matters may be made, on the basis of a limited number of tests, by professionals and others with different interests in education.

Let us tease out some of these characteristics. Some of them are concerned with the student's *performance* in relation to the syllabus (1), or in relation to an abstract view of general competence (8). Some of them are concerned with making judgements on the basis of performance about characteristics that are relevant to future study, aptitude (2) and attitude (5). These may feed into more obviously *predictive* issues, like how good at the subject the student will become (7), and these may be used in administrative gatekeeping for the selection process (6). Others are *diagnostic*, attempting to use test results to determine particular strengths and weaknesses (10 and 11), which may contribute to a student profile of competence. Several of these may also be used to assess the success of the teaching process, so that judgements may be made, on the basis of students' performance in relation to the syllabus (1), on whether teachers are keeping to the syllabus (3), or using appropriate procedures (4); thus test results may feed into discussions of *accountability* and of teacher *appraisal*. At the same time, the diagnostic element for learners may also be used to diagnose weaknesses in teaching procedures (9).

Now these processes are all approximate and uncertain. Let us consider them one by one.

Performance

A test can measure a student's performance only on the basis of the particular task that has been set, and only at the time the task was performed. We have to interpret the performance to tell whether it has any value as a generalization about what the student can do. Thus a bad essay may reflect a particular student's ability at all times, but it may also be a product of shortage of time in a formal examination, of hunger or tiredness, of inadequate teaching, or of laziness or lack of motivation, so that the performance does not reflect the competence of the learner at all. A good essay provides less scope for interpretation, but we still need to be sure that it could not have been learnt by heart, or copied (though most learners who do either of these reveal themselves by errors and misunderstandings untypical of competent performers). In general, though, performance will give us some direct access to a learner's ability, but we cannot tell how typical of that learner the particular performance is.

So performance has to be measured against a specification of what skills, knowledge, or feelings are desired.

Prediction

When we start using tests to predict such characteristics as future competence and attitude, or to define aptitude, we are dependent on further abstraction from any data we collect provided by a particular learner. We base such judgements on previous experience of learners in similar tests, and the ways they performed subsequently. Such judgements depend on previous research by psychologists, and on the belief that people follow more or less predictable patterns that do not vary greatly across different cultural groupings. The extent to which this belief is justified is a constant subject of academic debate. But we need to be very careful, as teachers, that tests are not used in inappropriate circumstances, so that assumptions about relevant cultural knowledge for Britain, for example, or the US, or about the role of literacy in society, etc., are not applied to societies where cultural knowledge is different, or literacy less widespread. The further our judgements are abstracted from performance, the greater the opportunity to introduce unjustifiable judgements in the process of interpretation.

So prediction has to be a measure of performance against previous performances by previously successful learners; thus a specification of behaviour by people who later became skilled performers is necessary as a starting point.

Gatekeeping

Yet many tests do tacitly predict, by gatekeeping. The small numbers of places in secondary school, or in higher education, make tests perform a social function in determining who can enter the gates and who cannot. Such tests—at best—are based on a prediction about potential performance at a later date. Unsatisfactory as this may be, it is preferable to alternatives such as bribery by buying places, or using personal influence. But gatekeeping is a means of rationing access to further study, or to particular professions, and as far as possible needs to relate to appropriate skills and abilities, if it is to be fair or efficient. It is not in itself a question of literary competence or of assessment, but of the uses to which these may be put—a political or social question. But once it is accepted that such selection is either desirable or necessary, to be fair judgements will have to relate to the best available professional opinion. So our understanding of literary competence and of assessment becomes crucial.

So gatekeeping has to be a measure of performance of candidates in some form of order, so that the most effective are let through the gate, and the less effective excluded—thus a specification of varying degrees of effectiveness is necessary.

All three of the interpretations discussed so far, performance, prediction, and gatekeeping, are interpretations for external purposes, to tell us what learners can do, what they will be like later, whether they are the best or the worst of their group. What about the process of learning itself?

Diagnostic purposes

Interpretation for diagnostic purposes has a value for the student during the process of learning. Here the test is used to define strengths and weaknesses of learners so that they can have their future experiences adjusted in ways that give them what is most useful for their particular needs. Such testing is not concerned so much with whether they can do something, as with what parts of the total field need more attention, and what can be left because learners are already competent. But again, of course, teachers have to make major judgements on a small amount of evidence, because we cannot possibly test the whole of the material that a learner has experience of. We have to interpret small examples of performance and generalize from those.

So diagnostic testing measures strengths and weaknesses, and is dependent on a specification of what these should be at a particular level of competence in a particular field. Thus good diagnosis depends on our understanding of how learners learn within any particular subject area.

Appraisal and accountability

On top of all the functions already described is testing that results from the fact that teachers and schools exist to enable learners to be successful. So—inevitably—people will judge schools and colleges by the success of their learners, and tests will have a tacit appraisal function for individual teachers, and an accountability function for institutions. This is most unfair, for such judgements rarely if ever take into account differences in the level of intake of particular classes, colleges, or schools, nor can you measure the quality of the experience of learners simply by measuring their performance. Yet performance is important, and part of the process of accountability should recognize this. For these reasons, tests of performance should never be the sole measure of teacher competence.

So any statement of institutional accountability or of individual teacher appraisal must depend on an explicit statement of what excellence as an institution or as a teacher should consist of, and measurement should directly reflect such a statement, as far as it can.

On top of these requirements testers need to ensure that their tests will actually work for their purposes. This means that unfairness should be avoided. Tests should not give irrelevant advantages to some learners, so a test of literature should not reward spelling unless it is felt that spelling is an essential requirement for competent understanding of literature. Otherwise good spellers without literary competence will benefit at the expense of bad spellers with it. Tests should not concentrate on one aspect of competence at the expense of others. Thus, the ability to recognize patterns of imagery in poetry may be valuable, but cannot be the sole feature of an examination without penalizing those who may be good at other equally worthwhile activities, for example, response to rhythmic variation. In other words, the test should be a *valid* reflection of the significant aspects of the subject being taught.

Discussion of principles of testing also assumes that the same person should achieve the same results whoever marks the paper, and—ideally—whether they take the paper today or tomorrow. The test should be *reliable*. However, for most teachers this is not a major issue, though it is for those who set large-scale examinations for many candidates. Within one class, in a close relationship with a particular teacher, the issue of reliability is less important—but validity, the extent to which the test really tests what you have been teaching, can be very important.

Establishing reliability is never easy, and often demands a statistical sophistication for formal examinations that literature teachers may well wish to leave to professional testers. But it is important that underlying principles are understood, for unless we are clear what each test requires us to measure, we are liable to produce (or worse still allow others to produce) unsatisfactory interpretations. To take one basic example: a test of attainment does not require us to discriminate between learners—if you want everyone to be able to understand the irony at the end of Shakespeare's 'My mistress' eyes are nothing like the sun ...', you can produce a test which everybody, or nobody could perform. And that would tell you who has and who has not attained that target. A gatekeeping test, however, needs to stretch out the list of candidates to discriminate between them as fairly as possible, so that the best go forward and the less good stay behind. For that purpose a much more sophisticated notion of attainment is necessary.

All of this should make clear that processes of testing are unavoidably bound up with definitions of the nature of the subject and what it is to be competent in it. Different commentators disagree among themselves not so much because they disagree about testing processes, but because they have different conceptions of their subject. 'Literature' is a term which is constantly argued about and redefined. How does it relate to general reading (is it different at all?)? Is it a reading, or a reading-and-writing activity? Is there a canon of essential works, or not? Is there a national (British), a linguistic (English), or an international tradition including translations? Is its goal personal growth, or the creation of writers, or the development of critical taste, or empathy for others through the reading of imaginative fiction, or what? All these questions are being debated, along with questions of the nature of meaning, and whether texts have privileged meaning or not. How you locate yourself in relation to these questions will partly determine how you devise tests for learners, and how you will react to those imposed by external authorities. But whatever our own views on the process of teaching, the issues outlined in this chapter will inevitably recur whenever we are faced with the need to devise, or to prepare for tests and examinations. These have to be seen as social constructs, cultural artefacts designed for purposes that we constantly redefine.

Testing literature

In this section I shall state some of the particular difficulties that arise for literature, in relation to the general testing criteria discussed in the previous section.

First, performance issues pose the fundamental problems mentioned at the end of the previous section. What are the skills, what knowledge, what attitudes and affective states are expected to be 'learnt' in a literature course? Among the many views that have been held at different times are the following:

- knowledge of: the English literary tradition, western literature, a local literary tradition, literature as a human activity, terminology for the analysis of literary texts, particular texts in detail
- attitudes to: literature, the world in general, including tolerance and respect for particular literary traditions, for cultural differences, for the imagination and the intellect
- skills in: criticism of literature, analysis of texts, critical ability with ideas in general, using the imagination, writing personally and creatively
- response to: creative work (literary and non-literary) both receptively, in reading, watching or listening, and productively, in writing, painting, composing or performing.

No doubt there are other possible factors to be identified in particular education systems, but even this initial list indicates the complexity of specifying what exactly we may mean by competent literary performance for our learners.

If we are faced with the need for predictive tests, we shall need to draw upon the accumulated experience of teachers in judging what are the appropriate goals for particular levels of literature teaching, and how far these may be attained by students at particular points in the education system. Although this may sound a more formidable task than that for performance testing, in fact teachers' judgements are often very reliable in predicting future competence. The biggest difficulty lies more in establishing the characteristics of good literary performance in general terms—the task required for performance testing as outlined above. Once there is clarification of what exactly are the agreed purposes of teaching literature, the practical issues of prediction are made easier by the skills that teachers have acquired from past experience. However, there is a major research question for those of us who want to understand what happens in teaching, to determine the nature of the different judgements made by teachers at different stages in schooling and to make these explicit. While this research question is of great interest, it does not need to be answered before teachers can teach competently—fortunately accumulated professional expertise can be effective without necessarily being explicit. But if we wish to pass it on to others through teacher education, or if we wish to make comparisons with other countries, explicitness becomes central to our project.

Gatekeeping tests for literature raise major questions. Particularly, they raise questions about the relationship between holistic and analytical responses.

Holistic responses will involve use of the complete set of skills that someone has developed, all the relevant knowledge, all their understanding. In traditional examinations, the essay response is the best example. Here, the student is asked to perform in the same way as the competent critic or commentator, in responding to a problem, or to a text. As a selector for academic work, this kind of exercise has certain advantages, because it aims to explore learners' capacities to perform like mature readers of literature. However, it does assume that the goals of literature courses are necessarily to produce readers of this kind, and it leads to substantial personal judgement in the marking process. Experienced markers can obtain a high degree of reliability by grading a range of free-response, holistic answers in order, establishing the agreed best third, and worst third of the scripts, then looking closely at those in the middle, and rank ordering all scripts in each of the three groups. Judgements may be as explicit as possible with criteria being extensively discussed, and markers may acquire the ability to produce results that are very close to those of other markers (indeed with this procedure it is usual for each script to be judged by at least two markers). The effect will be to produce an order, more or less agreed, from the best to the worst script. The problem in practice is not that major injustices are done in the ordering, so much as that the cut-off point (where the 'gate' is shut) is usually in the middle where the candidates bunch themselves closest together, and where it is arbitrary whether a particular candidate is above or below the people closest. If you add this to the fact that some performers under achieve under examination conditions, or may have been having a bad day when they sat the particular examination, you will see that some unfairness is inevitable. On the other hand, we should not attribute this unfairness to the testing procedure. People are not stable performers to that degree of sensitivity, and no one will ever devise a test that measures complex competences reliably once and for all, in any set of capacities. Gatekeeping tests provide a once-for-all chance in many education systems, but this provision is imposed by political decision, and those involved with testing cannot be blamed for the consequences of such decisions. Far better is a range of different types of test across a period of time, with candidates being judged as good as their best performances. But such procedures are more expensive and time-consuming, and are therefore harder to argue for.

Finally, diagnostic testing again depends heavily on a specification of what we are teaching literature for. Once we have clarity about that, we can start seriously addressing the issues of the strengths and weaknesses of particular students. And since diagnostic testing is part of much work in literature, it reminds us that testing must be seen as part of the overall teaching–learning process. The purpose of any curriculum is to help learners learn something worthwhile. Only in so far as testing assists this process is it valuable. Since testing is inevitably 'unreal', because we do worthwhile things for their intrinsic worth, rather than to be judged by some outsider, too much domination by tests destroys the reality and value of the activity. The pressures for testing outlined at the beginning of this chapter are all legitimate, and we cannot avoid some testing if we are to be allowed to teach literature at all. But testing is not itself teaching, though doing a test must relate systematically to learning, as my argument has tried to indicate. The relationship between the two is complex, and doing a test is not itself learning. Learners, teachers, and outsiders are right to insist that there should be some testing; but teachers are also right to be wary of the dangers.

PART FIVE

The politics of language teaching

9 British cultural studies

Introduction

In this chapter I want to demonstrate the overlap between personal belief systems and participation in international education. To do this I explore the educational background to the rise of interest in 'British studies' in the early 1990s. I examine some tensions between arguments for a nationally-based curriculum area and for teaching as an emancipatory activity, and then consider such issues in the light of recent approaches to research on the curriculum. Finally, I consider the teacher's role as mediator in an attempt to define the most appropriate methodological stance for an inevitably contentious subject area.

First, though, it may be helpful to express some of the concerns that many teachers feel about the new interest in this field. The concept 'British studies' raises a number of problems for educators, particularly those brought up, like myself, within the liberal tradition that has dominated intellectual thinking in the second half of the twentieth century. The generation that was educated in the years after the Second World War acquired a number of tacit assumptions that proved highly productive in the optimistic period of international regeneration, but which are severely challenged by the pessimism underlying contemporary conservative culture (including 'New Labour', which is surprisingly uncritical of recent conservative tradition). Among these assumptions was a belief in the power of formal education to overcome the fundamental problems of poverty, ignorance, and disease and (in the strongest version) to create a peace-loving and creative community of egalitarian altruists. Such naive hopes required a liberation from the local loyalties that had led us all to two world wars, to bureaucratic tyranny, and racist dogma. Education was internationalist, optimistic, mildly anti-wealth and suspicious of national governments unless they were engaged in freedom struggles against the major imperial powers.

This picture may be a stereotype, but it is by no means a caricature. In the 1960s, volunteers from the 'developed' world poured into 'developing' countries to teach in schools and universities, and do their bit to dismantle their own empires, or (as with the Peace Corps) to undermine others'. In Africa and Asia national ideologies were promoted, as a means of overcoming more local loyalties, usually paying lip-service to some form of socialism, each aiming at greater independence, greater equality, greater international anti-imperialist collaboration, and (though less explicitly stated) greater power over their own destinies. Conservative prime ministers welcomed the winds of change, and nations like South Africa which resisted were consigned if not to the dustbins of history, at least to those of the United Nations. And central to the realization of these goals was the education system, designed to a western European pattern, senior-staffed by western trained teachers or by imported western expatriates (frequently written as 'ex-patriots', as indeed they often were), superimposed on the vast traditional network of ordinary people's cultural relations, with which it scarcely interacted at all.

Nor was this model solely a response to the fragmenting twentieth-century empires: it drew on a long-standing European tradition. Nationalism, emancipation, and increased educational provision had contributed massively to the collapse of the European empires following the First World War, and to earlier nineteenth-century freedom movements (see Hobsbawm 1962: 164–71). The rhetoric of the succeeding power configurations, whether for the Communist International or for the League of Nations, reinforced beliefs that the wider the collaboration, the safer the world would become.

Teachers were the minor missionaries of this process. What they did to their pupils in Europe, their pupils did to theirs in turn, both at home and abroad. Education and progress rode together, hand in hand.

It is easy to ridicule this model, for the conflict between these internationalist aspirations and nationalist *realpolitik* was plain to see. But it offered a potent ideal to education: an opportunity, it seemed, to contribute to the improvement of the world both by overcoming petty nationalisms and by advancing equality between nations. Ironically for western exponents of this view, the substantial shift in economic power away from the west, arising from what the west calls the 'oil crisis' of the early 1970s, coincided with (and perhaps contributed to) the popularization of the conservative and the postmodernist critiques of such optimistic hopes. But these criticisms have been increasingly questioned as the 1980s have moved into the 1990s, and the aspirations of the 1960s may prove to have worn better than their critics anticipated. For, while not entirely disinterested, the cause was certainly not ignoble. Not only were children's lives sometimes saved, the negative effects of technology sometimes mitigated, tyrannies sometimes defeated (even if others arose), but the side effects of the free-market economies springing from the right-wing critique (perhaps allowed to develop more aggressively by the acceptance of impotence implicit in the cultural relativism that was central to the left's critique), have been the predictable emergence of virulent nationalist movements whose ideologies will inevitably conflict with the pluralistic tendencies of mass communication, air travel, and increased educational opportunity. While we cannot avoid sharing the disappointment at the continuing poverty, the continuing violence and instability of the countries for whom a generation of professionals worked (it seemed) so hard, it is difficult any longer to accept that intervention by professionals was the problem rather than the response to a need. The World Bank has been increasingly attacked for its insensitive implementation of monetarist policies, and the pressures of major crises in Africa, Europe, and the Middle East force social intervention back into the centre of the west's agenda.

In such an atmosphere, the competing ideologies, the post-1945 left-liberal consensus explicitly opposed by Thatcherism, and the monetarist identification of democracy with the free market espoused by the right, are engaged in a more equal struggle than they were a decade ago. Education once again has international relevance. The 'universal subject', the emphasis on what is shared by human beings rather than the cultural oppositions that create difference, is again important. As universality has been abandoned for particularity, transnational loyalties have become parochial or ethnic, and the negative effects are visible in each day's newspapers.

Thus any discussion of the teaching (or learning) of British culture poses, acute ideological problems. If we are being asked to accept the ethnic or cultural reductionism of the 1980s embedded in the curriculum in the form of nationalist studies, we need to examine our principles with great care, for it would be easy to slip into triumphalism in an effort to simplify and clarify complex historical processes for learners. On the other hand, if we are in fact responding to a demand by offering a set of values that can be defended in terms of universal needs, we have a responsibility to make as valuable a contribution as we are capable of. Either way, since we are considering a curriculum area, we are obliged to relate its justification to broad educational concerns. In the rest of this chapter, I shall consider the implications of educational research for a responsible role for British studies, and particularly for teaching methodology.

Britishness in a liberal perspective

The educational assumptions attributed to the 1960s reflect a view of British culture, a view based on a confident political and social tradition. In this tradition Britain's most distinctive contribution is a willingness to wash its dirty linen in public (because of a self-confident pride in the effort to improve through public and accountable criticism), and a civic life that values incorruptibility, public service, and lack of concern for personal gain. At its best it risks priggishness, at its worst hypocrisy; but it incorporates ideals that were popularly and justifiably celebrated by atheoretical libertarian writers from Milton and Fielding to Orwell. If the worth of such values for British studies now appears less self-evident than it might have done in the past (and such assertions are notably absent in discussion of the area), it is because British studies are being promoted when the concept of 'Britishness' is much disputed. The term became popular at the same time as the then Conservative government, elected by a minority of voters, explicitly repudiated compromise and national consensus and produced a unilateral assertion of what national values were (see, for example successive disputes over history and English language in the National Curriculum for schools in the years 1988 to 1993). Consequently, discussions of British studies that recognize the historical changes underlying recent arguments cannot avoid consideration of the relationship between national identity and oppositional politics. Nor would the situation necessarily change with a different government, for the tension identified in this argument will apply wherever individual teachers have to teach elements of a belief system based on nationalism.

In addition to these concerns, internal to Britain, there are concerns about the international context. Promotion of British studies has developed at a time when assertions of national values against supranational groupings have become politically significant in several parts of the world. 'National' here becomes defined as ethnic, set against governmental, as in the break up of Yugoslavia, Czechoslovakia, and the USSR. But 'Britain' is supranational in the same sense as those countries were. What makes Britishness defensible if the others are not?

Because of the complexity of such problems, it is easiest to take the view that there is a market for British studies, and there is a legal entity, Britain, and to offer no more than description and analysis. Hence we have the eclectic sets of materials recommended by interested agencies (the 1991 British Council list of library materials for British studies included books on art, economics, education, geography, language, law, literature, politics, science, religion, sport and theatre along with customs, food, the monarchy, television and other less weighty topics). This is Britain as a set of given facts, or, as an organism, but not Britain as something to believe in. Yet a set of given facts does not constitute a serious curriculum area. Without a carefully thought-through teaching methodology, such an approach risks being no more than intellectual tourism, or, high-grade stereotyping.

Any serious curriculum analysis forces us to ask 'What is this field of study for?', and that takes us back to the ironies of our earlier discussion. If we teach values as 'givens' how do we distinguish ourselves from the most reactionary 'blood, language, and soil' nationalism? If we teach values as 'process', we have to locate ourselves in a critical spirit within or outside the national and nationalist values referred to above.

So there is a fundamental irony that we cannot escape. If we approach teaching about Britain in a cautious, liberal, consensus-seeking manner, looking for what is best for civilization, and defending approaches because they are as right as we can make them, not because they are British, we are in direct conflict with both internal and external ideologies. We can no longer defend this view as a product of a particular British tradition (popularly, the myth that 'this was what we fought the Second World War about'; academically, a pragmatic, sceptical, and reformist philosophical and social tradition incorporating Locke, Mill, Popper as well as Wilberforce, Gaskell, Orwell, Beveridge *et al.*). Yet we can only teach what we are, and when we devise procedures, design curricula, and define new courses, we cannot avoid questioning and problematizing 'Britishness' if we belong to an academic British tradition. Perhaps the only way to proceed is to be explicit about this paradox.

Key curriculum concepts

'British studies' is a curriculum innovation which has been developed outside the mainstream of British education by practitioners who have not usually been closely involved in the debates in Britain of the past 20 years on the nature of the curriculum. It is therefore worth briefly describing some of these issues, for they have direct relevance to questions about British studies which are central to our discussion.

Much formal education has not in the past seen the content of education as problematic. Subject material might be adjusted and updated, but the range of subject areas, the generally accepted knowledge associated with each subject, and the hierarchy of prestigious areas essential for social advance is not typically questioned except in periods of crisis. None the less, curriculum discussion may be directed to a range of different goals. Skilbeck (1976) discusses classical humanist, reconstructionist, and progressivist ideologies. Each of these places emphasis on a different aspect of the educational process. Classical humanism emphasizes the knowledge and content inherited from the past, reconstructionism the needs of society for social improvement, and progressivism the development of individual potential in all its diversity. Golby (1989) develops Skilbeck's categories to include several different curriculum traditions. He calls the tradition that is concerned with implementation of an allegedly agreed and uncontentious body of knowledge technocratic, links it to reconstructionism, and argues that the British National Curriculum (introduced for England and Wales only by the Education Act of 1988) combines humanist and technocratic assumptions. He calls for a new cultural analysis curriculum which draws on recent understanding of educational sociology. This approach, which Golby only sketches very briefly, reflects a substantial shift in academic thinking about education, arising from experiences of the 1960s and 1970s.

In Britain, partly as a result of the major structural readjustment caused by the introduction of comprehensive, rather than selective, secondary schooling in the 1960s, many curriculum assumptions previously taken for granted were isolated, examined, and probed during the 1970s and 1980s. A key text in this process was Michael F. D. Young's edited collection *Knowledge and Control*, published in 1971. In this book a number of contributors questioned, with varying degrees of polemic, the beliefs about the stability and neutrality of the knowledge that schools made available to learners. For many in British education, this offered the first serious engagement with ideas that had been emerging throughout Europe in the decades following the Second World War. But it also pushed discussion of the curriculum away from a prescriptive and confident assertion of what the adult world ought to be doing to those in receipt of compulsory schooling, towards a more serious sociological concern with current practices as they were realized through action in classrooms, and the processes by which knowledge was filtered through the education system to learners. This shift marked a striking departure from the concerns about the different forms of knowledge of philosophers of education like Hirst (1974), who were interested in structures that were independent of social context; it was also distinct from the curricular traditions of psychological schools such as behaviourism, as in Bloom's (1956) taxonomy of knowledge, skill, and affective elements in the curriculum. As Hammersley and Hargreaves (1983) point out, the new sociology of education encouraged suspicion of too clean and rationalist an approach to the curriculum and a greater recognition of 'the unavoidable daily "messiness" of teaching' (p.4).

Following this shift in academic educational interest, a number of commentators have examined the processes of social construction: the history and sociology of school and university subjects (generally, see Becher 1989; for English, Doyle 1989; Protherough 1989; Evans 1993; for modern languages, Evans 1988). Similarly, curriculum practice has been re-examined (Hammersley and Hargreaves 1983). From the technocratic view of the curriculum as essentially an administrative issue, perspectives shifted to a concern with its unobserved working processes—a shift reflected in metaphors like 'the hidden curriculum' and references to the curriculum as 'the secret garden' (Lawton 1979).

The technological tradition of curriculum discussion concentrated on key structural issues, of scope and coverage, of ordering, of aims and objectives. The sociological approach was concerned far more with processes and behaviour rather than plans and specifications. But the two approaches are inevitably complementary. Without a structure and demarcation, there is no field within which to behave, and educational institutions, being institutions, inevitably produce statements for planning and administrative purposes. Such statements cannot avoid questions of structure and coverage.

Objectives for particular student groups

The curriculum issues referred to in the previous section raise a number of questions for 'British studies' which can be related to the traditions discussed there. On the one hand, we need to consider the prime objectives of the subject: are we exposing students to a liberal-humanist perspective, Britain as part of a particular tradition in western civilization, Britain at its most humane? Are we using Britain as an instrument in social reconstruction, the basis of free markets, the bastion of democracy? Are we providing an example of a particular form of constantly deconstructing, constantly criticizing and analysing, constantly problematizing, approach to cultural phenomena, in which it is the academic approach that is distinctively British, rather than the content, which is incidentally British, but really need not be? On the other hand, we need to consider the internal structure and organization of material to be included: how much are we concerned with 'knowledge about Britain'? How explicitly are we concerned with affective factors, encouraging students to admire and respect Britain? Are there skills that we would expect students of British studies to acquire? What should be the scope and coverage of the course? In what sense can there be progression? What are the appropriate modes of assessment?

Answers to these questions are crucially dependent on the needs of particular groups of students. Yet the educational issue cannot be reduced to any simple identification of topics with student interests or anticipated needs. In the British Council's newsletter *British Studies*, Montgomery (1993) contrasts the concern with British institutions characteristic of German *landeskunde* and French *civilisation* courses with the cultural analysis approach inspired by the work of the Centre for Contemporary Cultural Studies at Birmingham University. This is a similar contrast to that advanced by Golby between technocratic/humanist and cultural analysis curricula. Yet, in the context of British studies, the latter approach is developing a methodology which still requires decisions to be made about which aspects of British life to concentrate on, and consequently a selection of 'institutions' for investigation. If the choice of institutions results in a sociology of British society becoming the subject of investigation, potential students will presumably be those who need to understand the nature of contemporary life in Britain. If the choice is more historically or institutionally based, there is still a choice to be made between 'typical' institutions, and those events, such as literary or scientific achievements, that have held their place in contemporary interest because of the value that subsequent generations have placed upon them. Thus we have a matrix:

Past	e.g. Henry Mayhew Mass Observation	e.g. Isaac Newton Virginia Woolf
Present	e.g. Private schools Leisure pursuits	e.g. Tom Stoppard? Thatcherism?
	'Typical'	*Valued*

Figure 9.1: Cultural studies curriculum matrix

But as the entries for the present illustrate at once, decisions about what to include immediately raise questions of whose values are being promoted by the selection of topics for study. While there may be a general educated consensus on major events, intellectual movements, and significant individuals in the past (though of course the debate on 'the canon' in literature discussed in Chapter 7 is specifically about the contentiousness of such claims for consensus), no such agreement is likely about contemporary social phenomena.

This disagreement is only partly a matter of distance. Montgomery comments that outside Britain institutional study is valued, while inside it cultural analysis is preferred. Certainly, for many learners, Britain is in some sense a 'given' culture which needs describing, while inside Britain, individuals are engaged in the sometimes painful process of creating Britain through struggle. But while curricular decisions made by insiders will reflect participant ideologies in a different way from those made by outsiders, both will be claiming typicality, for both will be selecting significant items from a much wider range of possible choices. None the less, this difference in perspective raises serious questions for foreign learners who are taught by British teachers. Participants in the culture will inevitably present an insider, and partisan view which foreign teachers of British studies may hope to avoid.

Montgomery, however, sees the two approaches more neutrally as options for any teachers, and attempts to find a principled way of relating their two sets of concerns. He sees such a way in the study of language as a social institution. Variation according to user is, he suggests, variation of identity, defined particularly by class, gender, and region. Variation according to use is more closely tied in to institutions. The study of dialectal variation will contribute to a concern for cultural analysis, while institutional analysis will be supported by a concern for genres and registers. But this is to associate both approaches with the data as 'given' while proponents of the cultural studies approach often have a more fundamental agenda, associated with the critical discourse movement (Fairclough 1989). For such advocates of cultural studies, part of the teacher's role is to expose the power relations underlying varying social discourses, and to show the workings of competition and political manoeuvre that underlie apparently innocent linguistic and social relationships. Again, the tension between ideological stance and a body of content shows itself.

British studies as a curriculum area

It will be clear from previous discussion that any curriculum area will simultaneously show some characteristics of all earlier traditions. Institutional constraints in education are strong, and however radical teachers wish to be, they are forced by their professional environment to operate within unavoidable constraints. Among these are the following:

1 A selection has to be made from the mass of possible subject matter
2 The process of teaching and learning requires that the selection is given some organizing principle(s) to enable learners to come to grips with it at all
3 Criteria for the selection and organization will include explicit (or, frequently, implicit) goals for the learners to achieve; these goals must reflect a realistic assessment of what learners bring to the study at the beginning: if they do not the curriculum will be so unrealistic that it will be doomed to failure
4 Failure to make the processes in 1–3 above explicit to teachers will result in wasted effort and inefficient organization.

It is striking how little discussion of learning issues actually appears in accounts of British studies. Yet our understanding of processes of learning is now both sophisticated and sensitive to variation caused by variables such as age, cultural expectations, and previous experience of learning. A number of key points about processes of learning can be made from the experience of formal education in the past. First, learners construct their own meanings by a process of engagement with appropriate data. They must, therefore, he offered opportunities to interact with data. Second, their construction of effective meaning depends on being able to integrate their new understanding with the sets of categories they are already using to deal with previous experience. Thus learning depends on interaction between the new and the old. Because of this, the procedures used in teaching, and the selection of issues for study, will need to recognize not only motivating and appropriate material, but also means of integrating comprehension of Britain with the knowledge and understanding that students already have.

This brings us to a key paradox. Most discussion of British studies has concentrated on ways and means of 'presenting' one or other of the many possible critical perspectives on Britain. Yet unless we are able to clarify exactly what kind of study activity a particular course is practising, and how this relates to the previous understanding of the learners, the presentation risks being educationally ineffective. It seems to be widely agreed, as Dunn remarks, 'that the "Studies" part of the title has come, over the last twenty years, to be understood as a code for interdisciplinarity' (Dunn 1994: 11), but, as he points out, there may have been a retreat into traditional discipline structures. However, it is not so much the discipline structure that is likely to pose educational problems; most subjects, and particularly social studies, become interdisciplinary when they are taught to relatively inexperienced learners. Rather, it is the difficulty of relating the classroom processes called upon by teachers to the knowledge and experience of the learners. Understanding such knowledge and experience will cause us to examine the obvious issues of how to connect knowledge of British constitutional structures, scientific and literary history, or sporting practices with learners' knowledge of their own countries. It also enables us to explore the relationship between critical approaches expected by British-based teachers and those expected of learners at home, and the epistemologies that learners take for granted (knowledge as authoritative fact versus knowledge as best available hypothesis versus knowledge as vested interest of the powerful, to stereotype some contemporary positions). It also forces us to take into account the relationship between the skills and practices for the consideration of cultures that learners have already acquired and those needed for British studies. All three of these general areas are of course closely bound up with each other, in ways that are culturally grounded, and difficult to analyse, so it is scarcely surprising if the solution is often a tendency to rely on the content and to slide past other issues with eyes averted.

The most sophisticated attempt to deal with these other aspects is described in the work of Michael Byram (his published works from Byram 1990, to Roberts *et al* 2000, and references in those, give a full picture of his work). He started with a concern for the role of culture in foreign language learning, but his studies have far wider implications, because of his interest in developing students' abilities to analyse and comment on culture, both in their own and in the foreign environment. None the less, turning learners into ethnographers in their own right (which is his solution to some of the problems) is not an easy option on courses in which overseas travel is unavailable, so modified versions of cultural sensitization will be necessary on many courses. What makes Byram's approach significant for us, though, is the central role of learners' understanding of their own cultures. The main way through most of the paradoxes that have been identified in this chapter seems to be a recognition that British studies must in the end be a comparative activity.

Once the specification of what learners can be expected to understand already about their own culture has been completed, the traditional concerns of technological curriculum design become primarily administrative issues, relating to resources, time, and space. But that first specification has wide implications. It will suggest, for example, the extent to which the British studies curriculum should concentrate on a historical approach, perhaps drawing upon liberal-humanist assumptions of quality and value, or on a contemporary analysis, either 'critical' or sociological-descriptive. It will suggest, of course, the extent to which artistic, scientific, economic or popular culture may be prominent, and it will indicate realistic approaches to assessment (where relevant), student participation, and teaching mode.

Yet to describe the curriculum task in this way is not to deny the importance of the individual teacher. The educational principles discussed in this chapter provide a background for what is always, in the last resort, a personal relationship between teacher and taught. Such a relationship depends upon the teacher feeling that the approach adopted is not just appropriate to the learners, but also honest to the teacher's beliefs. Consequently, whatever understanding derives from the kinds of analysis referred to here must be modified by careful interaction with the teacher's own expectations. At the same time, as I have tried to argue here, the teaching role when dealing with British studies is subject to ideological and attitudinal tensions which other subjects such as language and literature possess in a much more muted form. For British native-culture teachers working overseas, some of these problems may disappear if they can always teach and plan jointly with a local person. But many of them are inherent in the subject, and constitute both its risks and its challenges.

10 Teaching English as a world language

Introduction

This chapter surveys the recent history of English teaching from an international perspective, choosing Africa as a representative point from which to consider key issues about the immediate past and the next few decades. As in previous chapters I emphasize the uncertainty and unpredictability of factors which will influence planning, while attempting to show that we can still operate in principled and consistent ways. Of course, in the teaching of English, our perspectives change from place to place and from time to time. Yet it is unlikely that the interpersonal skills needed by the best teachers have changed fundamentally over the centuries. The technologies change and new skills become necessary—but the ability to relate to learners, the role of enthusiasm for the subject, and the interaction of these with a sense of purpose and organization were as relevant in 1500 as in 2000. None the less, the ways in which individual teachers conceptualize and talk about their task do change, and it is sometimes helpful to consider contemporary issues from particular, located positions in other periods. For example, if we examine the history of the teaching of English in Africa, we shall see many interesting reflections of the ways in which it has been taught in other parts of the world. In about 1950, for example, the teaching of English language in Africa, offered as it was to a small and elite minority of the population, was not seen except by a few individuals as fundamentally different from the teaching of English in Britain. Indeed, many of the syllabuses at that time for the teaching of English in Africa were syllabuses virtually identical to those which were produced for the teaching of English in the UK, and there was an assumption that the purpose of teaching English was certainly to provide communication, but also to provide an education in a literary and classical tradition similar to that which native speakers had. Subsequently this view was modified by a number of shifts in perspective which led us now to be less confident about the nature of language, the role of the English language itself, and the roles of native speakers.

English in the world

The idea that English had a destiny beyond Britain has an extensive lineage, at least as far back as Samuel Daniel in 1599:

> And who in time knowes wither we may vent
> The treasure of our tongue, to what strange shores
> This gaine of our best glorie shal be sent,
> T'inrich vnknowing Nations with our stores?
> Which worlds in th'yet vnformed Occident
> May come refin'd with th'accents that are ours.
> (Daniel 1950: 96, quoted by Bailey 1992: 97)

The following three centuries of imperial and economic expansion found English increasingly seen as a vehicle of an often insensitive triumphalist culture. By 1950 Britain had just emerged from a war in which it had commandeered the English language as part of the war effort. In 1942 George Orwell had written in a book review in *Horizon*:

> In this war we have one weapon which our enemies cannot use against us, and that is the English language. Several other languages are spoken by larger numbers of people, but there is no other that has any claim to be a world-wide lingua franca. The Japanese administrators in the Philippines, the Chinese delegates in India, the Indian nationalists in Berlin, are all obliged to do their business in English.
> (Orwell 1970: 250)

Yet the confidence that the English language is a weapon of value to English people was already being undermined by the very processes Orwell referred to. The massive spread of English teaching in the years after the war led to the position that is now true: that the English language no longer belongs numerically to speakers of English as a mother tongue, or first language. The ownership (by which I mean the power to adapt and change) of any language in effect rests with the people who use it, whoever they are, however multilingual they are, however monolingual they are. The major advances in sociolinguistic research over the past half century indicate clearly the extent to which languages are shaped by their use. And for English, the current competent users of English number up to seven hundred million, living in every continent (Crystal 1985), of whom less than half are native speakers. Statistically, native speakers are in a minority for language use, and thus in practice for language change, for language maintenance, and for the ideologies and beliefs associated with the language—at least in so far as non-native speakers use the language for a wide range of public and personal needs.

Perhaps fortunately, neither native speakers, nor non-native speakers, are coherent, homogeneous collections of people. Within each group diverse interests lead to alliances and co-operation, but equally to conflict and disagreement. But if a substantial number of non-native speakers did come to see themselves as a single group with major shared interests, the impact on the international language would be considerable, and native speakers would be directly affected, for changes in world language English would necessarily affect the sub-dialects of native speakers' Englishes.

Another widely accepted belief of 50 years ago was that the distinction between first and second languages had considerable value in the processes of curriculum development and of teaching. Now, we are much less sure that the boundaries between first, second, and foreign language are discrete, and certainly it is not clear exactly what it is that one is saying in talking about somebody as a second language user. The traditional distinction, in which second language users learn in a society which adopts the target language for some public functions, and foreign language users do not, is increasingly hard to maintain. For many purposes English is becoming (no doubt temporarily) a lingua franca within Europe and in other traditional foreign language settings, while in traditional second language settings, such as West Africa and India, there is a lively debate over the relative independence from English of the regional varieties. When the Nobel Prize for Literature has been awarded to Soyinka, and British-based prizes for fiction regularly go to authors whose works reflect a multilingual background and a multilingual experience (Rushdie, Mo, Ishiguro, Desai), over the heads of writers who are monolingual English users, the usefulness of the hard distinction is difficult to defend. Further, even as a basis for teaching methodology, it is unwise to distinguish techniques suitable for second language work from those for foreign language work. Indeed, the teaching methodologies of the communicative movement in language teaching (Johnson 1982; Brumfit 1984; Prabhu 1987), together with associated humanistic movements (Stevick 1976), may be seen as attempts to introduce second or first language teaching assumptions into traditionally foreign language contexts. Certainly, my own biography shares with Munby, Widdowson, Wilkins, Davies and Johnson (to name only a few of those who published in the field of CLT in the late 1970s) the sequence of initial experience in ESL contexts, and a later interest in EFL concerns accompanied by dissatisfaction with the aridity of many foreign language techniques.

It thus becomes clear that concepts like second language or first language teaching only have relevance when associated with certain kinds of organization in the school system. But of course it is not only the notion of a second language and the notion of English which have become problematic. The concept of 'teaching' is not the same as it was in 1950. The shift from the teacher as an instructor to the teacher as a facilitator, with a corresponding increasing emphasis on learner strategies is well documented (for language teaching by Stevick 1976, among others). And since the high point of progressive ideas in the classroom, probably sometime in the 1970s, there have been determined attempts by governments to return to the notion of teacher as 'instructor'. So we tend to think about teaching as a contested activity with forces pulling us in both these directions.

Not only has 'English' become international in the last half century, but scholarship about English has also become international as interest in studying English has spread across different countries. We are no longer a language community which is associated with a national community or even with a family of nations such as the Commonwealth aspired to be. We are an international community and there is not a human being alive in the world who does not have some interest in the future of English, primarily because of the economic dominance of the US.

There are substantial arguments continuing about the extent to which English may or may not be valuable in the economy of countries in different parts of the world, for (as Coulmas 1992 demonstrates) language issues are closely bound up with economics, as well as with politics. Consequently, questions about the relationship between language policies and power pose serious arguments to which in the next 50 years we are going, between us, to have to work out answers. But for the moment, let me try to chart some of the shifts of the last 50 years.

English teaching since the Second World War

In language teaching, we have seen a series of informal policy movements. There has been a shift from literature to language, and a shift from language to learners. The shift from literature to language I have already briefly referred to. Many people interpreted the fairly immediate goals of language teaching as access to a literature, perhaps because the most powerful model of language teaching was the teaching of classical languages, Latin and Greek, in nineteenth-century schools. Now dead languages are very convenient of course, because the culture is defined and relatively static and to teach a language as if it is dead perhaps prevents the people learning it from seizing it for their own purposes. Throughout the first years of the twentieth century, it was clear that there was tension between people who wished to have syllabuses that were based on a heritage model, whether in Britain or overseas, and people who had experience overseas trying to fight their way through to linguistically more sensitive, better researched bases with communication as the prime goal. Whether it was the earlier vocabulary movements associated with Michael West (1953), or the development of a sense of the structure of the English language through Harold Palmer and A. S. Hornby (see Howatt 1984: Chapters 16–18), or whether it was the movement that led ultimately to a recognition of English for Specific Purposes (ESP) in the late 1960s and early 1970s (Swales 1985), the tendency was to move towards a specification of the nature of language in communication. All of these shifts in perspective were attempts to undermine the idea that the prime role of language teaching was literary (even though literature is itself a significant mode of communication), and hence to move towards what came eventually to be called communicative competence. It could be argued, though, that the shifts of the last 50 years owe more to three very different sources, none of them primarily concerned with education. First of all, there is the rise of linguistics and sociolinguistics. We are now much better informed about the nature of language. That is not to say, of course, that in 1950 there were no linguists of great sophistication (though it was only in 1944 that J. R. Firth was appointed to the first British professorship in general linguistics). But the 50 years since then have seen a movement, very significant for our argument, towards recognition of the enormous variety of dialects, codes, and styles, and the enormous range of ways in which these can be operated. No language is a single language, and this is much more clearly documented now than it was, partly of course because the technology to record and store spoken language is now available freely as it was not 50 years ago. That is the first substantial shift.

The second substantial shift is not linguistic at all, but relates to oil, and the economy associated with it. We can recognize the change in financial relationship between the rest of the world and the countries that industrialized in the nineteenth and early twentieth centuries very clearly. This change is seen in the symbolic as well as the actual effects of the early 1970s fight for higher prices for the oil that kept the old industrial economies running. Indeed, you could argue that many of the changes and innovations in English language teaching in the 1970s owe their origin to the fact that there was an international market of people who wanted English (especially in the oil-rich gulf states), wanted it immediately, and for the first time had the means to pay lavishly for it. So somehow experts, teachers, curriculum developers, needs analysts, publishers, and cultural organizations from the countries with a strong interest in English all responded; there was a ferment of ideas and activity in the aftermath of the oil crisis. In contrast, the 1980s were years of consolidation, when the profession tried to make sense of, rather than advance from, that rich body of 1970s ideas. So my second major cause of change is the economic shift following the oil crisis.

The third major change of very recent years is the impact of a philosophical tradition which originates mainly in the non-English speaking world. In an inchoate, but none the less powerful shift of sensibility, a consensus has developed from the work of a succession of philosophers writing mainly in French, to some extent in German, and to a smaller extent in English in the US. This movement has roots in a variety of sources including major writers such as Bakhtin and Vygotsky in the first decades of the Soviet Union, and the structuralist programme of Saussure (see, among many surveys, Hawkes 1977; Wuthnow, Hunter, Bergesen, and Kurzweil 1984). These 'post-modernist' philosophical ideas dispute many of the clear-cut assumptions that underlay professional attitudes towards language and language teaching as much as they challenge beliefs about the value of science and the idea of progress. Foucault particularly has influenced people looking at classroom and pedagogic language and led researchers to ask questions like: 'Who is empowering whom?'; 'In whose interest is the language being used?'; 'If language is knowledge, and knowledge is power, who should decide what languages are taught and how?'; 'In whose service is the concept "native speaker"?'; 'In whose service is the concept of "teacher"?' (See Cameron, Frazer, Harvey, Rampton, and Richardson 1992; Fairclough 1989.)

The view that language is substantially a matter of power relations has had a major impact on several strands of contemporary applied linguistic thinking. The claim made is not so much that there is no knowledge, but that recognized knowledge is a more or less straightforward reflection of the exercise of power. In spite of the political risks implicit in this position (for a vulgar interpretation leads to politicians happily accepting the view that as they have the power they also have all necessary knowledge), it is none the less a doctrine which in the 1970s and 1980s has undermined popular acceptance of what were regarded as certainties—including some of the certainties about English language teaching that we had inherited. It is, for example, a particularly happy argument in addressing the privileged status of the 'native speaker' in language teaching (Rampton 1990; Davies 1991).

I do not myself believe that knowledge is merely power, but I do believe that language use, and knowledge about language (including linguistics) has a specifiable relationship to power (see Joseph and Taylor 1990); hence debates about the future of English, in any part of the world, are arguments in part about the potential for power of the use of English. That is why within Africa discussions about the appropriate language for African writers to adopt (Ngugi 1981) are so significant in defining future cultural options. Consequently the question of who is entitled to 'own' English becomes very important because, once one acknowledges the diversity of purposes, ideologies, and political or social roles that English can perform, the stated principles underlying the introduction of English into schools, colleges, and universities require much fuller democratic discussion than when they were previously accepted as self-evident. Hence the spirit of the times leads towards emancipation and empowerment in the use of English, with moves away from literature (with its emphasis on a tradition, and a controllable curriculum) towards speech to which everyone has access, with effective oracy as a substitute for effective literacy. There is a shift away from English as part of an education that inducts you into a humanistic tradition, to an education that facilitates your communication for whatever you want with whoever you want: a shift therefore towards a notion of a communicative competence where the communication is defined by the capacity of individuals of different cultures to interact. Hence the relationship between the language and the culture requires careful analysis by local teachers and writers.

However, while we have to acknowledge that languages are used as symbols in cultural argument, we cannot accept a complete identification of language and culture. Language codes are always capable of variable meaning; if they were not, we would be unable to construct new messages out of existing codes. So the meanings which constitute our cultures cannot be exclusively identified with the language which expresses them. Indeed, the fact that translation can be achieved, however partially, indicates that culture can transcend language. Ever since the independence movements of the 1950s, debates about the interaction between national and world literature, local and international spoken English, the needs of a very large multilingual community and its connections with the world community, have been widespread in Africa (see, for general African policy issues, Bamgbose 1991; for Nigeria specifically, Omodiaogbe 1992). It is very interesting to note that debates of a generation ago in Africa are in some ways only now becoming significant in current discussion in Europe and in Britain (see, for example, discussions of emerging language policy in Mitchell 1991).

But these debates are central to the definition of individual and group identities, and the relationship between language and identity is extremely complex. Taking on a new language adds to one's repertoire of identities, but also complicates and destabilizes what we were aware of before. Sometimes, a kind of subjective schizophrenia develops, but this process of developing multipersonality options is not limited to linguistic choices for an individual. It is characteristic of the educational process, and not just in an international context, but in all education. Any cultural movement that takes you away from the security of your local base towards a wider national, or international, or pan-world set of concerns, is threatening as well as stimulating. It may be exciting but it may also be frightening and it will almost certainly be destabilizing if it is effective. What we have to recognize is that English in the next 50 years will be strongly in the forefront of a process of destabilization which other technological forces are pushing us unavoidably towards: unavoidably, because this destabilization, the process of becoming bicultural or multicultural, of being bilingual or multilingual, is imposed on us by television, by the jet plane, by the fact that we can be in London yesterday and almost anywhere else in the world today. It is imposed on us by the fact that if something happens in Beijing, people in Eastern Europe look at it and decide on how they are going to respond or not, as governments, as individuals, as people; by the fact that there is constantly available commentary on world events in a number of world languages, including English; by the fact that we are constantly arguing about what language we are going to use and where.

Yet the process is not actually as simple and automatic as I have implied, because of course, even if we acknowledge the power of these changes, we also create structures that control and guide them, and these may be instruments in the tacit competition between different languages of wider communication. There are mechanisms through which the practice of English teaching is developed, specifically created to try to control and steer the process. National and international initiatives develop through government organizations, or through professional associations like TESOL and IATEFL, and these initiatives operate within a set of larger social and political concerns. In the 1960s, the British Council ran a scheme called Aid to Commonwealth English as part of its efforts to support and promote English. The shift in discussion from the notion of empire to the notion of commonwealth was a shift also determined and dictated by the kinds of relations that states wished to have with each other, and accompanying that another ideological shift was influencing attitudes to education systems in general. Reading a writer of the 1940s like George Orwell, you become acutely aware of the push towards a welfare state socialism in response to the 1930s fascist movements. At this time education was seen as a right to be offered to everybody, and language education as a right came along with it. But soon education was seen in the context of a cold war confrontation, with international aid money tending to go to the places where the rich states needed to preserve influence. Later, there was a shift away from the model of welfare state cold war based exported education to a concern for north/south relations. Whether economic structures were actually contributing to or detracting from the successful development of states within the south block became a concern for the World Bank. Western aid stopped resisting communism and started promoting capitalism and free markets. And education systems, of course, continued to operate, but adjusted their meta-discussion to current ideas. International funding depended on what were the oppositional forces that the donors perceived, and education, and within education language teaching, tended to reflect the contemporary rhetoric. Thus rhetoric shifted from language as a liberating and democratizing instrument in the 1970s, to communication for international trade in the 1980s.

The next 50 years from an African perspective

It may be felt that this concentrates too much on non-language teaching factors, but the point I am building up to is that the next 50 years of English teaching will actually be subject to factors we cannot define through an understanding of language or of language learning/teaching. Let me provide one or two possible scenarios that might be good or might be bad, but which may well affect us profoundly.

Let us predict, for example, that South Africa consolidates itself as a stable, peaceful democracy in the next 30 years; this will be an immense, complex, very difficult task, but not an impossible task. If South Africa works well, there are in that country infrastructures, a body of talent, all the bases for major investment, in education as in so much else. The resulting changes in Southern Africa will have impacts throughout the whole of the rest of Africa that we cannot predict at all. It could be that the major direction of new developments in African language teaching may be spread from South Africa, or from other sources within East or West Africa, or from none of them. But what happens in South Africa will probably have a major impact on educational funding in Africa, including English teaching, more than any decisions made by English professionals alone. And supposing South Africa were to adopt a non-English policy, or were to reduce its role in education very substantially, that would affect the thinking of all states in the continent.

What happens in Europe may have a major international impact. There are people who believe that English is dying in Europe and that German will take over its international role as the European Union welcomes more East European members. Some view this with pleasure, some with scepticism, some with fear, some as a challenge: personal views vary. But the key factor is that we cannot tell in advance what is going to happen. *De facto*, English is a very widely used language in the European Union. That may imply that English becomes increasingly the major means of external contact for Europe, but it may also happen, of course, that other languages become more important as power relations within the European Union change.

If you look at the possibilities of the next few years, it is clear that outside Europe, Arabic, Japanese and Chinese are going to be immensely important international languages, not just because of the numbers of speakers, but because in Australia and New Zealand and increasingly in the Americas, Chinese and Japanese are the languages that they are taking most seriously, while Arabic will spread as Islam continues to gain influence.

The impact of the economy in the Pacific basin on the future of English could be very important. The knock-on effect to English of a major rise in Japanese as a foreign language or in Chinese as a foreign language, either of which could become a far eastern lingua franca, could be very considerable in the next 50 years. How we shall respond to that, we cannot predict, but it is clearly a possibility that we have to be ready to anticipate. From an African perspective, the future of the Pacific rim may seem less immediate than the future of South Africa, but far-eastern economies have already had a significant impact on the west, and a global economy makes detailed prediction an unwise act.

None the less, we can probably expect that much more important in Africa will be international attitudes to schooling, access to publishing, the questions of who controls the publishing, who invests in the publishing, where the markets are, who produces the teaching materials, how local the materials can be, where the teacher supply comes from, how much teachers are paid in relation to equivalently educated professionals in other spheres, and where we develop the research and the understanding we need. All of these are issues in which there will be shifts in the global view, just as much as there will be shifts in the local view. I predict that in the next 50 years we shall not see as much confidence in processes of schooling, internationally, as we had in the last 50. But what I cannot predict is how we will cope with education in that situation. It is already apparent that assumptions about the value of compulsory education are breaking down; whether this will lead to major changes in policy or not cannot be predicted.

One of the scarcely noticed features of the violence of Eastern Europe in the 1990s is that it follows 50, 60, 70 years of strong moralistic, political, and egalitarian indoctrination in schools. If there is ethnic conflict, it is not because schools have failed to try to combat that possibility. Inevitably, critics of compulsory education will conclude that schools have not been as effective in creating peace-loving citizens as they were expected to be when they were established. On the back of that, there may even be the view, arising out of similar conflicts, that multilingualism, the shift towards a combination of local languages and world languages, is not as effective an educational goal as it previously was thought to be.

People coming together in the European Union have tended to come together via the major languages. But one of the effects of coming together is a revival of many of the minority languages in various countries. What is not yet clear is whether the tendency of the early 1990s in Europe, which is that more and more small countries with a single dominant language are emerging (Slovenia, Latvia, the Czech Republic, for example), is a tendency which will continue in Europe, or indeed be imitated outside Europe (see Harris 1994).

All of these are very broad issues, but they serve to show how there is much in the future which we cannot predict, but which may have substantial impact on our thinking about language education in the next 50 years.

The final major area I want to refer to is the communication revolution. English is seen by many as the means by which we shall all have access to information technology. Certainly, as a metaphor, it has been immensely powerful in our field.

In linguistics, information technology was the quiet undercurrent of the revolution in linguistics led by Chomsky. Behind that paradigm shift was the question, 'If you looked at language as if it was programmable, what would that imply?' And many of the defects, as well as many of the strengths of that linguistic revolution, since 1957, have been defects and strengths associated with that metaphor. But of course that metaphor also reflects a real change in technology. There is easy knowledge transfer now in quantities and at speeds unimaginable in the past; there is real communication, not just through television, but real communication of massive databases. We can in principle, anywhere in the world, connect to databases that are traditionally preserved in Paris or in Oxford or in Washington. Information availability is there for the stealing, as well as for the borrowing or buying. And inbuilt into this technology are threats to freedom as well as opportunities for creating freedom. It may or may not lead (I suspect myself that it may not) to massively improved ways to assist language learning by means of IT (Information Technology), but it will inevitably enable us to exploit the knowledge associated with our language teaching much more effectively because knowledge in itself is much more freely available. More substantially, it may render much language teaching unnecessary, as programmes of translation enable knowledge transfer across languages more cheaply and more efficiently than long-term and expensive language teaching systems. And if that happens, the relationship between the small elite of polyglots, with direct access to the languages of science and technology, and the receivers of knowledge who do not have that, will be a major political concern.

It is almost a cliché that the communications revolution will define the next 50 years. But completely different social and political events, which cannot be predicted, will lead to attitude changes and ideas that we cannot attempt to anticipate. Who would have predicted the significance, 50 years ago, of several of the major themes that underlie much international discussion now? Who could have predicted AIDS for example? Who could have predicted the oil crisis in quite the form in which it came? Who could have predicted the way the Soviet block collapsed?

Because we cannot know this future, we could be tempted to opt out of the demanding task of thinking and planning. That would be most irresponsible, for we mould and sometimes create the forces that make the future. The interaction between technological change, changes in general attitudes, and our personal roles is going to be what determines where we go as individuals and as members of professional groups. We have to make ourselves available to each other. Nobody can plan in detail for the kind of chaotic future that internationally entwined economies necessarily cause for themselves. Nobody can say 'I know what will happen in the year 2010'. (We do not even know whether it is going to be called the year 'twenty-ten' or 'two thousand and ten', let alone what is going to happen.) In that year, we cannot say exactly where we expect to be. But we can equip ourselves with structures that will enable us to be responsive. Wherever we are, there will always be a demand for some international languages; there will always be a demand for some trans-group languages and we can create structures so that we are able to respond in informed and responsible ways to new events, where we empathize, where we react and understand, and sympathize and feel for the learners in whose service much of the work that we do has to be placed. So, at a personal level we need regular communication.

We need structures for analysis too, through research, through clarifying and theorizing practices, even if this is not actually directly in the service of the learners; we analyse in order to reach fuller understanding of the processes. We can organize to create the conditions in which we can do these things and we can publicize the things that we have done.

Now of course it is very easy to say that this is what we have to do. But we can be sure that the need for international communication through direct personal contact will never be greater than in the next 50 years. The Internet cannot be a substitute for the holistic understanding that comes from direct meetings with individuals; knowledge transfer cannot be a substitute for seeing, smelling, hearing and walking through unfamiliar settings. There will no doubt continue to be large numbers of varied and different agencies of international communication, so that we can continue to learn from each other, to share our experiences, and respond to the forces (many of which, as I have been arguing, will not be themselves linguistic or pedagogic) which shape our personal and professional lives. What must happen is that these are used as instruments of co-operation, not competition, for humane and not exclusively for technical purposes. For if we drift much further towards market-driven and technology-based contact alone, it will be a poor look-out for Africa, and an even poorer one for the world as a whole—for a globalized world is only as good as its poorest communities.

11 The English language and language rights

Introduction

When I first addressed the ideas outlined in this chapter, I was speaking to the International Association of Teachers of English as a Foreign Language (IATEFL) in the northern English city of York. As it happened, it was a strikingly appropriate place to discuss multilingualism and power, for York is the birthplace of Alcuin (735–804). From York Alcuin, author of a grammar of Latin, set out to spend the last 20 years of his life educating Europe. As the *Dictionary of National Biography* states, in York he 'acquired a training as many-sided as was possible for the time and with more of a literary tendency than was then usual, except in the Northumbrian and Irish schools' (Stephen, 1885, Vol. 1: 239). Historians used to refer to this period as the 'Dark Ages', with the implication that Roman culture had faded and died. But it had not, it had simply moved to the geographical periphery, to Ireland, to Northumbria, to the Eastern Empire. And from the periphery European culture was reinvigorated, by means of language switching, as Anglo-Saxon, Irish, and peripheral-language speakers took over Latin for their own cultural extension and for the restoration of past intellectual traditions. Later, in the fifteenth century (using the Christian calendar) it was Islam, through Greek and Arabic interchange, that restored the continuity of European culture, as Latin fragmented into a variety of mutually unintelligible dialects, many of which readers of this book no doubt now speak and write.

So the phenomenon I examine in this chapter is not new. Though it is complex and needs to be addressed through philosophical principles, it is highly relevant to the situations in which most second and foreign language teachers work. And that, of course is why recent years have seen increasing interest in the relationship between language and power, an interest that has unavoidably directed attention to the international role of English. Both at home and abroad, the English language and those who promote it have been under attack. For the prosecution we can read books like Fairclough 1989; Tollefson 1991; Crowley 1991; Phillipson 1992; and Pennycook 1994, whose titles *Language and Power*, *Planning Language*, *Planning Inequality*, *Proper English?*, *Linguistic Imperialism*, *The Cultural Politics of English as an International Language* illustrate the agenda they address (and sometimes the answers they offer). From the middle ground of attempts to provide coherent policy and the research to underlie it have come studies such as Roberts, Davies, and Jupp's *Language and Discrimination* (1992), and planning documents from a number of countries, for example, Australia's *National Policy on Languages* (Lo Bianco 1987) or South Africa's National Education Policy Investigation (NEPI 1992). For the 'defence' of English have emerged various responses, including the English-only movement in the US (Baron 1990), much of the discussion around the British National Curriculum for English (for example, Marenbon 1987), and a range of political statements from governments and their representatives.

As part of this debate, a claim has been made that individuals have language rights, and it is this claim, and its implications for EFL teaching, that I would like to explore in this chapter. To do so, I shall be forced to look at the work of a number of political and social theorists and philosophers who have no direct interest in language or education. However, it is important to see that discussion of power, rights, and legislation in language or education is weakened if it ignores general discussions of those concepts.

Language rights

Phillipson quotes Article 27 of the 1966 International Covenant on Civil and Political Rights:

> In those States in which ethnic, religious, or linguistic minorities exist, persons belonging to such minorities shall not be denied the right, in community with the other members of their group, to enjoy their own culture, to profess and practice their own religion, or to use their own language.
> (quoted in Phillipson 1992: 94)

He then considers a review of international conventions and decrees (Skutnabb-Kangas and Phillipson 1989) indicating that:

> No declarations ensure the maintenance of the mother tongue, despite the many clauses condemning discrimination. A valid conclusion is therefore that the *existing international or 'universal' declarations are in no way adequate to provide support for dominated languages.*
> (Phillipson 1992: 94–5; italics in original)

He also quotes the United Nations *Draft Universal Declaration on Indigenous Rights* 'as it establishes as fundamental human rights that indigenous people should have' (Phillipson 1992: 96):

> 9   The right to develop and promote their own languages, including an own literary language, and to use them for administrative, judicial, cultural, and other purposes.
> 10   The right to all forms of education, including in particular the right of children to have access to education in their own languages, and to establish, structure, conduct, and control their own educational systems and institutions.
> (Document E/CN.4/Sub.2/1988/25)

In October 1987, at Recife in Brazil, the UNESCO organization AIMAV (now the Association Internationale pour le Développement de la Communication Interculturelle) called on the UN to adopt a universal declaration of linguistic rights. Tollefson cites a statement from this seminar which glosses the implications of the call to the United Nations:

> Every social group has the right to positively identify with a language or languages and have its identification accepted and respected by others.
> Every child has a right to learn fully the language or languages of his/her group.
> Everyone has the right to use any language of his/her group in any official situation.
> Everyone has the right to learn fully at least one of the official languages in the country where she/he is resident, according to his/her own choice.
> (Tollefson 1991: 172)

Such claims have support from commentators outside formal conferences also. Tollefson himself notes (1991:211), in summarizing what his book stands for, 'A commitment to democracy means that the use of the mother tongue at work and in school is a fundamental human right', and later:

> This perspective views language as parallel to race, gender, and other factors as deserving of legal protection, and it measures social justice by the extent to which societies ensure that individuals may use their mother tongues for education and employment.
> (both quotes Tollefson: 211)

In 1989, the FIPLV (Fédération Internationale des Professeurs de Langues Vivantes) endorsed the call for a language rights declaration, and devoted a number of newsletters to the issue, with a substantial range of rights proposed. These went beyond the demands so far made to include, for example, a right 'to be taught within the framework of state education' at least one language 'to extend ... social, cultural and intellectual horizons, and to enhance international understanding' (no.9 in a statement approved by the FIPLV General Assembly in Pécs, Hungary, August 1991, quoted in FIPLV 1992: 2). Even further, FIPLV moved on to look at the linguistic needs of particular professionals and to discuss these as rights: 'The linguistic rights of scientists' (FIPLV 1993: 2–3).

At the same time there have been several national and supranational attempts to impose greater variety or depth of language learning. Even the British government which blocked a 1989 European Community proposal to enforce the teaching of two foreign languages extended the role of foreign language teaching by making it compulsory for all in the 1988 National Curriculum proposals, though this position has been weakened somewhat in the 1990s so that foreign languages do not have equal status with other major subjects in the curriculum.

It will be clear from the brief survey above that a number of different issues are embedded in the language rights documentation. Concerns for the rights of minority communities are linked with concerns for a more equitable range of multilingualism among the dominant taught languages. Concerns about educational provision are associated with the rights of individuals to practise mutually agreed modes of behaviour, and concerns about government support are linked with concerns about the cultures individuals identify themselves with.

At the same time, anyone involved in teaching the world's most dominant languages cannot ignore this discussion. Whether it is teachers of other dominant languages being concerned about the threat of English (discussed by Phillipson 1992: 97), or speakers of minority languages feeling under cultural threat, the major villain is likely to be English. Pennycook's attempt 'to seek out ways of thinking about the position of English in the world that will help myself and other teachers to understand our work differently' (1994: 5) is necessary for all who identify professionally with English.

What are 'rights'?

'Rights' have a long history, but in contemporary discussion they are usually related to post-1776 constitutional argument. But even here, as the Ghanaian Robert Gardiner pointed out years ago, their role was in practice strictly limited:

> ... the principles of the American Constitution, the French Declaration of the Rights of Man—these were all designed for domestic consumption only. In the United States of America, even the home market was limited; the 'fundamental creed' which states that 'all men are born equal and are endowed by the Creator with certain inalienable rights' was not allowed to embrace the Negro slave.
> (Gardiner 1966: 80–1)

Nor, we should add, did women figure prominently at that time in the drafting of such rights.

Discussion of 'rights' is still of course extensive in philosophical and legal literature. In this section I want briefly to consider key issues in defining inclusive 'rights'.

First, we can consider 'rights' either as objective statements of fact based on a pre-agreed position, or as personal assertions of a claim that ought to exist. Thus, that I have a right not to be discriminated against in employment on the basis of my gender or ethnicity is a fact in relation to British law which can be established by reference to parliamentary legislation. The linguistic 'rights' that are being claimed, however, are not of this kind but the second type: assertions of a claim—but a claim that their advocates no doubt hope will eventually be enshrined in law.

Second, we have to recognize that while legal rights are relatively straightforward, providing there is an agreed legal system to refer to, moral rights are much more complicated, because there is no single moral code accepted by all human beings, and assertions of 'right' usually reflect points of conflict between different codes.

We see this, for example, in the current debate about the extent to which animals have rights. Thus moral rights are usually stated as if they are facts in terms of the (individual) moral system of a specific speaker, or as part of an assertion of a claim against those who represent other sets of rights (for example religious leaders who maintain a different moral system from that of the complaining individual).

Third, discussion customarily distinguishes between negative and positive legal rights. Negative rights enable us to do anything that is not positively forbidden. Thus we have a right to free speech except where the law forbids it (we may not libel individuals or abuse racially). Positive rights depend on the law, and we could not exercise them if the law did not exist (we have a right to a defence counsel if accused of an offence and put on trial, but only because the law says so). And in both cases we as members of the community have rights to do (or not to do) anything not forbidden by the law, and the same for anything specifically permitted by the law. In so far as we have accepted the legal control of the government, we are covered by the law.

But with moral rights we are in a competitive situation. An assertion that there ought to be a moral 'right' is establishing the moral situation of people who may not agree either with the right itself or (more importantly) with the moral claims or code of which that right is a part (so animal rights protesters want to establish rules for those who think animals have no rights, as well as for those who do, and people against—say—euthanasia are demanding that their moral code applies to people who would commit themselves to a quite different moral code). Hence the lobbying of moral rights to become in some sense legal rights requires the existence of an agreed legal body that has jurisdiction over all parties, whether they agree with the right being claimed or not. Some would say that this also entails a relationship between obligations (to other people or to the legal body) as a condition of possessing rights—but that is clearly incompatible with views that animals or young children have rights, and it is easiest to treat rights as entitlements because we exist rather than because we behave well!

Discussion of rights is also bound up with discussion of justice, and our 'contract' with the state. The contemporary liberal position is exemplified by John Rawls (1972) who has advanced two baseline principles:

> First Principle Each person is to have an equal right to the most extensive total system of basic liberties compatible with a similar system of liberty for all.
> Second Principle Social and economic inequalities are to be arranged so that they are both:
>   (a)   to the greatest benefit of the least advantaged ... and
>   (b)   attached to offices and positions open to all under conditions of fair equality of opportunity.

(Rawls 1972: 302)

However, this view has been attacked as concentrating on the individual, as if each individual is isolated from all communal ties and cultural associations. As the political scientist John Dunn comments, in an analysis of the principles of nationalism, in such an argument 'there is no place for the nation or indeed for the sovereign political body as a unit of conceptual account' (Dunn 1979: 57).

This is not the place to explore the technical details of the Rawlsian and communitarian debate, but the relationship between individual and the community is none the less important for us. This is because language rights cross the boundary between individual and communal or group behaviour, as becomes clear if we look at the statements on rights which have been quoted in the section on language rights above.

Language is performed 'in community with other members of their group' (1966 Covenant), 'Every social group' has a right to identify with a language, 'Every child has a right to learn fully the language or languages of his/her group' (1987 AIMAV). So it is to considerations of the role of community that we must now turn.

Community

The Canadian philosopher Charles Taylor, in a careful discussion of 'multi-culturalism', notes the relationship between claims for recognition for marginalized groups and the notion of 'dignity', as in the phrase 'dignity of human beings'. The underlying premise, he comments, is that dignity is not differentially distributed—everybody shares in it. This emphasis on the dignity of individuals has been an increasing feature of social discussion since the late eighteenth century, and is associated with the sense that I as an individual have an identity, unique to myself, that I should be true to (Taylor 1994: 27–8).

This 'authenticity' to oneself (to join with Taylor in using Lionel Trilling's 1969 term) derived from Rousseau, but is most powerfully articulated by the German philosopher, Herder. As Taylor puts it (1994: 30):

> Each of us has an original way of being human: each person has his or her own 'measure'... There is a certain way of being human that is *my* way. I am called upon to live my life in this way, and not in imitation of anyone else's life. But this notion gives a new importance to being true to myself. If I am not, I miss the point of my life; I miss what being human is for *me*.
> (Taylor 1994: 30)

Taylor then goes on to point out that two very different conclusions have emerged from this tradition. On the one hand is the politics of universalism, which emphasizes the equal dignity of everyone. On the other is the politics of difference, which emphasizes the uniqueness of each individual. The first concentrates on a universal human potential, which entitles us to respect in virtue not of what we have done but of what we have the potential to do. The second concentrates on our capacity to be uniquely ourselves, again a universal human potential, though a potential to be different from others. However, because we become 'ourselves' in the process of communication, including using language, this may easily extend into a recognition not just of unique individual difference, but of unique cultural (or, as we have seen, language-using) grouping within and through which we realize our distinction and our difference. Thus 'a stronger demand has recently arisen: that one accord equal respect to actually evolved cultures' (Taylor 1994: 42).

It is this claim that raises complex problems for all of us. For a start there are difficulties in holding the two positions simultaneously. The universal human potential that deserves respect deserves it in relation to some universal capacities for good which can be judged 'good' against universally relevant criteria. Equal respect for actually evolved cultures, on the other hand, implies accepting all culturally created difference as equally deserving respect, thus denying the relevance of culturally determined external categories for judgement at all. The first demands that we are blind to human difference and respect the universally shared potential in each person; the second that we recognize and respect human difference, manifested in cultural groupings, as inherently and universally valuable precisely for the qualities that are unique and unshared.

Second, there are clear problems over what constitutes an 'actually evolved culture'. Taylor tries to arrive at a possible solution by suggesting we could believe 'that all human cultures that have animated whole societies over some considerable stretch of time have something important to say to all human beings' (1994: 66), but even this muted and cautious statement is very difficult to convert into practice. How long do you have to be a 'recognized' culture to qualify? And if all cultures deserve respect (as distinct from toleration), what does 'respect' mean? It cannot mean genuine admiration if it is offered to everyone's culture equally; indeed it risks becoming simply patronizing kindliness. But worse than being patronizing, it is likely to diminish cultural differences by forcing cultures to be judged as all examples of the same (vaguely defined but 'positive') phenomenon.

> If all cultures have made a contribution of worth, it cannot be that these are identical, or even embody the same kind of worth ... In the end, the presumption of worth imagines a universe in which different cultures complement each other with quite different kinds of contribution. This picture is not only compatible with, but *demands* judgements of, superiority-in-a-certain-respect.
> (Taylor 1994: 71, footnote, my italics)

But, and Taylor insists on this, such a view may be a presumption reflecting good will, but it can only be an *a priori* presumption based on our own moral commitment. Furthermore, we may add that if it is a presumption, it is a presumption based on the fact that cultures evolve, that is they are the product of individuals working together and changing their shared ideas in the process of working together through dialogue and interaction—as we see, for example, in the models of social theorists like Mikhail Bakhtin (most accessible in Holquist 1990) or of George Herbert Mead (1934). Whatever conditions we support, they must be conditions that allow cultures to evolve in this way; otherwise there will be no mechanism for change, adaptation, or learning.

It is arguments of this kind that have led Habermas (1994) to distinguish between the (individual or group) culture which will be different potentially for all citizens, and the common political culture without which they cannot live together peaceably, and which must be shared. The state can only maintain the conditions in which individuals may develop cultural practices; it cannot guarantee the maintenance of the practices themselves:

> For in the last analysis, the protection of forms of life and traditions in which identities are formed is supposed to serve the recognition of their members; it does not represent a kind of preservation of species by administrative means.
> (Habermas 1994: 130)

Habermas defends a position which is surprisingly similar to that of Rawls, but by approaching it not from the individual but from the cultural perspective. He points out that:

> Cultural heritages and the forms of life articulated in them normally reproduce themselves by convincing those whose personality structures they shape, that is, by motivating them to appropriate productively and continue the traditions.
> (*Ibid* 1994: 130)

Consequently:

> The constitutional state can make this hermeneutic achievement of the cultural reproduction of lifeworlds possible, but it cannot guarantee it. For to guarantee survival would necessarily rob the members of the very freedom to say yes or no that is necessary if they are to appropriate and preserve their cultural heritage.
> (*Ibid* 1994: 130)

Some commentators have moved to a similar position to that taken by Taylor for individuals, or by Habermas for a single state, claiming that similar considerations could be brought into play internationally. Charvet (1994), particularly, considers the implications of a cosmopolitan ethical theory, and concludes that 'we should not think, because we cannot have a world state, we cannot be members of a world-wide ethical order' (p.189).

Problems with these formulations

There are a number of aspects of the language rights discussion that require careful consideration. This section raises the issues that I see as most important, though it cannot explore them in the detail they deserve without taking up half the book with this single issue. First is the status of language users as communities; second, the domains in which rights may protect the use of a language; third, the role of formal education; fourth, the interactional nature of communication; fifth, the meaning of terms like 'mother tongue'; sixth, the economic implications of 'rights' commitments. Each of these reflects an aspect of language as the possession of a community, and the discussion of community above is therefore directly relevant.

Language users as communities

Language use only becomes problematic when there are languages or styles to choose from. Then, selection of language and style may result from, and also become a badge of, social differentiation. Indeed, we may go even further, and argue that whenever there is social differentiation, linguistic variation will reflect it. Thus, language users operate as communities through the linguistic choices they make.

Now, in some contexts there may be very little freedom of choice. Social pressures, often reinforced by a legal system, may constrain our linguistic options quite substantially. We may not interrupt freely in a church, a law court, or parliament, without observing complex and enforced linguistic rules. If we disobey them we can be subject to punishment, and even more—as for example in a church—we may be subject to peer pressure to conform.

But even in these circumstances we can (if we are willing to incur the risk of displeasure or sanction) opt out. We have some freedom of choice about the community we identify with. Hence, we can consider the issue of linguistic community as part of the issue of freely joinable communities in general, and our response to a liberal or restrictive view of responsibility to community will relate to our view about whether we should (or should not) enforce or encourage or otherwise influence through the legal system the free association of individuals. In this sense, Tollefson's view that language is analogous to race or gender is disingenuous, for race and gender categories and the social position they imply are imposed by others (though they may be willingly accepted by members also). The world is full of people who have opted out of linguistic roles that they were born into (we are not born with a language, but into a language community). The objection to racism and sexism is that they turn allegedly biological categories, acquired genetically, into cultural ones without the agreement of members of those groups. But membership of a particular language group has no biological basis whatsoever, and language is an entirely social/cultural category. Language users are thus more or less voluntary members of a community, and legislation about language use requires the law to take a view on how voluntary such membership ought to be. The right to practise as a member of a speech community would then be justified as the right of an individual to choose to practise an association. But the right would have to include (if it was to be a genuine right) the right to choose not to practise and associate as well as the right to do so. In this respect, language affiliation is more analogous to religious affiliation than to ethnic or gender characteristics.

Protected use of language

There is a big jump from my last statement to Phillipson's statement (1992: 94) that 'no declarations ensure the maintenance of the mother tongue', for accepting that declarations should ensure the maintenance goes beyond ensuring the right of the individual to practise as a member of the speech community to saying that (some of them at least) must practise. Protecting the freely chosen use of language is one thing; compelling (i.e. protecting the unfreely chosen use) has social implications that require careful analysis of the underlying politics.

But it will be clear, I hope, that I am confirming the need for protection of the right of individuals to practise the language they choose. In fact, this is not what some of the 'rights' statements ask for. They ask (and the references I cite here can all be found in the discussion of Phillipson 1992, and Tollefson 1991, above) for protection for members to enjoy 'their *own* culture … religion … language' (1966 International Covenant), 'their *own* languages' (1988 UN), 'languages of *his/her* group' (1987 AIMAV), etc. Here, individuals are being assigned to linguistic groups in much the same way as racists or sexists assign individuals to groups. I am sure that it was in no way the intention of the drafters of such documents to identify with racist or sexist practices, but to restrict the rights of language users to the language group within which they were born implies that in some sense we are inalienably members of a particular culture, expressed through a particular language, and that we should have a greater commitment to that than to any other cultural or linguistic grouping that we may wish to opt for. Mobility is implicitly seen as threatening. Once again, we are caught up in the problem that Charles Taylor noted, and we may well ask whether 'my' authenticity is the authenticity of the individual or of the group. And above all, if it is of the group, who is to determine which group I can or should authentically identify with? There may be a case for children being able to make claims on the language in which they were brought up for education—but it cannot be because they have a special loyalty to that unless we believe that our cultural inheritance is more than accident. Yet to link us authentically and exclusively with any particular culture is to deny freedom to choose, and indeed to deny a role for education, which is about extending and changing cultural repertoires. (Though we should in fairness note that some formulations, such as AIMAV's 1987 'Every social group has the right to positively identify with a language …' do recognize this problem.)

Thus if we believe in any sort of freedom to choose (however constrained) we have to be suspicious of rights which assign individuals to language groups by definition, whether those groups are widespread and threatening languages or small and threatened. On the other hand, we have to protect individuals' right to practise their language if they wish to. But the right has to be permissive, not compulsive in effect, unless it is a right at the expense of the freedom of individuals to choose. Hence the position of British National Curriculum proposals for Welsh (which must be learnt in Wales whether individuals or groups wish it or not, but will not be supported outside Wales even if groups do wish for it), or for ethnic minority languages (which are either not approved at all or must be taught only as 'foreign' languages) pose major problems in a mixed society. How the new South Africa deals with its eleven official languages in statutory provision will be interesting to observe, and many other countries have similar problems in defining policy in a multilingual environment. Certainly, the tendency to identify language with nation and region has an uncomfortable ring of 'blood and soil' about it, by blurring the issues of 'blood' (genetic), 'language' (culture) and 'land' (power).

Formal education

Some of the rights claimed make specific statements about formal education, and indeed about 'administrative, judicial' (UN 1988) and other organizational arrangements. Some, indeed, like FIPLV 1989, make claims on 'state education' which would fall foul of some current governments' right-wing policies on withdrawal of education from state funding. These claims raise difficult issues of the extent to which 'rights' have to underpin the specific legislative programmes of individual governments and individual countries. If 'rights' lie within constitutions, and are in some sense the criteria by which the well-formedness of laws are judged, then their claims cannot be too particular in relation to mechanisms for implementation. Anyway, any claim on educational practices runs into severe definitional problems, because there would have to be a list of administratively approved languages (as there is in England and Wales for the foreign language National Curriculum), and rights would then be fought over on financial grounds, because factors like teacher supply and training, production of teaching materials, etc., come in to play, as we shall see in the discussion below of economic factors. The key point to note here is that a 'right' on administratively organized social practices is a very delicate one if it is to be more than 'feel-good', wish-list aspiration. Because the number of mother tongues is potentially infinite, an infinite administrative commitment is being made by a promise to provide educational support. This may be possible (the right to a defence counsel in English law is also potentially infinite), but it does depend crucially on a judgement about the likely demand and the capacity of the larger community to supply what is needed. A legal right that could not be supported administratively is not worth the paper it is written on.

Communication as interaction

Underlying many of these problems is a key feature of language: it is inherently interactional. Individuals 'use their mother tongues' (Tollefson 1991: 211), 'in community with the other members of their group' (1966 International Covenant). But they also use them in community with members not of their group, to varying degrees depending on the range of contacts available. Languages are used to create solidarity, but also to threaten solidarity, to conceal, but also to reveal, to claim identity both within and outside particular cultural groupings. And this is important, because languages are not the same as cultures. Languages reflect the cultures of people who use them, and in some communities (typically isolated and relatively small) the isomorphism between language and culture may be very considerable. But none the less, inherent in language is a transcendence of any particular culture, because interaction is inherently cross-cultural. In order to see particular languages as identifiable with particular cultures it is necessary to reify culture, to fix it in some sense with finite boundaries. But because we make it, by interaction (not exclusively but substantially linguistic interaction), it has infinite capacities to respond to the challenges of new contacts and new relationships. Any single 'culture' is a collection of individual cultures, both fundamental (ideological commitments, epistemologies) and more superficial (bird watchers, statisticians, baseball addicts, and stamp collectors all share cultures). Each of these produces linguistic, semiotic, and conceptual variation, to which we adapt when we participate and from which we depart when we leave and associate ourselves with other cultural practices. In all of us (and especially in the contemporary international deracinated world) there are numerous cultures, each expressed in different community associations and different linguistic repertoires. Whole philosophies have been built round these processes of interaction (see for example Bakhtin 1981; Habermas 1984 and 1987; or Popper 1994a: 33–64). I do not need to explore the implications of these philosophies further, but we should note that each of them uses the communicative and interactional properties of language, freely engaged in, to establish the prime basis of cultural and intellectual development.

What is a 'mother tongue', etc.?

I have already raised some of the problems in defining or enumerating exactly what 'their own languages' (UN 1988) means, or how they can be incorporated into education and practice. Many, certainly a majority of the world's population, grow up in environments where several distinct languages are typically used in home and in the immediate neighbourhood. Multilingualism and multidialectalism are human norms, not deviations. The problems that many of the rights movements are addressing may be seen as by-products (significant and worrying ones) of state power in industrial countries. The question is not whether minority and ethnic rights need protecting, but what are the best ways of doing so. It is unclear that oversimplifying the roles of language (apparently to suit a Eurocentric model in which everyone has a tidy mother tongue and is identified with a particular, administratively definable culture), necessarily serves that purpose well. Even in the European context it is based on an impoverished view of individuals' linguistic repertoires (see Rampton 1990; Davies 1991).

Economic issues

Again, we have already raised many of the problems in our discussion of education. Because we all move in and out of styles, dialects, and languages (how diverse they are depending on our starting point), a commitment to equal involvement with all languages (dialects? styles?) raises complex problems of definition and a constant commitment to more and more financial investment, for the number of potential claimants is as large as the population itself. This is probably why territoriality is in practice used more often than language as a basis for language rights provision: it is organizationally tidier.

But provision has implications for materials, teacher education and supply, parental contact and many other expensive support mechanisms. Whereas a 'right' to shelter or health care could in principle be provided relatively equitably (though, as we know, most countries are not prepared to fund even these) because everyone's minimum needs are similar, an individual linguistic 'right' in education has structural repercussions that are almost unimaginable in their range and quantity. If we conclude that the 'right' has therefore to be awarded selectively, we may reasonably ask in what sense it is really a right at all. Yet no conceivable responsible government could actually commit itself to economic support for all claimants to linguistic maintenance. The only economic response that makes sense is to maximize, not to guarantee linguistic freedom.

Nor are such problems exclusively about education, of course, for interpreters, public signwriters, publishing houses, research programmes, and legal enforcement systems will be necessary if linguistic rights are to be guaranteed.

At the same time, we need to be clear that we cannot base resistance to a notion of language maintenance rights solely on economic grounds. Arguments such as those I have just outlined may contribute to the debate on practicalities, but the core criticisms have to be the earlier ones about individual freedom.

What about English language teaching?

The first point to stress is that people concerned with ELT cannot ignore the issue. Whatever reservations I may have expressed, we have to be clear that it is a very, very serious issue, and the extent of the demand for language rights only reinforces the need for teachers of powerful languages to address these concerns sympathetically and carefully. But we should not be ashamed of being in ELT either. The world needs languages of local, national, international and world-wide communication. If English did not have the dominant position (because of political and economic power far more than because of any conspiracy to promote the language), some other language would—because mass communication necessitates mass languages, and mass communication cannot be avoided or rejected.

But power, even unintentional power (and English brings with it a mixture of exploitation and altruism, just as any strong force does) needs control. We too need to participate in the control, and in the resistance to power abuse. How can we do this?

First, we can ensure that teacher development, teacher education, and teacher training is sensitive to the larger context. Teaching does not take place in a vacuum, and too few certificating courses address the underlying ideologies and philosophies of current practice. For language teachers especially (and perhaps even more for those who travel the globe in search of their language teaching) the need to consider issues raised in the books listed earlier in this chapter is crucial.

But to be grateful to those books for raising the issue does not entitle us to accept weak, sentimental, or glib argumentation. There are parts of several of the books which implicitly support illiberal, patronizing, or inconsistent positions in the name of freedom. Teachers need to be equipped to consider such arguments as part of their professional development—but also to recognize that this is a debate in which we have to address fundamental political problems with care and seriousness.

Second, we can establish what a desirable linguistic agenda should be. Rather than attempt to guarantee unrealizable sets of 'rights' we should distinguish the essential from the desirable, and the desirable from the dangerous. The right to practise the language of one's choice (not 'one's own language') with other members of the speech community is an example of an essential right. Using such languages for administrative and judicial purposes may well be desirable for some groups providing safeguards are maintained to prevent coercion of individuals who wish to repudiate a language. But it cannot be guaranteed because languages institutionalize in *ad hoc* ways, responding to non-linguistic political and social imperatives. Cultures must have the freedom to define the extent of their linguistic institutionalization. Giving the right to use a language enables such negotiation to take place; committing us to institutions is to provide the answer while preventing the questions from being asked. What is desirable for some groups may be dangerous for others.

But while we cannot answer these questions for the whole of society, we can provide a language teaching agenda that supports the position I have outlined. We might call this a 'charter' or an 'agenda' or a 'statement of desirable practice'— anything except a guarantee of the impossible, for guaranteeing the impossible simply makes us, and our legislatures, look foolish. Such a proposal has already been outlined briefly in Chapter 1 and more fully in Chapter 6.

To adjust our international English language teaching, so that it fitted into a framework of this kind, would involve thinking about the individual language (which could, but probably would not be a variety of English) (1), the national language(s) (which could include English) (2), the nature of language in personal and social activity (3), and foreign language(s) (which will often include English) (4). (See Figure 6.1, Chapter 6, p.82)

The implications of such a commitment will affect classroom methodology, including attitudes to majority and minority mother tongues, the role of translation, multilingual talk and so on. They could also affect curriculum planning, materials design, and assessment. But of course such considerations must also take into account our understanding of language learning and teaching, and our awareness of best practice.

This is not the place to explore these implications in any detail. What this chapter has primarily asked us to do is to consider language as a genetic endowment to construct and use a cultural product. 'Rights'-based discussion has to be treated with care, because it risks attributing to communities the power to repress individuals' freedom of choice more than is functionally desirable for the advancement of civilization. A belief in human beings demands a less restrictive celebration of language. Alcuin's multilingualism 1200 years ago is a useful reminder both of the richness of language and of the transitoriness of languages. We should celebrate language, but we should also acknowledge that languages are born just as languages die. In the last resort, individuals will make their own choices whether legislators like it or not—but repression of linguistic choice is as bad as repression of languages. At the moment we cannot predict how individual language communities will respond to the impact of global technology, and whether in the long run the reduction in the number of spoken languages of the past centuries will be halted or reversed. But in the short term we are no doubt right to be pessimistic. Either way, there will always be as much language in the world as there are human beings. Taking the long historical view, we have to recognize that languages are born and languages die, but language can be neither created nor destroyed.

PART SIX

Research and understanding

12   Research in the language classroom

Introduction

The view I have taken of language, knowledge, and culture implies a particular attitude to research. This chapter introduces the basic arguments for research into language in the classroom, describes the major kinds of research that may be undertaken, and outlines briefly the main procedures and techniques available to researchers. The rationale for research relates to the general view of the nature of language and the nature of systematic enquiry which underlies this book.

Approaches to research

Researching may be defined as 'systematizing curiosity'. Its ultimate purpose is to provide better and better explanations of phenomena.

Research is essentially a cumulative process, building on what has gone on before. Unfortunately, the term 'research' has become debased, so that anyone enquiring into the necessary background facts for a television programme will be listed in the credits as a 'researcher'. However, it is worthwhile to list some of the features that should distinguish serious research from simply the search for information.

Competent research will involve:

1 Careful formulation of the questions to be investigated, to ensure that they are not phrased in such a way as to confuse major issues with minor ones, or to embrace many different questions within one vague, general topic which is incapable of being investigated systematically
2 Careful exploration of the best means of investigation for the particular question being addressed
3 Consideration of the major previous attempts to explore the same and closely related questions, in order to borrow and adapt appropriate formulations of the questions, and appropriate modes of investigation
4 Explicit accounts of the process of question formulation, the criteria for selection of the research techniques, and the reasons for the questions being felt to be important in the first place

5 Full documentation of the procedures used, the means by which information has been gathered, and the methods of interpretation and analysis which have been adopted
6 Explicit acknowledgement of all previous work which has contributed to the conceptualization, means of collection, and procedures for analysis of the data collected
7 Specific interpretation of the data collected, to assess its usefulness in relation to the initial research questions
8 Evaluation of the extent to which the project has achieved its aims, together with an account of the ways in which the process of research has led to changes in the initial formulation of questions—and any other relevant judgements that the researcher may wish to pass on to interested readers
9 A willingness to publicize the research, so that it can contribute to further development by others to the exploration of the same, or related questions.

By the definition I am proposing, research is characterized by being a public, systematic, and useful activity. It is public, because it needs to be distinguished from simply improving one's own private understanding: it is not another name for personal study. It needs to be public because private work is necessarily inefficient. Public work benefits from having procedures throughout being open to scrutiny by others who will lack the biases of the original researchers (though they will have others of their own), who will bring further understanding to bear on the same problems, and who will be able—above all—to offer public criticism as a result of which methods and formulations can be improved upon in subsequent work. Private research would not benefit from this, and would thus risk being tied to the idiosyncracies of one set of researchers, being limited to what one person or group of people knew about, and being sympathetic to the interests of those who formulated the proposal, and thus possibly unintentionally biased.

Research must be systematic, because it needs to be explicit about its procedures if it is to be distinguished from mere hunch. What kind of systematicity will be sought depends on the question being investigated, but for every question, the means of exploration will be examined exhaustively to ensure that it is the best that can be devised for the time and resources available, and the formulation and interpretation of the research will be systematically examined as rigorously as possible.

Research must be useful, in a particular sense. It will not necessarily be useful in its immediate results—otherwise we would be committed to producing the results which most fitted with what we most wanted to find out! But the question to be investigated must have some useful point to it; it must be something that we need to know. A recognition of where particular problems are is a necessary control on irresponsible mind games. While irresponsibility, divergent thinking, and imagination will all contribute to the wide range of potentially fruitful ideas that researchers may exploit, funding, time, and expertise are limited. Justifying a particular area for investigation involves necessarily showing how the study will contribute, directly or indirectly, to improving our understanding of language teaching.

But for this understanding to be useful, we do not need to adopt a narrowly utilitarian point of view—all we need to do is to show that we have thought clearly about why we should indulge our curiosity (in a way that is relatively expensive in time and effort) on this topic rather than another. The benefits are the public scrutiny which should improve the effectiveness of what we do by laying us maximally open to advice and criticism. But the right to these benefits needs to be argued by a demonstration that we are not merely being self-indulgent.

Within this framework, there are three main types of research. Often researchers may be dependent on external funding, but individual investigations may fit into these categories also.

'Pure' research

The prime intention of this will be to increase our understanding of the most important unclear areas of current study. For language teaching these may be questions in psychology, sociology, linguistics, or any other relevant field—or questions of pedagogy which are motivated by a concern to understand what it is that makes certain procedures appear effective in the classroom. This tends to address questions like 'Why do things happen as they do?' and 'How do we explain particular events and particular relationships?' The cumulative effect of research of this kind is to build up a more or less agreed picture (or 'model') of how things work in a particular field. Such agreed understanding influences the ways in which politicians and decision makers plan, so such research has relevance to any conceivable future activity in the area being investigated.

'Action' research

It is frequently argued that teachers should devote their time most fruitfully to this type of research. The argument usually made is that this is most useful because it is aimed at a particular situation, without the concerns for replicability and generalization which characterize pure research, and without the policy having been previously defined by others as in policy-orientated research. It is further argued that action research aims additionally at educating teachers by helping them to become self-aware about their work, and that this is as important an aim as evaluating or information gathering. Certainly, research by teachers, for teachers, on their processes of teaching, can only be a good thing. But if obtaining a clearer understanding of teaching processes requires care and rigour in other modes of research, there is no good argument for action research producing less care and rigour unless it is less concerned with clear understanding, which it is not. The real point about action research is that it is closely tied to the particular interests and needs of particular teachers—but these require the same kind of careful support as any other serious investigation.

Policy-orientated research

Such research is concerned with monitoring the effects of policies which have already been decided upon. To know whether a particular programme is realizing its stated aims and is therefore effective, whether it is being effective but in unexpected and unanticipated ways, or whether it is being ineffective, is clearly valuable for sponsors and planners. It enables future planning to be more effective, and sometimes enables adjustments to be made to programmes which are failing to achieve their intended effects. Such research may lead to a questioning of underlying theory, and contribute to formulation of better explanatory models, but that is not its initial intention. Its main purpose is to monitor the effect of policies. In practice, indeed, many sponsors prefer to discover that their policies are working, especially if a lot of money has been invested in teaching materials, for example, or in a new mode of examination. Thus there are potential political risks in reporting this mode of research which need to be consciously guarded against. If the research is to make a genuine contribution to the advancement of knowledge, in however limited a way, the independence of the researcher is crucial.

What distinguishes these three types of research is not so much the procedures used, as the context in which they operate. Typically, pure research will be performed by professional researchers (who may also work simultaneously as higher education teachers), perhaps in collaboration with practitioners. The formulation of the problem will depend on the work of scholars and researchers, and the work may be funded by research councils, private charitable trusts, or government agencies, and will usually carefully describe its relationship with all previous relevant research.

Action research will be performed by practitioners, on topics formulated by practitioners. If there is external funding, it may well come from sources whose main concern is with activating the teaching profession rather than with a prime interest in whatever results are obtained.

Policy-related research will be performed by professional researchers, sometimes in formally set-up research institutes attached to official organizations. The work may be collaborative with practitioners. The formulation of the research topic will usually be defined by the policy, and the funding agency will usually be the policy-making body. Relationships with previous research may be made explicit, but this is not regarded as essential.

None the less, in spite of these contextual differences, if the research is to be of more than personal value (and hence to justify the term 'research' at all), they will all be the same in following the general procedures I have outlined above.

Ways of doing research

The fullest and clearest account of ways of approaching educational research is Cohen and Manion (1994). Quantitative approaches to applied linguistic research are explained in detail in Hatch and Farhady (1982) and Brown (1988). Other books on classroom research include an authoritative survey of empirical work on language instruction and its relationship with learning outcomes (Chaudron 1988), an account of the historical development of classroom research with key texts (Allwright 1988), and examples of qualititative approaches in Bailey and Nunan (1996). Brumfit and Mitchell (1990) provide accounts of language-classroom research from a wide range of eminent practitioners, and a shorter summary of major issues in classroom research can be found in Mitchell (1985).

In this section I shall briefly describe the general types of research available to teachers. These themes are explored at greater length in Cohen and Manion (1994), and are taken up for language classrooms in Brumfit and Mitchell (1990).

First, it is useful to distinguish between description, intervention, and experiment.

Descriptive research will aim at providing as accurate an account as possible of what current practice is: how learners do learn, how teachers do teach, what classrooms do look like, at a particular moment in a particular place. In itself such work will only be illuminating if the description is carried out with a particular intention in mind. A description that included everything conceivable that happened in a classroom would be unwieldy and incomprehensible. We have to determine what is and is not relevant information, and to do that we need to know what the purpose of our description is. In practice, then, descriptive studies will usually look at classrooms in relation to particular sets of criteria. These may be, for example, to compare practices of teachers at different levels of schooling, to compare practices with different target languages, to see whether there are differences between native-speaking and non-native speaking teachers, or to see the relationship between what textbooks recommend and what actually happens in classrooms. The argument for concentrating on description is that expectations of teachers, recommendations of teacher educators and theorists, and the demands of administrators, are often rightly concerned with what ought to be. However, there is little point in constantly pushing for an ideal without any understanding of what in fact happens. We actually know remarkably little about typical practice in language learning, and there is a great need for additional comparative studies. On the basis of these we can then provide some explanations of teacher and learner behaviour.

Interventionist studies are those in which some aspect of teaching or learning is deliberately changed, so that the effects can be monitored. Thus new materials may be introduced, new types of learning activity may be devised or used in an environment where they were not previously used, or teachers may be asked to smile more, use the target language exclusively, or participate in small group discussion. The setting is the normal one for teaching and learning, but the research monitors the effect of changes which have been deliberately introduced. The examples given here relate to research into language teaching as a process— but classrooms are also used as sources of data about language learning in general, with interventions designed to reveal learners' internal strategies or psychological processes. These have a less direct relationship with teaching, though they may of course contribute to our understanding of general processes of learning, and this in turn will be reinterpreted to result in experimental teaching procedures.

Experimental studies are similar, but usually involve a much more formal control of variables, thus stopping the classroom from being at all typical. Learners may be put into a language laboratory, or be given highly controlled tasks to ensure that the only factor that they are responding to is the one in which the researcher is interested. Experiments of this kind often operate with a 'control group' of learners who do not receive the special treatment, so that their behaviour can be contrasted with that of the 'experimental group'. Whether these procedures have ecological validity (that is, whether evidence from such studies has a direct bearing on normal behaviour in typical classrooms) is a matter of considerable debate. Certainly, their results require careful and intelligent interpretation before they are translated into classroom use. But they may contribute usefully to clarification of key issues in associated disciplines.

Descriptive studies are a necessary, and rather neglected, base from which discussion of innovation can proceed. However, they do not in themselves result in improvement of teaching or learning, and some researchers consider them an inefficient way of exploring theories of teaching and learning (see Cook 1990). Others (for example, van Lier 1988) would argue that the apparent rigour of interventionist and experimental studies obscures the close relationship between learning and social context, and that 'rich' descriptions of learning experiences are an essential element in building up a satisfactory theory of language acquisition. Certainly, any understanding of teaching must take into account the social context, and I would myself accept the view that studies of language acquisition should proceed simultaneously along routes concerned with psychological and internal processing and those examining external and cultural factors such as those found in typical classrooms.

People who wish to construct idealized models of internal processing will be more attracted to interventionist and experimental procedures. It is certainly the case that such procedures have been developed over a long period, and produced an extensive and sophisticated literature to enable researchers to avoid basic errors in claiming relationships between observations when none actually exist. Courses teaching research methods often include detailed statistical techniques for the analysis of data, and large-scale work usually calls upon the skills of statisticians in interpreting the large bodies of data collected. One risk in such work is that only what can be rigorously measured is examined. Some argue that such procedures restrict us to examining the trivial and simple, and ignoring the complex but much more important real world in which teachers and learners have to operate. In its strong form this is a foolish debate, because we use simplification all the time in ordinary life in order to be able to cope with the mass of impressions that confront us. We are constantly making judgements about relevance and irrelevance, and interfering with random activity in order to structure a more directed and useful context for change. This after all is what teaching consists of, and in this sense formal research is only doing the same thing. But just as teaching can develop its own routines which lose touch with the needs of the outside world that it partly serves, so too can research procedures. A constant debate is necessary about the connection between tidy and structured activity and the more complex and untidy world it is meant to illuminate. Indeed, one of the major contributions that teachers will make to this debate is a close acquaintance with the untidiness of language learning contexts, and an awareness of the successes that can be achieved among (and even possibly because of) the theoretical untidiness.

The debate referred to above is often couched in terms of 'quantitative' versus 'qualitative' research. However, a careful consideration of these concepts will make it clear that they cannot really be opposed to each other. If we are examining something that can be objectively described (either numerically, or by explicit and economical records of other kinds), there is no sense in not making use of such data. On the other hand, if the questions we are interested in cannot be quantified simply, we should not avoid them solely on those grounds. We cannot limit observation to what can be measured without ignoring most of the areas that teachers and learners are interested in. It is much more important to break down our questions into those parts for which objective and measurable categories are appropriate, and those for which such categories cannot neatly be devised. As long as the status of our observations is made clear in our reporting, and as long as objectivity is achieved where that is possible, the research will be valuable.

But 'objectivity' is a relative concept. If ten witnesses agree, we will consider something more objective than if only two out of ten do. The view of someone close to the action will be preferred to that of someone a long way away—but someone too close may only see part of what is being observed, while someone a little further away may see the whole picture. Any measurement must clearly be relevant to the question being asked, and subjective impressions of a complete experience may be more valuable than objective measurement of a small and unimportant part. Ultimately, interpreting the value of particular research, and sorting out the best procedures to use, must depend on determined common sense by practitioners.

The major options in language classroom research include the following:

1　Studies of language learning based on the observed performance of individuals in typical classes. These may be longitudinal studies of individuals throughout their school careers, or studies of achievement of classes as groups. Much curriculum work makes assumptions about typical progress, with a very small base of knowledge to refer to

2 Comparisons of learners' language experiences inside and outside the classroom setting

3 Analyses of the relationship between theoretical ideas, teaching materials and syllabuses, and classroom practices

4 Analyses of different teaching styles, relating to factors such as materials used, types of learner, size of class, etc.

5 Analyses of the beliefs of teachers about their practices and needs, related to actual classroom practice

6 Analyses of the beliefs of learners about their practices and needs, related to their degree of success

7 Case studies of classrooms in particular contexts, attempting to draw upon and synthesize elements of all the above.

For each of these, descriptive studies may be justified on their own, or relationships may be explored through process-product studies relating learners' progress in language learning to different aspects of the classroom learning environment. Such studies may be highly focused, exploring the impact of particular types of interaction on learning, or more comprehensive in coverage (as in Fröhlich, Spada, and Allen 1985).

Major studies, for example Naiman, Fröhlich, Stern and Todesco's study of the good language learner (1978, reprinted 1996) may combine many of these procedures in an effort to obtain a comprehensive picture of a particular problem. Above all, this list should not be seen as exhaustive. Good researchers will be constantly thinking of new procedures to address new (or old) problems.

Techniques used in the study of language classrooms have included:

1 Documentary analysis, relating textbooks, for example, or curriculum documents either to analyses of classroom practice, or to the suggestions of teaching methodologists

2 Recordings or actual live classroom lessons analysed according to category systems devised for particular purposes (see Mitchell 1985 for further discussion)

3 Maps of classrooms showing the distribution of, for example, teacher questioning, learner response, teacher movement, etc.

4 Quantified statements of types of contributions of particular learners as groups, or of individual learners over a long period

5 Diaries kept by researchers over an extended period of observation, consisting of both systematic and impressionistic observation

6 Lessons discussed retrospectively by observers, teachers, and learners and the different perspectives analysed

7 Semi-structured interviews in which a core of questions are addressed in a relaxed and improvised way by researchers talking to learners, teachers, or other relevant people such as parents or administrators

8 Diary studies (see Parkinson and Howell-Richardson 1990) by learners or teachers
9 Tests (of language competence or other relevant knowledge or skills) administered to learners (or teachers)
10 Questionnaires exploring attitudes and beliefs about different aspects of classroom experience
11 Focus group discussions by teachers or learners, recorded for analysis without the researcher being present.

The above list is far from being definitive, however, and techniques are constantly subject to criticism and change. At present, two of our most striking unresolved methodological problems are (a) how to identify appropriate units of analysis for classifying and categorizing behaviours observed in the language classroom (linguistic and otherwise); and (b) how best to access the intentions, plans, and strategies of classroom participants which underlie observed behaviour. Classroom research, if it is to remain productive, must retain a questioning attitude not only towards the objects of study, but also towards its own procedures and assumptions.

Being a teacher and being a researcher

It would be unwise to pretend that the processes of researching and teaching can be combined without effort. There is a particularly strong contradictory pull in that research is a type of contemplation (however systematic) while teaching is a type of action. Pure research will require explicit hypothesis creation, with clear and falsifiable statements that can be rigorously analysed and tested. This process will involve simplifying from the rich context of particular classrooms that teachers are specially trained to respond to. All teachers know that classrooms are confusing places, with different agendas being pursued by different participants, with many different activities and thought processes happening simultaneously, and with different needs being addressed in different parts of the classroom at the same time. Few lessons follow plans exactly, and few plans follow principles as precisely as theorists intend. Teachers work in a world of real people, real motives, and conflicting interests, and their prime task is to survive in this world, in order to influence learning and direct it towards the most profitable activities and routines for success. Distancing yourself from this experience enough to be able to see it in relation to the experiences of others in similar situations is part of maturing as a teacher—but it is not easy, and demands sensitivity and commitment.

At the same time, it is vitally important that this distancing is practised by teachers, and that research is not carried out exclusively by outsiders. Understanding what it is to be a teacher, from direct and substantial experience, is different from understanding teaching processes from outside. Knowing how to teach, knowing as an outsider what teachers do, and knowing from experience the practice of teaching, are three different modes of understanding. By combining them, a fuller picture of the teaching process will be built up than by relying on one only. And exactly the same points can be made about knowing language learning processes. The risk for teachers is that research will come too much from outside the profession, so that the contingent and contradictory experiences actually encountered in schools and classrooms are neglected in the efforts of outside researchers to be tidy and concentrated.

For these reasons, the health of research into educational matters is dependent on combinations of research from external perspectives, collaborative research by teachers and outsiders, and research from within teaching itself. By interpreting research from all these sources, we may hope to develop the fullest and most coherent understanding of the teaching process.

Further, work of this kind is not only justified by the need for research to be sensitive to the social experiences of teachers and learners; it is also justified as a contribution to effective teaching. As with any important activity, teaching will benefit from being reflected on and examined systematically. We should not forget, however, that many competent teachers reflect very little in this way without failing to be teachers. Good teaching is entirely possible without a researching perspective on the part of the teacher. Similarly, we would not define as a teacher someone who reflects or researches all the time. Participant research involves accepting some degree of tension between different modes of thinking and acting. The justification rests in the indirect improvements to practice which will result from increased understanding, and the sense of understanding and control of our environment which comes from seeing it more clearly.

Why do research?

There is a sense in which serious practitioners, in any field, will expect to monitor their own performance as objectively as possible. In this sense, language teachers should always be engaging in 'research' if they are to work responsibly and professionally. In Britain, the Teacher Training Agency has this at least partly in mind when it calls for teaching to be a 'researching profession'. But there is a wider issue too, for a whole tradition of linguistic and educational research needs to be exploited if research in the language classroom is to make genuine contributions to our understanding.

For many learners, teaching provides the main context for their language learning, so teaching and its environment are as important objects of research as the learning process itself. We can also control teaching processes more readily than the internal mechanisms of learning, so understanding how teaching works in practice and how its workings relate to successful learning is a necessary adjunct to effective education.

But at the same time, we have to acknowledge that we lack empirical support for much of what is known about teaching methodology. Such a lack does not invalidate the understandings of teachers, teacher trainers, and language methodologists—there are many valuable practices in language teaching which will never be capable of rigorous falsification in a scientific sense, any more than the success or failure of a particular marriage will be capable of investigation in terms of a single neat and falsifiable explanation. No major area involving human relationships can be addressed truthfully by such a mechanistic approach. But that does not mean that we should neglect empirical study as shamefully as we have done in the past. There is a great deal that we do not know, but could in principle know, about practices in classrooms. Until we have built up our knowledge base much more substantially, methodologists and theoreticians will be open to the attack that they are basing their proposals too much on hunch, the peculiarities of their own personal experience, or a lazy acceptance of tradition. Scholarship and empirical study must combine, but—particularly in the British tradition of language teaching—there has been far more scholarship than empirical investigation. The result of this is that exciting recommendations have abounded since the 1970s: functional-notional syllabuses, procedural syllabuses, needs analyses, authentic materials, and graded objectives, to name only a few. But there has been remarkably little analysis and replication of analysis of their effects, or even of classroom practice in relation to these. The exceptions to these generalizations were until recently in Britain more concerned with languages other than English, though their work provided models which could be adapted by teachers of international English. Examples from the 1980s are Mitchell, Parkinson, and Johnstone 1981; Sanderson 1983; Kasper 1986; Peck 1988; Mitchell 1988. For more recent international work on English, see Bailey and Nunan 1996.

Yet the substantial empirical work carried out on second language acquisition and associated areas, predominantly in North America and mainland Europe (surveyed in Mitchell and Myles 1998), does not enable us to answer many of the important questions that concern language teachers. We need many more studies before we can even begin to produce a coherent, empirically-based account of all the important factors in language teaching.

Furthermore, we do not as yet exploit the many small-scale studies which have been carried out by doctorate students in many universities throughout the world. We need authoritative surveys of high quality doctoral work which identify the trends in understanding which have been developed in a wide range of good unpublished studies.

Thus there is much to do before we can consider language teaching to be well-founded as an activity. In addition to high quality analysis of ideas, to be found in a wide range of books by (to give only a few examples) Finocchiaro, Rivers, Widdowson, Stern and Howatt, we need mechanisms for the synthesis, analysis, and evaluation of a wide range of empirical projects, procedures for the re-evaluation and replication of studies to enable us to make robust statements about what is and is not sound knowledge, and a steady flow of well-trained and committed researchers, who genuinely keep abreast with ideas on language teaching, and who desperately want to understand its processes and procedures. Few if any countries provide the infrastructure for such a research base to develop, but language teaching benefits from an international market, and international organizations such as the Association Internationale de Linguistique Appliquée (AILA) have for years provided an infrastructure which the profession exploits less than it should.

Educational research, 'disciplinary' study and interdisciplinary study

Language teaching is a form of education, and educational research is inevitably interdisciplinary. Indeed, it is clear that education is a very important field for research, partly because so much money is invested in it, and partly because it raises key issues about the nature of human experience. Human beings are by nature educating creatures, for they are unique in their ability to pass on culturally acquired characteristics to their descendants, and the medium for doing much of this in the contemporary world is explicit education. Understanding educational processes is thus an important part of understanding what makes us distinctive creatures. And central to the educational process is the role of language, and the learning of new languages, dialects, and modes of discourse. Understanding language teaching and learning will contribute to our understanding of language, of education, and of the human condition.

But to say that education is a crucial area of human endeavour is not to say that it is a single, formal discipline. Rather, it is a field of study which may be explored from a variety of disciplinary standpoints. Philosophers, psychologists, sociologists, historians, linguists, anthropologists, or economists, indeed any human scientist, may choose to examine educational institutions or educational processes. It is clear that psycholinguists, sociolinguists, teaching methodologists and sociologists all feel they have understandings to gain from examining language learning, and useful contributions to make to the theory of language in education.

Some of the traditions represented in these disciplines will be predominantly experimental or observational in character. But some disciplines (for example, history) have traditionally been concerned more with documentary evidence than with direct observation; others (for example, philosophy) have been concerned with the construction of clear arguments from evidence provided in other disciplines such as psychology or political science, or with the creation and analysis of hypothetical but illuminating scenarios, rather than with empirical study. Within traditions such as these, 'research' means something very different from its meaning in the empirical sciences.

'Education', however, needs all these kinds of research, and in so far as much of it is concerned with education, so too does applied linguistics. Serious methodological discussion of language teaching may be regarded as the equivalent of philosophical discussion in other spheres. Just as lawyers gain from the study of jurisprudence, literary critics from critical theory, historians from historiography and scientists from philosophy of science, because these provide them with the tools for avoiding blind following of tradition, so too language teachers gain from methodological discussion by people who understand language teaching from direct experience, and can interpret and assess the significance of appropriate theory and research.

But we may acknowledge the need for all these types of research, and at the same time feel that the proportion devoted to some types is too great for the good of the profession. Too much empirical study and too little interpretation may result in nothing being discussed that cannot be measured by the current available technology, or only the currently fashionable research areas being considered relevant to the process of language learning; too much interpretation and too little empirical study may result in myths being perpetuated without being tested against recent observation or experiment. An ideal balance should be sought—but the balance will be dependent on the social conditions in a particular place at a particular time. The quantity of empirical work that is attainable now in the US, where research students require a PhD degree to qualify for many professions and consequently are willing to work on projects at this level (though even this may be changing), will be harder to attain in countries where a PhD is less necessary for career advancement. What is attainable in one decade, when governments or commercial interests are interested in funding education-related work, may not be attainable in another when external funding agencies divert their attention to work in other areas, or reduce the gross amounts of money available for research. What is possible in countries where teachers have a high academic training in research methods may not be possible elsewhere without major, expensive changes in training policy.

Yet, in spite of the different social contexts of language teaching, a research perspective towards our work will always be desirable, in all places and under all conditions. To say this is simply to restate the requirement that language teaching should be carried out responsibly and professionally. How that perspective is realized in practice will depend on funding, the training and experience of teachers and administrators, the relationship between the professional research community (if any) and schools, and other factors that vary from place to place. What is undesirable, though, is the exclusion of some types of enquiry, limiting research to that within one tradition only, and denying recognition, and funding to others. Variety of approach is essential if the richness of language use and educational opportunity is to be adequately understood.

At the same time, the enormous lack of descriptive work in classrooms makes this still the most neglected area. Because successful learners and successful teachers often carry their successes from culture to culture, we know that there are universal characteristics for effective language learning and teaching. But both learning and teaching are also culturally constrained, and until we have a vast data-base of knowledge about practices in different places, we shall not be able to establish what is universal and what is local and contingent.

Comparisons are sometimes made between medical and educational research (Hargreaves 1996; Hammersley 1997 in response) to suggest that educational research is inefficient or incompetent. But medical research rests upon a far longer tradition than educational research, with far more replication, and far larger numbers of researchers. Compared with some areas of the curriculum, language teaching has made a strikingly successful start to empirical study in the last third of the twentieth century. It is certainly time to begin taking stock of what we have learnt (see, for example, Ellis 1997 for a valuable overview of one part of the research tradition). But researchers need to keep up the momentum through the current climate of educational cutbacks if our understanding is not to fossilize.

13 Teaching, researching, and knowledge

Introduction

This chapter attempts to take the discussion in the previous chapter further forward, exploring some of the paradoxes implicit in phrases like 'research for teachers' and 'teacher–researchers'. By doing this, I hope to define more clearly what the relationship should be between researchers and those who practise the art of teaching.

Conventionally, the relationship between applied linguistic theory and English teaching theory may be represented as in Figure 13.1. It is of course possible for applied linguistic theory to be relevant (with appropriate changes) to theory in any other area where language is a major issue for practitioners, for example translation, speech therapy, or lexicography. But language teaching is forced to be an interdisciplinary activity in the ways indicated by the figure, and any teacher must necessarily adopt a perspective in relation to all these disciplines.

Such a perspective is not necessarily conscious. But teachers who become aware of arguments in any of these contributory disciplines will recognize their relevance to the beliefs and values that underlie their practical teaching.

The problem for the researcher is that there is a contradictory pull. I argued in Chapter 12 that the best research requires explicit hypothesis creation, with clear and falsifiable statements which can be analysed rigorously and tested ruthlessly. This process involves simplification of the contingent and contradictory impressions that are perceived by anyone who is forced to operate in a world of real people, real motives, and conflicting interests. In order to cope with this state, teachers (and learners) have to accept and reconcile simultaneous understandings which can be analysed, at different times and in different ways, by psychologists, linguists, educational theorists, philosophers, sociologists, and anyone else who may choose to study education as a phenomenon. We all manage to cope with this kind of combination of interests whenever we act as practical people—but the point about teaching is that it is intrinsically active and interventionist, not intrinsically reflective and 'disinterested'. Like all important activities, it will benefit from being reflected upon, but the prime purpose is not reflection—and someone who reflects or researches all the time will not be defined as a teacher at all.

Yet there is a danger in thinking that only linguists, psychologists, and the others should conduct research into teaching or learning. If this were allowed to

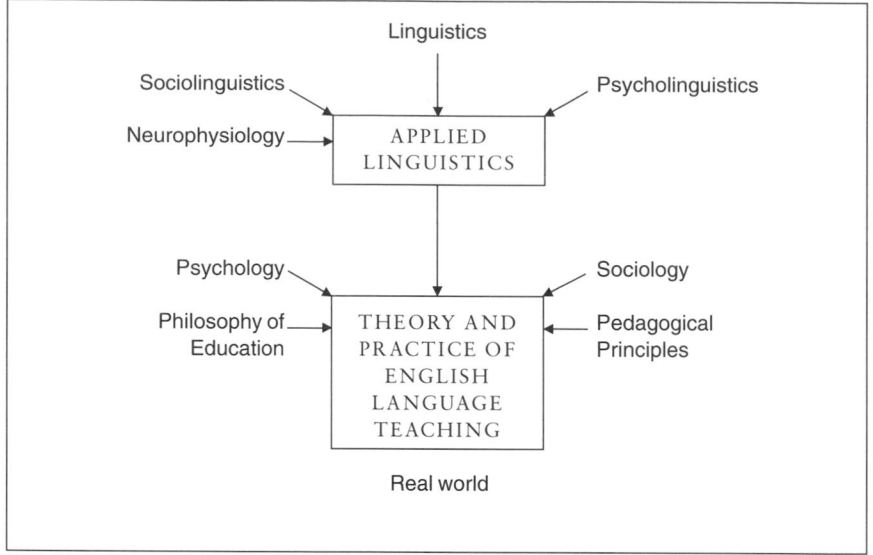

Figure 13.1: Applied linguistics and ELT

be the normal practice, teaching would constantly be theorized or examined as an activity which was a branch of philosophy or whatever feeder discipline supplied the researcher; it would never be examined from the point of view that actually made it teaching (rather than psychology, etc.), and consequently could never be reflected on in itself, but only as a version of something else—and an inefficient version, because it would have different goals which rightly divert its activities away from psychological or philosophical concerns.

What I am arguing for is a recognition of the study of language teaching methodology as the most rigorous possible examination of the process of teaching from the point of view of the language teacher. This examination will be partly empirical, partly interpretative, partly reflective, partly philosophical—but it will always be self-examining in the light of insights that must inevitably be drawn from work by practitioners of other disciplines as well as by teachers.

The state of contemporary research

The implication of this argument is that effective research relevant to the language classroom depends on at least four essential activities:

1 Interpretation by teachers of empirical work from traditions not primarily concerned with classrooms (for example, much Second Language Acquisition—SLA—research)
2 Empirical work within any tradition carried out and interpreted by people who are, or have been teachers, and can therefore adopt a teaching perspective through their experience

3 Empirical work carried out by non-teaching researchers in close collaboration and consultation with practising teachers

4 Synthetic examination of work from all these traditions in the light of teaching needs, and sensitive to the experience of being a teacher.

All of these are necessary modes of research and scholarship if teaching is not to become unbalanced in its relationship with research. In most countries the perceived power of people with the status of 'researcher' is so strong in comparison with the power of people with the status of 'classroom teacher' that a conscious process of correction is always necessary to prevent biases towards research or disciplinary needs distorting accounts of pedagogic needs.

At the same time as expressing these warnings about the risks, we should also be defending the need for research equally vigorously. There must be few enterprises costing so much that are as little monitored and studied (in most countries) as educational processes. We desperately need to base our teacher education intuitions on firmer descriptions of typical practice, and to relate our proposals for improvement more systematically to the kind of synthesis referred to above.

Yet, we need to be careful of over-interpreting results. Language teaching has changed over the years whether or not researchers have provided support. Competent teachers are always looking for areas where their practice can be improved upon. Such people will initiate changes by trial and error that may eventually become influential. The fashion for group-work is not primarily the product of research, but a shift which thousands of teachers felt the need to make away from the teacher-centred class. More negatively, the movement towards teaching French, and reducing the choice of other foreign languages, in Britain, has proceeded through administrative and teaching requirements against the recommendations of all theorists. Teaching has its own dynamic, and part of the researcher's task is to record and interpret a phenomenon which exists independently of the researcher.

Further, there need not be, in logic nor in principle, a necessary relationship between research and the practice of teaching. Improved anatomical studies of elephants are valuable to veterinary surgeons and biologists, but do not logically entail changes in the elephants' behaviour, however much advance there may be in the understanding of causes of that behaviour. Nor is there any necessary relationship between improved understanding of research and the practice of teaching. Indeed, we might wish to argue that the capacities which made a good teacher in 1929 would make the same person a good teacher in 1999—the fundamental qualities are not dependent on articulated and rationally argued awareness of language, but on unarticulated and intuitive awareness that any language user has potential access to, at any time and in any place.

I shall return to this point later, and will modify it in part, but it is worth stating starkly at the outset, for there are external needs to justify both educational research and the professionalism of teaching which lead to arguments in the other direction—yet to insist on a simple, direct relationship is to commit researchers and teachers to positions which are unhelpful to both.

Researchers are pressurized to produce deliverable results to 'improve' teaching when understanding principles and practice—without any direct practical spin-off—is a necessary precondition of this; teachers are made to feel guilty for not 'implementing' research findings when practical and intuitive craft knowledge is just as important as research in enabling teaching to improve. In the long run, there will be a relationship between these, but the 'direct relationship' argument risks rewarding short-term panaceas and simplistic solutions.

Contemporary language teaching

In the *Annual Review of Applied Linguistics* for 1987, I attempted to classify the main characteristics of the major language teaching movement of recent times, Communicative Language Teaching, drawing upon the writings of a range of commentators. This list of 11 characteristics will provide a convenient starting point for a view of current research.

Briefly, these are (with relevant theoretical discussion referred to where appropriate):

1 Concern for the needs of the learners, and attempts to define them (Munby 1978)
2 Emphasis on the content of an activity rather than on specific language learning (Prabhu 1987)
3 Specification of syllabuses in terms of functions or notions (Wilkins 1976)
4 Tolerance of language variation in the classroom
5 Individualization
6 Toleration of errors as inevitable and part of the process of acquisition (Corder 1981)
7 A desire to provide a supportive and guilt-free learning environment (Stevick 1976)
8 Techniques which provide naturalistic language use: pair-work, simulations, information-gap activities, etc. (Widdowson 1978)
9 Language items presented in contexts of typical use
10 Authentic or semi-authentic materials
11 An unwillingness to constrain language production or interpretation, so that teachers cannot predict exactly what, language will occur in the performance of a given task (Brumfit 1984).
(List drawn from syntheses in Johnson and Morrow 1981: 1–12, 59–66; Littlewood 1981: 85ff; Stern 1983: 258–62; Savignon 1983: 199; Finocchiaro and Brumfit 1983: 91–3; Brumfit 1985: 3–32; Richards and Rodgers 1986: 64–86.)

This constellation of features, combining old techniques in new ways, emphasizing some previously undervalued techniques like role-play, adding some principles previously not adopted at all like refusal to correct, and defending the general argument by appeals to new theoretical constructs like communicative competence, is typical of change in language teaching: it develops by piecemeal accretion, and only after the event do commentators observe the consistencies in the historical movement.

None the less, it is striking how small a role specific research played in these changes. The works listed in association with the specific items are without exception interpretative rather than based directly on specific empirical research—though they are usually based on intensive study and analysis which resembles historical, literary, and philosophical research. Very few of them, though, refer directly to classroom observation, and most are making arguments for what ought to happen without specific reference to observation at all. (The only exceptions to this listed above are Prabhu 1987; Stevick 1976; and parts of Brumfit 1984.)

It is also worth noting that, although 'communicative language teaching' has been discussed as a phenomenon for a long time (Candlin 1971 is the first reference to the term that I have found) it was only after about 15 years that descriptive research examining its practices began to be published (for example, Fröhlich, Spada, and Allen 1985; Mitchell 1988).

The claims made in the previous section of this chapter may seem unjustified when we consider that three books about research in classrooms appeared in the same year (Allwright 1988; Chaudron 1988; van Lier 1988). However, it is clear that all three of them recognize major gaps in the research tradition; indeed van Lier puts forward an argument very similar to the one in this chapter—that second language research takes insufficient notice of general educational research, and has failed to note the arguments for ethnographic research in the classroom. Such research, he argues, is defensible not in order to provide hypotheses to be tested, but as an end in itself. He calls for a bottom-up data-driven development of theory-rich contextualized descriptions of classroom activity, and the active involvement of teachers and learners in the research process.

Chaudron's authoritative survey of the empirical literature reflects the other, more positivist tradition. He aims to review 'confirming or disconfirming evidence for claims about the influence of language instruction and classroom interaction on language learning' (1988: xv). None the less, this book does raise difficult questions for researchers. Particularly, Chaudron points out the wide range of category systems in use, and the consequent difficulty of comparing different research projects and classroom data. The practice in most academic disciplines of building on the research of predecessors is made particularly difficult by the local intentions of many researchers. There are major variables about which we have hunches in our practice: we perceive differences between mother tongue, second language, and foreign language teaching; between teaching beginners, intermediate, and advanced students; between teaching younger and older learners; between the behaviour of non-native and native-speaking teachers. We do not have firm evidence to show that such factors impose constraints across different national and cultural traditions of teaching—yet we expect to export teacher training and methodology across cultures. Categories for analysis of language classes across cultures would help us to build up a far clearer empirical picture of what actually happens in typical classes, so that recommendations can eventually become more fine-tuned to particular situations.

But there is a deeper issue to confront as well. If teaching language, like other kinds of teaching, develops partly by the accumulation of professional wisdom, what are the conditions in which that 'wisdom' develops. Even if it is not always wisdom (because it may not always lead to the wisest practice), it is certainly craft knowledge, and demands investigation. The area we have called 'method' in language teaching is part of the culture of the language classroom. In general education the 'culture of teaching' has been the subject of much research; yet this aspect has been almost entirely neglected in discussions of language teaching. Research of this kind poses problems, as Feimen-Nemser and Floden have described:

> Three methodological problems have special significance for research on the cultures of teaching. First, the focus on culture implies inferences about knowledge, values, and norms for action, none of which can be directly observed. Second, the existence of many teaching cultures raises difficult questions: Which culture or cultures does a study address? How can differences among cultures and similarities within cultures he documented? Third, researchers must neither evaluate a culture by inappropriate external standards, nor fall into the relativistic trap of asserting that every aspect of that culture is good. Judgement is unavailable in research on the cultures of teaching, where pragmatic questions about directions for change are always in the minds of researchers and policy makers.
> (Feimen-Nemser and Floden 1987: 506)

This is of course simply to say that researchers into classrooms as social entities have to accept the problems that anthropologists have been addressing for a long time. But if we see teachers and learners as crucially socialized by the educational process and the educational setting of which they are part, such studies are essential. It is at least arguable that language teachers are teachers first and language teachers second. Certainly, learners' behaviour may be constrained as much by their learner role in a school as by their lack of language knowledge. Neglecting the culture of teaching, researchers may have concentrated, understandably, on what is more easily accessible to research, and what attracts funding from agencies who do not understand schools and have little sympathy for educational research, rather than on what is strictly of direct relevance to our understanding of learning and teaching.

A further point needs to be made. If teachers and learners are socially situated, and if their situation is a major element in their linguistic and pedagogical behaviour, we need to explore their perceptions of their role much more fully than we have in the past. Input and turn-taking, question types, and classroom organization are all outward manifestations which researchers have been able to describe and quantify. But they are impossible to interpret as motivated behaviour without consideration of the views of those who structure such activity.

Allwright (1982) and Mitchell (1988) are among the few language researchers who have moved some way in this direction. We need to examine the beliefs of teachers, their subjective views on methodological issues, their claims about what they are doing, and to set these beside the views of learners, policy, and observations of classroom practice (see Brumfit, Mitchell, and Hooper 1996). Apart from any other consideration, our awareness of language as a means of identity creation must lead us to see such studies as crucial for understanding language use. We say that language is meaning, but refuse to consider its social construction in much second language acquisition work. Further, a rich examination of classroom culture should include consideration of the views of parents and administrators as well.

The role of teachers

It will have been apparent that I am referring more often to teachers than to learners. In these learner-sensitive times, this should be defended. In formal language learning the interests of learners and teachers are complementary. But in practice we can do more about teachers than we can about learners. There are fewer of them and they are certificated, and controlled by the state. They plan overtly, and are subject to social and cultural constraints in the classroom that we need to understand if we are to enable teacher education to operate effectively.

But teachers also have a major influence on language learning. The quality of teacher is a determining factor in learners' perceptions of the value of their task. Teachers (1) structure the exposure to the language, (2) provide many of the opportunities for language use, and (3) mould the conditions in which motivation to learn will develop—they thus have a major role in all three of the pre-conditions for successful language learning which cannot be dodged. These pre-conditions are unnegotiable; without decisions being taken about all three of them, instructed language learning cannot take place. So understanding teachers is just as important as understanding learners.

But understanding teachers means understanding ideologies, as well as identities. It means understanding attitudes to literacy and to literature as socially constructed entities in different cultures. And teacher education requires that teachers themselves see the role of such constructs in society, as well as understanding language in its more defined aspects. All of these concerns take us a long way from existing research, but closer to relevant research.

Ultimately, we have to see teachers as contributors—unavoidably as well as desirably—to the creation of language learning theory: 'unavoidably' because a theory that teachers do not affect will have no effect on teachers—in the process of operating with it, they will change it; 'desirably' because the evidence drawn from the people who spend more of their working lives with learners than anyone else does must have value as evidence to be interpreted in the light of our theoretical understanding.

And this leads me to reject as inappropriate the metaphor of the elephant and anatomical studies which I referred to at the beginning of this chapter. Elephants do not read anatomical texts and cannot argue with researchers. Theories of the anatomy of classrooms, and of the language learning in whose service they are constructed, must come from those who live in classrooms in collaboration with those who research them. They cannot come solely from those inside classrooms, for their view is partial and limited to a relatively small number of teaching situations, with themselves as a key figure. They cannot come solely from those outside classrooms for they have not experienced fully 'what it is to be a teacher' and lack that crucial type of insider knowledge (see Brumfit 1984: 7). They can come from collaborative work, from work with those who have been, or are, both active teachers and active researchers. But the two roles need to be equal. Research requires a substantial knowledge base as well as substantial technical training. Teaching equally requires both these, but different knowledge and different training for the different purpose. Teachers who dabble in research and researchers who dabble in teaching will not solve the problem of creating coherent and powerful language teaching methodology. Learning to do either involves a struggle through a demanding apprenticeship. But individuals who have done both for significant periods of time, and sympathetic groups of collaborators whose collective experience spans both, can indeed construct the principles without which action remains blind, inconsistent, and ineffective.

14 Educational linguistics, applied linguistics, and the study of language practices

Introduction: the scope of applied linguistics

In this final chapter I try to broaden the discussion by linking it to the concerns of applied linguistics as a supporting science, and thus consider the place of scientific discourse in discussion of real-world problems like those confronting educators. In the first half I chart in detail the history of attempts to define applied linguistics, linking these where appropriate with practice in British education. In the second, I examine some of the current pressures to extend the scope of applied linguistics, particularly postmodernist views, and propose a conceptualization of our task which should not have to change with every shift in fashion.

Pit Corder in discussion once remarked that educational practice demands '*implied* linguistics' rather than applied linguistics. Certainly, many underlying concerns about the implications of linguistics for practical work are permanent features of discussion, particularly those about the relationship with language in education.

If we consider the formal constitution of the British Association for Applied Linguistics (BAAL), originally adopted in 1967, we find it reads: 'The Objects of the Association are … the study of language use, language acquisition and language teaching, and the fostering of inter-disciplinary collaboration in this study …'. Until recently the association's headed paper used its name against a backdrop of listed areas of study: 'language acquisition, language teaching, language disabilities, language varieties, language in literature, language policies, languages in social services, translation, interpretation'. Yet against this apparently centralizing claim on many fields we have to set the centrifugal tendency for other bodies to be formed to develop their own more precise specialisms. Associations for teachers of particular languages already existed when BAAL was set up with Pit Corder as its first Chair, but since then students of second language acquisition, poetics and linguistics, lexicography, French language studies, language awareness and no doubt other fields have established their own associations, operating simultaneously as rivals and collaborators with BAAL. It is interesting to note that (despite long-standing claims for 'educational linguistics', for example, by Spolsky 1978 and Stubbs 1986) there is no separate British association for educational language work, while CLIE (the Committee for Linguistics in Education) arose from joint meetings between

BAAL and the Linguistics Association of Great Britain (LAGB), and is under the joint control of the two associations. Its substantive function is 'to explore and evaluate ways in which linguistics and applied linguistics might contribute towards the school curriculum and the professional training of teachers' (1980 terms of reference, revised 1984), and it has produced a succession of valuable pamphlets to this end.

None the less, we could ask of applied linguistics, as J. D. Palmer did in Kaplan's 1977 symposium: 'Should we not discard the name? Let's call it language teaching, or stylistics, or dialectology, or phonology, or syntactic theory, or whatever it is' (Kaplan 1980: 26).

The purpose of this chapter is not to defend separate organizations for linguists, language teachers, or others. Indeed, one of BAAL's major justifications is, as the preamble to the membership list makes clear, 'to provide a common forum for those engaged in the theoretical study of language and for those whose interest is in the practical implications of such work'. None the less, the very broad conceptualization of its role that BAAL has adopted requires some defence, for it is not only vulnerable to the charge of academic imperialism; it could be charged with vagueness, incoherence, and confusion. Members of the association could be regarded as those who are left over when the serious or technically-minded have identified themselves elsewhere according to their specialisms; alternatively, it could be the forum in which theoreticians and researchers with a social conscience (including but not exclusively linguists) explain themselves to atheoretical practitioners; or as the forum in which 'performance', 'language in use', 'linguistic social practices' and similar themes are explored and studied. All of these views are represented in discussion (though the first is too offensive to have been said in writing!), and no doubt some elements of BAAL's activity could be related to all of these, even the offensive one. But they are, in my view, inadequate accounts of an appropriate rationale for a discipline/field/ subject such as applied linguistics. There is a much stronger case to be made, which is more abstract than those referred to above, but defensible (indeed I shall argue essential) for the well-being of our understanding of language, human beings, and education.

Applied linguistics as mediation

It is curious, when we have all recognized from Saussure the arbitrariness of the sign, how difficult we find it to free ourselves from the centrality of linguistics to applied linguistics, even when the function and practices of people who call themselves 'applied linguists' may have shifted. Yet decisions have to be made that reflect social structures (such as the functions of departments within higher education), and most would agree that applied linguistics makes more sense grouped with linguistics in the national Research Assessment Exercise for universities than with any of the single, and equally arbitrary, sub-areas within which most BAAL members work. None the less, in this as in other ways, it suffers from all the problems of inter-disciplinary areas, and all the problems of applied areas. Might it not be better, therefore, to accept a straight 'linguistics applied' perspective, to use Widdowson's formulation from BAAL's 1979 Annual Meeting (Widdowson 1980: 165), and follow the precepts of the association's founding fathers? If not that, might it be better to argue that applied linguists are the repository of what another former Chair of BAAL, Sam Spicer, called 'real understanding of real language', and to concentrate on the strong model of 'language in use'? Either of these would make our self-definition tidier—but I hope to show that either would also weaken the value of our work and result in lower quality research and theorizing than an alternative definition of applied linguistics. That defines applied linguistics as:

> The theoretical and empirical investigation of real-world problems in which language is a central issue.
> (Brumfit 1995c: 27)

Let me, then, consider some of the problems of major alternative definitions.

To start with, we need to recognize that much discussion of what applied linguistics is relates to parallel debates about what linguistics is. The distinction between linguistic and applied scholarship is of course very old, for classical rhetorical studies were clearly applied in intention. Robins (1967: 13) implies that linguistic scholarship in Plato and Aristotle relates merely to the skills of reading and writing, but Philebus (18b) shows Socrates clearly concerned with meta-classification:

> The unlimited variety of sound was once discerned by some god, or perhaps some godlike man; you know the story that there was some such person in Egypt called Theuth. He it was who originally discerned the existence, in that unlimited variety, of the vowels—not 'vowel' in the singular but 'vowels' in the plural ...
> (Hamilton and Cairns 1961: 1094; Hackforth's translation)

And the classification continues, with considerable subtlety.

It is harder to find meta-statements (as distinct from exemplifications) on the distinction between theoretical and applied language study. The eminent Danish linguist Rasmus Rask (1787–1832) is cited (Gregerson 1991: 12) as distinguishing between theoretical linguistics (discovering and formulating laws) and applied (explanations of words and grammar). But Howatt (1984: 265) follows convention in dating the term 'applied linguistics' to the launch of *Language Learning—a Quarterly Journal of Applied Linguistics* in 1948. Certainly the explosion of interest in linguistics-informed language teaching followed the wartime successes of linguists such as Fries in the US and Firth in the UK in developing language training.

Discussion of the nature of applied linguistics proliferated in the 1960s and 1970s, as the national and international associations, including AILA and

BAAL, were founded, and the themes which emerged remain relevant at the end of the twentieth century.

A seminal book, *The Linguistic Sciences and Language Teaching*, (Halliday, McIntosh, and Strevens 1964: 138) comments, 'applied linguistics starts when a description is specifically made, or an existing description used, for a further purpose which lies outside the linguistic sciences'.

Such early discussions were confident about the relationship between linguistics and applied areas like language teaching, though they anticipated many of the difficulties that are still raised about any simple relationship between linguistics and practice. Mackey, writing from a Canadian perspective, expressed the problems with exemplary clarity. His complete definition/historical note in 1966 was:

> **What is applied linguistics?**
> The term 'applied linguistics' seems to have originated in the United States in the 1940s. It was first used by persons with an obvious desire to be identified as scientists rather than as humanists; the association with 'applied science' can hardly have been accidental. Yet, although linguistics is a science, 'applied science' does not necessarily include linguistics. The creation of applied linguistics as a discipline represents an attempt to find practical applications for 'modern scientific linguistics'. While assuming that linguistics can be an applied science, it brings together such diverse activities as the making of alphabets by missionaries and the making of translations by machines. The use of the term has now become crystallized in the names of language centres, reviews, books, and articles.
> (Mackey 1966: 247)

But he raises several substantive difficulties:

> Contemporary claims that applied linguistics can solve all the problems of language teaching are as unfounded as the claims that applied psychology can solve them. For the problems of language teaching are central neither to psychology nor linguistics. Neither science is equipped to solve the problems of language teaching.
>
> It is likely that language teaching will continue to be a child of fashion in linguistics and psychology until the time it becomes an autonomous discipline which uses these related sciences instead of being used by them. To become autonomous it will, like any science, have to weave its own net, so as to fish out from the oceans of human experience and natural phenomena only the elements it needs ...
> (*Ibid*: 255)

Politzer provides a partial illustration of the issue raised by Mackey. He posits a fictional teacher, 'Mr Jones' to make his position clear:

> Mr Jones has utilized linguistics or has had recourse to Applied Linguistics in the sense in which the term is used in this publication, because Mr Jones has

gone through the following process: 1. He has recognized a pedagogical problem. 2. He has utilized his knowledge of linguistics to formulate an assumption concerning the precise nature of the pedagogical problem. 3. He has utilized his knowledge of linguistics to formulate another assumption concerning a way of dealing with the pedagogical problem. 4. He has devised teaching procedures based on this assumption and has tested it, at least in a very informal sort of way.
(Politzer 1972: 2)

But Politzer also refers to other areas (sociolinguistics, psycholinguistics), and other disciplines (psychology of learning, social psychology) in formulating his 'conclusion concerning teaching procedures' (pp.2–3). He reflects the psychologism of the period in asserting boldly 'Applied linguistics may be considered as a branch of psycholinguistics' (p.2), and recognizes that linguistics could be applied to areas other than language teaching.

None the less, this description suggests a technology drawing upon linguistics which is less humane and educationally sensitive than Mackey's. A year later, Pit Corder extends this notion to one of theoretical dependence:

The application of linguistic knowledge to some object—or applied linguistics, as its name implies—is an activity. It is not a theoretical study. It makes use of the findings of theoretical studies. The applied linguist is a consumer, or user, not a producer, of theories ... Language teaching is also an activity, but teaching languages is not the same activity as applied linguistics.
(Corder 1973: 10)

Thus by the mid-1970s the notion of applied linguistics, albeit limited to language teaching, was both marketable, and—by implication—unproblematic. For example, Wardhaugh (1974) allows us to interpret applied linguistics inductively by using the title *Topics in Applied Linguistics* for a book, but not making any definition; instead he concentrates on items of linguistically informed commentary on spelling, reading, and second language teaching, for example.

A definition deriving from Corder is still commonplace in basic dictionaries and reference books. Take, for example, Crystal, in *A First Dictionary of Linguistics and Phonetics*, 1980:

A branch of linguistics where the primary concern is the application of linguistic theories, methods and findings to the elucidation of language problems which have arisen in other areas of experience.
(Crystal 1980: 28–9, repeated with minimal modification in Crystal, *The Cambridge Encyclopedia of Language*, 1987: 412)

Another example is that given by Richards, Platt, and Platt, *Longman Dictionary of Applied Linguistics*, 1985:

1 the study of second and foreign language learning and teaching. 2 the study of language and linguistics in relation to practical problems, such as LEXICOGRAPHY, TRANSLATION, SPEECH PATHOLOGY, etc. ...
(p.15, and again in the second edition, 1992, retitled *The Longman Dictionary of Language Teaching and Applied Linguistics*, p.19)

Kaplan and Widdowson in *The International Encyclopedia of Linguistics*, 1992 provide a third definition:

> A technology which makes abstract ideas and research findings accessible and relevant to the real world; it mediates between theory and practice.
> (*Ibid*: 76).

Thus there seemed to be, as Buckingham and Eskey (1980) indicated in a 1977 TESOL symposium that preceded the setting up of the American Association of Applied Linguistics, 'General agreement that ... applied linguists perform a *mediating* function between theoretical disciplines and various kinds of more practical work' (p.2). However, the debate does not stop there, and even applied linguists who have drafted these definitions, such as Crystal and Widdowson, may, as we shall see, move beyond mediation in their practice. Buckingham and Eskey, indeed, go on to suggest that linguistics is reconnected with real world language by applied linguistics. Others in the same symposium follow Krashen in accepting a limited and top-down model. For him, applied linguistics is concerned with:

> The creation of materials and methods for second language teaching. Research in applied linguistics consists of comparisons of materials and methods, with student progress in L2 performance as the dependent variable ...
> (Krashen 1980: 13).

Applied linguistics as an (inter-)discipline

However, another strand of argument was visible. Peter Strevens had already, in a memo for AILA 1975 (published as Strevens 1980), pressed Corder's definition further. Applied linguistics involved both theory and practice, had multiple bases, not just linguistics, and was broader than language learning and teaching alone. Most interestingly, he observed that it 'redefines itself afresh for each task' (p.19), and is dynamic not static. This account is distinguished from others by its concern for sensitivity to context and awareness of the richness of potential source material.

Other linguists were also expressing doubts about the linguistics applied model. Spolsky made a clear statement of the case in 1978:

> ... the structural linguists applied their efforts to replace a system based on one limited view of language (the translation method) by an equally rigid and psycholinguistically invalid approach (the audiolingual method). When this

system turned out to be inadequate, there were many who thought that all that was needed was to come up with a new one based on the latest theory of language.
(Spolsky 1978: 2)

His solution is to propose an 'educational linguistics' in order to escape a perceived closer link to linguistics rather than to, for example, pedagogy.

But, building on hints in Strevens' paper, this position was superseded by a more ambitious programme. Widdowson, introducing his book *Explorations in Applied Linguistics*, still works within the language teaching model, but makes grander and more holistic claims.

> Applied linguistics, as I conceive it, is a spectrum of inquiry which extends from theoretical studies of language to classroom practice. The papers appearing here explore issues that can be located at different points on this spectrum: some with a focus on matters of a predominantly theoretical kind, others with a primary focus on matters of practical pedagogy. But in all cases the whole spectrum is presupposed as the context of discussion ...
> (Widdowson 1979: 1)

Furthermore, Corder's avoidance of theoretical concern is explicitly repudiated:

> Language teaching is necessarily a theoretical as well as a practical occupation. If this were not so, discussion on the matter would reduce to an exchange of anecdotes and pedagogy would be a mere pretence (pp.2–3) ... A communicative orientation involves a consideration of a whole host of issues—how discourse is processed, how interaction is conducted, learning styles and strategies, developmental patterns of language acquisition, the role of learner and teacher—all these and more.
> (Widdowson 1979: 3)

Even more grandly, Kaplan (1980a: 63) notes 'I would contend that there is virtually no human activity in which the applied linguist cannot play a role'. Certainly many British linguists had already engaged in an impressive variety of applied activity. Lyons' and Halliday's work on stylistics and the latter's on educational linguistics, Sinclair's on that and on lexicography, Crystal on language disability, Trim and Stubbs on teaching modern languages and English as a mother tongue respectively, may all be mentioned, to restrict the list to those who started primarily as linguists rather than (as most British applied linguists did) as teachers or other practitioners.

In a book that directly arose out of an invitation to address BAAL, Crystal writes:

> ... what one is applying is not so much knowledge about language, as a way of investigating language—a methodological, as distinct from an empirical, dimension for the subject.
> (Crystal: 1981: 2)

We already have, then, applied linguistics as a mediation, as an interdisciplinary interaction, as a technology, as a methodology, and as an autonomous theoretical and practical discipline.

We could see this diversity of definition as evidence that the discipline was alive and active. In practice, though, Stern's diagram (1983: 18, Figure 14.1) is typical, treating applied linguistics as a technology:

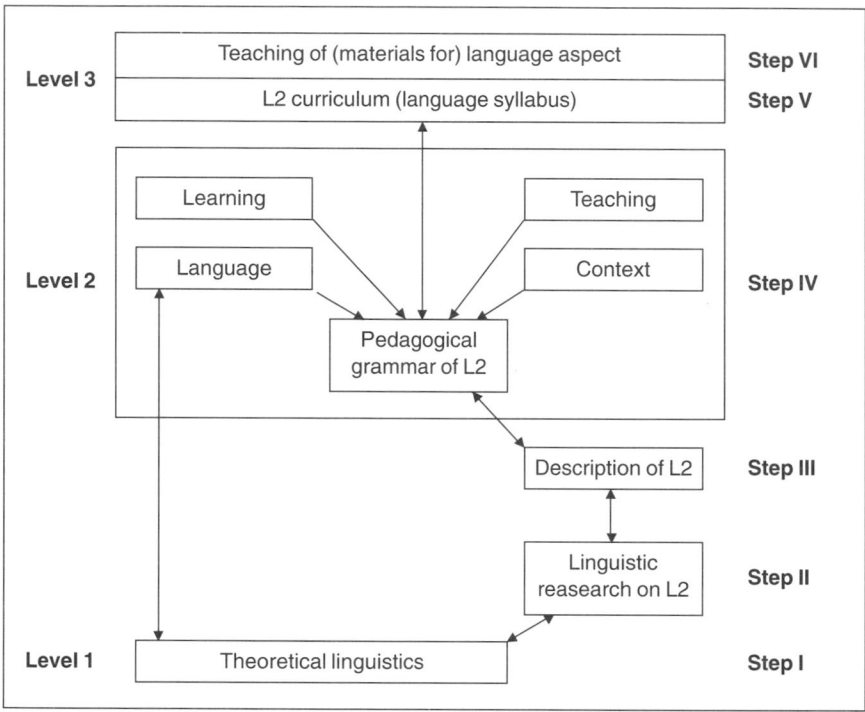

Figure 14.1: The interaction between linguistics and language teaching
(reproduced from Stern 1983. OUP with permission)

But it is important to point out that accounts like this are only metaphors. The psychological processes of teachers, materials-writers, and curriculum designers may reflect the categories of such models, but only as integrated and largely unconscious decision-making processes; the algorithm metaphor, which underlies such boxes and arrows, does not reflect an ordered series of discrete events. Furthermore, there are completely alternative accounts possible. Reflecting on my experience of writing English teaching materials in Tanzania in the late 1960s, I could have modified Stern's categories with some justice to produce the alternative model in Figure 14.2.

This is not to say that linguistics was ignored, nor that we lacked explicit language learning principles; only that the model below is a closer representation of our thinking in workshops in which nation-building and justice were the

Step VI: (as in Stern) Teaching materials

Step V: (as in Stern) L2 curriculum

Step IV: Subject matter choices/language/learning/teaching

Step III: Description of sociopolitical context

Step II: Political theory in Tanzania

Step I: Ethics/political theory

Figure 14.2: Language teaching and theory: one alternative model

uppermost thoughts in our planning processes. Were we engaged in practical applications of applied linguistic theory? I had certainly been strongly influenced by Halliday, McIntosh, and Strevens (1964) as a serious analysis of practical problems that I was facing daily in the classroom. But I was not in Tanzania because of teaching techniques, however principled, any more than language users habitually speak to display their syntactic skills. I was there because I believed in the Tanzanian government and wanted to create something good out of the remains of the dying British Empire. And similar motives drove many of my most professionally committed language-teaching colleagues.

You do not have to agree with these ambitions to recognize that motives are at least as important as linguistic applications in defining how we address practical problems in which language is a central issue.

Widdowson comments on the fictionality (in all sciences) of generalized statements, and remarks about application:

> You do not *apply* a theory which is a fiction, any more than you apply a novel. What you do is develop your awareness of what a useful model of behaviour might be for your particular purposes.
> (Widdowson 1980: 168)

He then goes on to clarify the interrelationship between linguistics itself and applied linguistics by suggesting that

> Linguistics applied works in one direction and yields descriptions which are projections of linguistic theory which exploit the data of actual language as illustration. Applied linguistics ... works in the opposite way and yields descriptions which are projections of actual language which exploit linguistic theory as illumination.
> (*Ibid*: 169)

This is a far cry from a mediating role. It implies a sophisticated technology of its own for applied linguistics. Crystal, too, moves beyond mediation, commenting (1981: 18) that applied linguistics has its own independent purpose: 'implicit in the applied linguistics enterprise is a comparative dimension.'

Thus applied linguistics is emerging as an integrated discipline, feeding into linguistics technically sophisticated statements about language in genuine social situations, on the one hand, and responding to the needs of practitioners, on the other. This implies that it has an authoritative body of knowledge to offer practitioners. Carter has characterized their needs, from the point of view of outsiders, whether politicians, the press, or linguists:

> ... if teachers have no formal training in linguistic awareness then they will lack categories and frameworks for thinking about and analysing crucial elements in learning and will therefore draw such categories from a common store of half-belief in which prejudice and fact combine indistinguishably.
> (Carter 1990a: 17)

And at least some practitioners accept such views, if Crystal (1981: 8) is correct in his assertion that 'Many professionals will listen to linguists because of "the ubiquity of failure"'. Certainly, there has been a widespread hope that linguistics might resolve some problems of 'failure'. Indeed, notwithstanding the suspicion of English mother tongue teachers towards linguistics, innovations like A-level English language, the Language in the National Curriculum (LINC) programme, and movements for Language Awareness and KAL (Knowledge about Language) have shown an increasing demand for greater understanding of language in the teaching of English as a mother tongue. It is noticeable, for example, that there are many more references to linguistics in Brindley's 1994 Open University reader for training future English teachers than in its sibling, Swarbrick's 1994 book on modern languages. This would not have been the case ten years ago, and research carried out in the early 1990s in Hampshire (Mitchell, Hooper, and Brumfit 1994) showed that the practices of experienced modern language teachers reflected the detail of linguistic analysis far more than similar English teachers' practices did.

Whatever the demand is, though, the richness of possible interpretation of linguistic data remains daunting, as Cook and Seidlhofer indicate:

> Language is viewed in various theories as a genetic inheritance, a mathematical system, a social fact, the expression of individual identity, the expression of cultural identity, the outcome of dialogic interaction, a social semiotic, the intuitions of native speakers, the sum of attested data, a collection of memorized chunks, a rule-governed discrete combinatory system, or electrical activation in a distributed network ... We do not have to choose. Language can be all of these things at once.
> (Cook and Seidlhofer 1995: 4)

Because so many scholars address linguistic matters from so many perspectives, the privileging of linguistics in applied linguistics is bound to attract criticism. Certainly, the claim has some force that close-to linguistics work is dominant in international research traditions. The rise of second language acquisition (SLA) empirical work, for example, dominated the journal *Applied Linguistics* in the late 1980s (19 out of 42 papers in volumes 8 and 9, with several of BAAL's 'areas' scarcely receiving any attention at all). But the 1990s have seen a more ferocious counter-argument developing, with a stronger underpinning in non-linguistic theory. Phillipson (1992), indicting applied linguistics along with other agents of 'English linguisticism', worries about the limitation to linguistics (for example, pp.175–6) and at the same time calls for a 'critical' applied linguistics (p.321). Similarly, Pennycook writes:

> One of the problems with applied linguistics … has been its divorce from educational theory and the tendency to deal with language teaching as a predominantly psycholinguistic phenomenon isolated from its social, cultural and educational contexts.
> (Pennycook 1994: 299)

Further, if the journal *Applied Linguistics* is typical, the concentration on first world scholarship (32 out of 40 authors from Europe or North America in volumes 8 and 9; 34 out of 45 in volumes 12 and 13, for example) suggests a heavy emphasis away from many centres of real-world practice. So Pennycook can justifiably claim that

> With the gradual consolidation of applied linguistics, furthermore, there has been a constant move towards educational expertise being defined as in the hands of the predominantly male Western applied linguistic academy, rather than in the hands of the largely female teaching practitioners … [This leads him to assert.] … we need a reconceptualization of the role of teachers and applied linguists that does away with the theory/practice divide and views teachers/applied linguists as politically engaged critical educators.
> (*Ibid*: 303)

Similar debates can be found in other fields (see, for example Blaug 1980 in economics; Gibbon 1989 in archaeology; Purvis 1992 in education).

Language and education

Proponents of 'educational linguistics' by analogy with educational psychology, etc., base their argument, as we have seen, on the disciplines outside linguistics that are relevant to language teaching. However, such an argument is relevant to any study of language in real-world situations, and is not peculiar to education. Further, there are many ways in which language interacts with educational activity. Apart from the direct teaching of languages (first, second, or foreign), language is a crucial mediating force in processes of learning (or arguably often *is* the process of learning, if we accept the notion that learning is substantially another term for entering a new discourse community), and is a major element in establishing the school itself as an institution. Thus school language policies rightly embrace the linguistic practices of teachers and administrative staff, as well as students, refer to language outside as well as inside the classroom, and ultimately need to relate to a conception of the role of language in the world, and hence the whole social philosophy that the school is an agent in promoting.

To separate these activities from sociological, philosophical, political, economic and psychological factors would be manifestly impossible, and once educational linguistics departed from linguistics proper, there would be no point at which the list of relevant further disciplines could be stopped. Yet the arguments for not stopping at linguistics are so overwhelming, as we have seen, that there is little point in rehearsing them further here, as they are now so universally accepted.

So in education, as in any other social practice to which language is centrally important, the floodgates are open. Whether we like it or not, we have to learn to swim.

A socially contextualized applied linguistics

A widely proposed solution to this apparent loss of focus is to reject the positivist tradition that has allegedly inhibited previous discussion, and to embrace alternative philosophies, to accept the postmodernist critique, and to deny the validity of previous procedures—thus rejecting the notion of 'focus' altogether.

Postmodernist critiques are in many respects liberating. We each stand at the intersection of many discourses, and the proposal that a single grand scheme is neither necessary nor attainable may relieve us of the burden of seeking it. But there are problems with wholesale rejection of previous practice. Such rejection fails to recognize our social and historical inter-connectedness: we are culturally different at the same time as we are culturally the same, and emphasizing either to the exclusion of the other obscures the crucial question of the relationships between similarity and difference. Any investigation of practice in the real world is confronted by both similarity and difference, and understanding how to incorporate them into our research practice must be a central question for applied linguistics.

The definitions that we have so far encountered are not so much incompatible with each other as successive steps on a journey towards autonomy. While they may be related to Evensen's (1995) comparison of general and applied linguistics, they may also be viewed as positions about scientific activity in general, with applied linguistics being distinguished by deriving from 'real-world' (i.e. problem definitions initiated by non-linguists) issues, but still engaged in explanation, generalization, and theorizing about these. The object of study is embedded in practice, but the purpose and epistemological concerns remain the same as those for any other science: the production of better and better explanations, as a necessary preliminary to solving problems systematically. In applied linguistics as characterized earlier in this chapter, we first have the technical argument, using linguistics for purposes beyond linguistics (Halliday, McIntosh, and Strevens, Politzer, Corder). Second is the interdisciplinary argument that any applied problem, while needing to call upon linguistic procedures, cannot be solved solely by those, as the nature of language requires an embeddedness in social and psychological action, so that these (and other) factors must come into play also (Mackey, Strevens, Spolsky). Third is the claim that theorizing and investigative methodologies have to be remade to encompass the larger task of theorizing and investigating linguistic practice as defined in the second (Widdowson, Crystal). Fourth is the demand for social accountability and for a value-laden acceptance of the ideological bases of the linguistic real-world problems that applied linguistics is required to address (Phillipson; Pennycook). This fourth move can be seen as a shift away from linguistics altogether, and not surprisingly it is particularly contentious. None the less, this progression can be seen as a continuous dialectic between an autonomous and idealized vision of language and a socially accountable view. First, the techniques of description are utilized; second, they are seen as restricted to only some features of language, so autonomy is questioned; third, the richer account of language has to be retheorized to reintegrate into a richer idealization; fourth, the value system of the whole process has to be questioned, to challenge the richer idealization.

We should note, though, the different questions that lead to the various positions outlined above. In the first, the question relates to an idealization, a reification of language, to enable it to be seen as a 'system of systems', 'a structure in its own right', etc. The techniques for describing this autonomous entity (itself necessarily a convenient fiction) can then be utilized, as appropriate, for descriptive, and thus for applied purposes. In the second, the definition of the nature of language underlying the first is questioned. Language, it is claimed, is instantiated in social and psychological behaviour and consequently autonomous descriptions are inefficient (particularly perhaps for typical applied—'real world'—purposes) because they are partial. In the third, a claim is made that a richer idealization (though still, and unavoidably a convenient fiction, an idealization) can be theorized from the cross-/inter-understanding. In the fourth, the processes of idealization are (as in the second) undermined by a claim that competing idealizations exist, that they serve the interests of individual and power groups, that idealization may not be necessary at all, and so on. It is to this postmodernist critique that I now wish to turn, recognizing that it provides the strongest current challenge to the tradition I have tried to define above.

Postmodernism and applied linguistics

The past decade has seen a large body of literature interpreting postmodernism for non-specialist audiences (a convenient encyclopaedic source is Lechte 1994). I shall draw upon a number of specific criticisms of earlier approaches that derive from postmodernism, in order to isolate those which are most significant in applied linguistics. Writers most frequently cited include a range of precursors such as Kierkegaard, Nietzsche, Bakhtin, Sartre and even Popper, but those who are presumed by commentators to be card-carrying postmodernists (though most would deny the value of such a concept!) are mainly French-writing cultural theorists such as Lacan, Derrida, Foucault, Lyotard, Bourdieu and

Kristeva. Applied linguists who have drawn upon some of their ideas include Bourne (1988), Fairclough (1989 and later writings), Gee (1990), Tollefson (1991), Cameron *et al.* (1992), Phillipson (1992), Pennycook (1994), Rampton (1995a), and Masny (1996). In associated disciplines, Walkerdine (1988 and later writings) in psychology, and Usher and Edwards (1994) in education have made explicit attempts to interpret postmodernism for other purposes.

It will be clear from the range and eclecticism of the writers cited that what is being discussed is more a general tendency in thinking, something in the *Zeitgeist*, rather than a single and coherent system; indeed one of the major tenets of this approach is the explicit repudiation of single or coherent systems. Thus it is appropriate to extract a number of key themes for consideration, without insisting on systematicity.

Fundamentally, postmodernism is a critique of the enlightenment project which has dominated post-Cartesian thinking and post-1776, or 1789, political and social theory—the very fact that the dates of the American and French revolutions are resonant for all of us testify to the durability of the beliefs that postmodernist critics are opposing. At its broadest level, the concern is reflected in Lyotard's (1984) attack on 'meta-narratives', on attempts to see human activity as part of a grand scheme, driven by notions of progressive improvement of any kind.

As we saw in Chapter 11, the Canadian philosopher Charles Taylor (1994) has drawn attention to two conflicting traditions that have emerged from the Enlightenment: on the one hand, an emphasis on the similarity between people, leading to concerns about rights for individuals based on our sameness in entitlement; on the other, an emphasis on the rights not of people but of peoples, of communities, leading to concerns for the authenticity of cultures and the rights of groups based on our differences, as cultures. The postmodernist debate, like the multicultural debate, centres round the impossibility of holding both these post-Enlightenment positions at once. The interests of a 'universal subject'—a human being sharing attributes with all other human beings, conflict with the interests of an individual uniquely grounded within a particular culture.

Now language, as a major mediating factor for the individual and the social group, is central to this conflict, so it is difficult for applied linguists to avoid positioning themselves, wittingly or unwittingly, in the debate.

My own interest in such problems emerged from a different route: an interest in the critical community theories of such diverse philosophers as Bakhtin (1981; Holquist 1990), Popper (1994a, 1994b) and Habermas (1984, 1987). Each of these, in different ways, tried to encapsulate variation in human experience through the notion of collaborating but different discourse communities. But each recognized that the process of communication is more important than the product of communication: products will always be subject to repudiation, modification, and reinterpretation—but the lack of an agreed process for comment and criticism will result in less satisfactory or false knowledge, dangerous when exploited to address practical problems.

From this tradition, we derive a multiperspective view of the world. As Bakhtin remarks, there are aspects of our selves that we cannot know by direct observation: only an outsider can present us with a view of how we look from behind. Thus, even with a firm positivist viewpoint, notions of triangulation of research position are necessary to locate evidence within a descriptive system. More substantially, though, participants, external observers, and interested parties ('stakeholders' in the current jargon) see different features of the same event not just because of their different positions, but because of their different ideologies, or theoretical viewpoints. The process of observation is value laden, and consequently different value systems lead to different views of the same phenomena. In so far as participants' (including researchers') views of phenomena reflect ideologies which are shared by individuals' different communities, the 'differing communicative discourses' tradition intersects with the post-Enlightenment conflict depicted by Taylor, for there is potential dispute over the different 'stories' that observers, participants, and other interested parties will tell, over which is the most 'authentic'—i.e. the most useful or applicable.

Similarly, postmodernist theory may draw upon the tradition of the social construction of knowledge, deriving for linguists from Vygotsky, for sociologists more recently from Berger and Luckman (1966). Again, it is interaction between the individual mind and the social structures within which other, differing minds operate that leads us to our individual views of how reality is.

All this is to question simplistic interpretations of unproblematic knowledge, deductive assumptions about our capacity to prove particular generalizations for all time, and views of the objectivity of science. Associated with such interpretations are views of science as a progressive approximation to the truth, and its association with the inevitable betterment of the human condition. Although postmodernism may be seen as a pessimistic response to science's (or indeed to socialism's or Marxism's) failure to deliver, Foucault sees the conflict as a permanent rather than contemporary struggle, present in any historical period, between a modernist and a postmodernist viewpoint (see Usher and Edwards 1994: 9). The extreme postmodernist view asserts a relativism about human knowledge, and even about moral systems, that certainly conflicts with traditional progressivism, but which is politically appealing in a world in which more and more cultures are in unavoidable political contact (witness, for example, South-East Asian criticisms of United Nations views of human rights as being symptoms of western individualism). Even devices that have been seen as instruments for liberation, such as the establishment of norms for assessment purposes, are seen as repressive. Foucault remarks (1979: 184) that normalizing provides for subjects 'a surveillance that makes it possible to qualify, to classify and to punish', providing 'a visibility through which one differentiates them and judges them'.

One response to the epistemological difficulties inherent in this conflict is to concentrate on the fragmentation and consumerism of contemporary post-industrial society. According to Featherstone (1991: 126) this is characterized by the view that 'there is no human nature or true self ... the goal of life [is] an endless pursuit of new experiences, values and vocabularies'. Such experiences are, on the one hand, subject to the politics of representation, in which consumerism ensures the power of the representative images that provide such experiences—and, on the other, reflect and contribute to a playfulness which is evoked in opposition to the puritan tradition of conventional science. Parody, irony, punning, become stylistic weapons in opposition to clarity, directness, and the notion of one meaning at a time. Sequential thinking is replaced with the simultaneous holding of several strands of thought, even the simultaneous holding of conflicting positions. Thus postmodernism can link with other major and minor strands in contemporary culture: opposition to patriarchy on the grounds of a richer, more imaginative, divergent, empathetic feminist ethos; support for subjectivity and the validation of subjective experience; distrust of 'expertise' and the 'myth' of disinterestedness, a rhetoric of 'empowerment' for the disempowered in opposition to a (largely unanalysed) tyranny.

Central to postmodernism (if 'centrality' is possible in such a devolved discussion!), is 'textuality'—language. Because of this, applied linguists unavoidably have to locate themselves in relation to the critique that post-modernism offers. Language is central partly because it offers a major means of obfuscation (see, for example, Lacan 1979: 207), so postmodernists are at pains to draw attention to the status of their writings as texts. This is mainly to challenge the notion of an unproblematic relationship between a text and what it 'represents'—hence the emphasis on parody and irony. There is no simple relationship between what a text 'says' and an external 'reality'; indeed the notion of a truth which 'corresponds' with reality is no more than a function of communication processes. So a writer who implies omniscience—or indeed any authoritative position—as an individual writer (and the discourse conventions of academic writing particularly reinforce this tendency) misleads readers by claiming an authority that no one can legitimately claim—and in a sense the clearer the writing the falser it is. Further, we are not necessarily in control of language at all. Rather, it is in control of us: we are positioned by the requirements of the discourse we think we adopt, and our metaphors of adoption hide the fact that it adopts us. (But is that 'fact' a fact? Postmodernist discourse requires us to put every word into 'inverted commas' in order to insist on its textuality, providing us with the paradox of communicating about the impossibility of communication—a point I shall return to later.)

Finally on language, we should note the significance of inter-textuality. Linguistic artefacts cross-refer to other linguistic artefacts, not just in literary studies where such relationships as those between works like the *Iliad*, the *Aeneid*, and the *Divine Comedy* or (more recently) *Lord of the Flies* and *Coral Island* have long been acknowledged, but in all linguistic behaviour. Not only do jokes relate to and expand on other jokes, parodies abound as part of casual conversation, and individuals constantly quote other texts, but normal speech uses parallelism, assonance, and other 'literary' devices all the time (Tannen

1989). Once again, linguistic constructs, including academic genres such as that to which this book belongs, have to be seen as artefacts responsive to and contributing to the structure of other linguistic constructs.

How should applied linguistics respond?

So how should applied linguists react to the postmodernist project? Perhaps we should start by distinguishing a strong from a weak form. The strong form is easy to dismiss, if only because it cannot have any application and condemns itself to uselessness by a self-defined irrelevance. If there are no privileged general statements to be made, the general claims on behalf of the movement have no status; to make a general critique of all general critiques is to tie oneself into a paradox. If knowledge is merely expression of power relations, the concept of knowledge becomes redundant, and only power is left (a view that is attractive to dictatorially inclined politicians resisted by intellectuals). Anyway, what is the status of the claim that knowledge is merely power? If all viewpoints reveal perspectives which are no more and no less valid than any other, then viewing, communicating about it, and understanding become impossible activities to conceive of, and the communication of postmodernist (or any other) ideas can be no more than a nervous twitch. Such extreme pessimism about human interaction is dysfunctional at best and quietist to the point of evil irresponsibility at worst. The total democratization of epistemological perspective suffers from the same defect as its political equivalent, the total democratization of power as in philosophical anarchism (Woodcock 1962; Joll 1979). Both positions have attractive and anti-hierarchical features which provide a valuable critique of elitist and potentially exploitative positions, but by devolving significance to the lowest possible position, they are vulnerable to the first opponent who claims 'higher' authority—in politics the bully, in knowledge the charlatan: 'Anarchy can never be hegemonic. Anarchists can occasionally topple crowns, but never enjoy the results' (Sassoon 1996: 399). By accepting the weaker argument that hierarchical models of science risk being self-serving, we are enabled to look for protection against the misuse of hierarchy, to benefit from a critique which in its strong form denies the possibility of benefit at all. As Popper (1994a: 33–4) argues, 'The proponents of relativism put before us standards of mutual understanding which are unrealistically high. And when we fail to meet those standards, they claim that understanding is impossible.'

The key point for any science is not the impossibility of shared experience, but the relationship between what can be shared and what cannot. Each of us is both universal and unique in our culture. We have to account for the ways in which our experience is triangulated many times over: when we read, let us say, Homer, Virgil, or Dante, we share experiences with other humans who may never read them in the language we read them in, and who may never live at the same time as us. Yet what Pope or Chapman make of Homer links with what Robert Fagles has made of the *Iliad* (Fagles 1990), and with what Gnedich in

Russia made of it in the 1820s, as well as with Tolstoy's aspirations to epic grandeur in *War and Peace*. If there is no universal subject, what happens when we read the classics, or when we talk to each other at all?

Yet our grounding in culture is also crucial. We cannot treat all philosophical questions as variants on a single set of deculturized logical premises. Reading the *Iliad* after the twentieth century's experience of war is different from reading it in 1910, reading it in Greek is different from reading it in English, and reading it having read Dante, Virgil, or Tolstoy is different from reading it without. Rereading differs from reading; every experience is both new and old, and out of the tension between the two we make our understandings and our experiences. Exploring how we do this is one of the tasks of applied linguistics.

Constantly concerning ourselves with clarifying what is shared and what is unique about human experience demands a willingness to problematize and criticize. The first task is valuably performed by much of the postmodernist critique; the second is inherent in traditional philosophy of science, particularly in the critical community frameworks of Popper and Habermas. Popper's late papers provide a number of helpful comments for applied linguistics.

Popper's classic model of research and scholarship is summarized in the formula

$$P1 \rightarrow TT \rightarrow EE \rightarrow P2$$

(First a problem, then a tentative theory, then criticism or error elimination, then a second problem emerges and the cycle continues.)

The papers published just before his death contain many discussions of applied, social science and practical investigation. Many of them show that he recognized some of the key problems faced by socially embedded activities such as applied linguistics or education. For example, in a discussion of evolutionary principles underlying behaviour, he makes a crucial distinction between social tradition and genetic disposition which is a necessary preliminary to theorizing the similarity/difference debate. He writes:

> I will speak of a tradition as a behavioural pattern which does not change over a considerable period of time, *although other behavioural patterns or solutions are available from the point of view of the genetic composition of the organism*. And I will say that a way of behaving has become genetically or hereditarily entrenched if *no other patterns are available*—that is, if the type of organism has become genetically specialized. Specialization may thus be a matter of a tradition that can be broken, or of a hereditary entrenchment that cannot ...
> (Popper 1994b: 60)

Teaching methodologies are good examples of tradition, in Popper's sense; defining linguistic specialization resulting from genetic inheritance is one of the goals of some branches of SLA—but distinguishing what is genetically necessary for language acquisition, and what is convention is crucial for serious analysis.

Furthermore, too much specialization in science may become dysfunctional, for criticism and hence understanding is dependent upon culture conflict, or at least cultural interchange:

> … a limited amount of dogmatism is necessary for progress. Without a serious struggle for survival in which the old theories are tenaciously defended, none of the competing theories can show their mettle … intolerant dogmatism, however, is one of the main obstacles to science.
> (*Ibid*: 1994a: 16)

And again:

> … culture clash may lose some of its great value if one of the clashing cultures regards itself as universally superior, and even more so if it is so regarded by the other: this may destroy the greatest value of the culture clash, for the greatest value of culture clash lies in the fact that it can evoke a critical attitude.
> (*Ibid*: 1994a: 51)

This may be read as a reinforcement of the Phillipson and Pennycook critique, except that it insists on the superiority of neither side: it is the interaction, argument, and debate between the different positions which leads to advancement of knowledge, and polarization risks making debate more, not less difficult.

Popper also argues:

> More and more PhD candidates receive merely technical training in certain techniques of measurement. They are not initiated into the scientific tradition, the critical tradition of questioning, of being tempted and guided by great and apparently insoluble riddles rather than by the solubility of little puzzles. True, these technicians, these specialists, are usually aware of their limitations. They call themselves 'specialists' and reject any claim to authority outside their specialities. Yet they do so proudly, and proclaim that specialization is a necessity. But this means flying in the face of the facts, which show that great advances still come from those with a wide range of interests.
>
> If the many, the specialists, gain the day, it will be the end of science as we know it—of great science. It will be a spiritual catastrophe comparable in its consequences to nuclear armament.
> (*Ibid* 1994a: 72)

We may feel that this is somewhat over-stated, for in many disciplines there can be close relationships between the solution of specific detailed problems and creating the conditions for major new advances. But we can acknowledge the force of Popper's concern not to lose the desire for understanding in the concern for technical solution: to pursue solutions without first pursuing understanding can only result in solutions which are (at best) accidental and *ad hoc*. Particularly within linguistic traditions, the tension between the 'wide range of interests' necessary to account for linguistic practices in the world, and the technical specialization required for specific problems needs constant monitoring (see Rampton 1997 for further discussion of this point).

What applied linguistics needs (and anyway cannot avoid) is a plurality of approaches. At the same time, this does not entail randomness of approach. Communication between approaches has to be maintained so that underlying premises may be seriously criticized: autonomy is the enemy of progress. For this reason, the tone and substance of a note on debate by Beretta, Crookes, Gregg, and Long (1994) in *Applied Linguistics* is to be regretted: debate has to start by presuming good faith, otherwise criticism is being avoided rather than responded to. Similarly, criticisms of 'critical' approaches (for example, Widdowson 1995; Hammersley 1996) need to be treated with respect particularly by those who most disagree with them. As Rampton (1995a: 249) suggests, 'one does not have to believe in an autonomous voice of reason or in the trans-mogrifying power of supposedly context-free research procedures to be critical of inconsistency, a disregard for evidence, and ignorance about alternative accounts'. What one does have to have—and what applied linguistics crucially needs—is a recognition of difference within a context of similarity, of alternative views that never completely identify with others, but which critique them through our willingness to address similar (but not always identical) questions while remaining in communication with each other.

Finally, I shall return to my original attempt at definition: 'the theoretical and empirical investigation of real-world problems in which language is a central issue'. 'Theoretical and empirical' require the same procedures and conceptual-izations as any other science, pure or applied—but these will constantly and unavoidably change as human knowledge changes. 'Real-world problems' are investigated partly as a counterweight to the disconnection of autonomous and idealized disciplines (though recognizing that any theoretical and empirical study involves principled idealization), and partly because serious and as far as possible disinterested efforts to understand are particularly crucial in activities that have been defined by politicians, administrators, and practitioners. The interplay between similarity (by connection with other contemporary research, historical awareness, and generalization) and difference (by groundedness, by reflexivity, by action or participant research) is central to real-world problems. 'Language as a central issue' ensures enough overlap with other work to enable communication, criticism, and hence improvement to take place, and enough connection with a well-established autonomous discipline for the interplay between linguistic and applied linguistic theory to be potentially fruitful for both. But the interplay is never exclusively with linguistic theory. Psychological, sociological, pedagogical, economic and political theories may also be subject to critique from applied linguistic perspectives—and as we have seen, they will themselves lead us to question our own traditions.

Thus applied linguists are distinguished from other practitioners (1) by their desire to be engaged first and foremost in a process of understanding, because that is the best way of improving and of solving problems; (2) by their concern for language in the world, as perceived by non-scientists and non-specialists, because that is how language reveals the working both of the human mind and of social forces; and (3) by their desire to see language as an activity which manifests itself through multiple events, all of which are potential sources of understanding the nature of any other linguistic event. Because all human beings produce 'a dialect of their own' within a genetic inheritance and a social structure, the interaction between these is a central subject for understanding what human beings are, and how they think and learn.

Those of us concerned with that branch of applied linguistics that concentrates on language in education are engaged in a long, complex, and infinitely rewarding study. But we shall betray the richness, creativity, and diversity of our subject matter if we imply that definitive solutions to practical problems are easy to arrive at, or that human motivation and behaviour can be reduced to a limited set of predictable dimensions.

As speakers, as thinkers, as learners, as teachers and researchers, we edge our way together to tentative understanding. And as we do so, we too reflect and contribute to our (and others') understanding, through the unique dialect of our own.

Bibliography

Aitchison, J. 1997. *The Language Web*. Cambridge: Cambridge University Press.

Alatis, J., H. H. Stern, and P. Strevens. (eds.). 1983. *Applied Linguistics and the Training of Language Teachers: Towards a Rationale*. Washington, D.C.: Georgetown University Press.

Alladina, S. and V. Edwards. 1991. *Multilingualism in the British Isles*. 2 vols. Harlow: Longman.

Allen, J. P. B. and S. P. Corder. (eds.). 1973. *Readings for Applied Linguistics, The Edinburgh Course in Applied Linguistics Volume 1*. Oxford: Oxford University Press.

Allwright, R. L. 1977. 'Language learning through communication practice'. *ELT Documents* 76/3: 2–14.

Allwright, R. L. 1988. *Observation in the Language Classroom*. Harlow: Longman.

Andrews, S. 1999. *The Metalinguistic Awareness of Hong Kong Secondary School Teachers of English*. Unpublished PhD thesis, University of Southampton.

Annual Review of Applied Linguistics: Communicative Language Teaching. 1987. New York: Cambridge University Press.

Ashworth, M. 1985. *Beyond Methodology*. Cambridge: Cambridge University Press.

Bachman, L. F. 1990. *Fundamental Considerations in Language Testing*. Oxford: Oxford University Press.

Bailey, K. and D. Nunan. (eds.). 1996. *Voices from the Language Classroom*. Cambridge: Cambridge University Press.

Bailey, R. W. 1992. *Images of English*. Cambridge: Cambridge University Press.

Bakhtin, M. M. 1981. *The Dialogic Imagination*. (Translated C. Emerson and M. Holquist.) Austin, Tex.: University of Texas Press.

Bamgbose, A. 1991. *Language and the Nation*. Edinburgh: Edinburgh University Press.

Barnes, D. 1976. *From Communication to Curriculum*. Harmondsworth: Penguin.

Baron, D. 1990. *The English-Only Question*. New Haven, Conn.: Yale University Press.

Becher, T. 1987. 'Disciplinary discourse'. *Studies in Higher Education* 12: 261–74.

Becher, T. 1989. *Academic Tribes and Territories*. Milton Keynes: The Open University Press.

Belloc, H. 1928. *The Cruise of the Nona*. London: Century Publishing.

Benton, M., J. Teasey, R. Bell, and K. Hurst. 1988. *Young Readers Responding to Poems*. London: Routledge.

Beretta, A. 1991. 'Theory construction in SLA: complementarity and opposition'. *Studies in Second Language Acquisition* 13/4: 493–511.

Beretta, A., G. Crookes, K. R. Gregg, and M. H. Long. 1994. 'A comment from some contributors to Volume 14, Issue 3'. *Applied Linguistics* 15/3: 347.

Berger, P. L. and T. Luckman. 1966. *The Social Construction of Reality*. Garden City, N.J.: Doubleday.

Bernstein, B. 1971. *Class, Codes and Control Vol 1: Theoretical Studies Towards a Sociology of Language*. London: Routledge and Kegan Paul.

Blaug, M. 1980. *The Methodology of Economics*. Cambridge: Cambridge University Press.

Block, D. 1996. 'Not so fast: some thoughts on theory culling, relativism, accepted findings and the heart and soul of SLA'. *Applied Linguistics* 17/1: 63–83.

Bloom, B. 1956. *Taxonomy of Educational Objectives*. Harlow: Longman.

Bloom, H. 1994. *The Western Canon*. New York: Harcourt Brace.

Bloomfield, L. 1933. *Language*. London: Allen and Unwin.

Bloor, T. 1986. 'What do language students know about grammar?' *British Journal of Language Teaching* 24/3: 157–60.

Blue, G. and R. F. Mitchell. (eds.). 1996. *Language and Education. British Studies in Applied Linguistics* 11. Clevedon: Multilingual Matters.

Boucher, D. and P. Kelly. (eds.). 1994. *The Social Contract from Hobbes to Rawls*. London: Routledge.

Bourne, J. 1988. '"Natural acquisition" and a masked pedagogy'. *Applied Linguistics* 9/1: 83–99.

Bourne, J. 1992. *Inside a Multilingual Primary School: a Teacher, Children and Theories at Work*. Unpublished PhD thesis, University of Southampton.

Bright W. (ed.). 1992. *International Encyclopedia of Linguistics* Vol. 1. New York and Oxford: Oxford University Press.

Brindley, S. (ed.). 1994. *Teaching English*. London: Routledge in association with The Open University.

British Council. 1991. *Core Lists of Library Material: British Studies*. London: The British Council.

Britton, J. 1970. *Language and Learning*. London: Allen Lane.

Brown, G. A. and S. Armstrong. 1984. 'Explaining and explanations', in E. Wragg. 1984: 121–48.

Brown, J. D. 1988. *Understanding Research in Second Language Acquisition: a Teacher's Guide to Statistics and Research Design*. Cambridge: Cambridge University Press.

Brumfit, C. J. 1978. 'The English language, ideology, and international communication'. *ELT Documents 102*, English as an International Language: 15–24.

Brumfit, C. J. 1981. 'Reading skills and the study of literature in a foreign language'. *System* 9/3: 243–48.

Brumfit, C. J. 1983. 'The integration of theory and practice', in Alatis, Stern, and Strevens (eds.). 1983: 59–73.

Brumfit, C. J. 1984. *Communicative Methodology in Language Teaching*. Cambridge: Cambridge University Press.

Brumfit, C. J. 1985. *Language and Literature Teaching*. Oxford: Pergamon Press.

Brumfit, C. J. 1986a. 'Towards a language policy for multilingual secondary schools', keynote lecture at CILT/European Community Pilot Project Seminar, University of London Institute of Education, September 1986, published in Geach, J. (ed.). 1989. 7–19.

Brumfit, C. J. (ed.). 1986b. *The Practice of Communicative Teaching*. Oxford: Pergamon Press.

Brumfit, C. J. 1987. 'Concepts and categories in language teaching methodology'. *AILA Review* 4: 25–31.

Brumfit, C. J. (ed.). 1988. *Language in Teacher Education*. Brighton: National Congress on Languages in Education.

Brumfit, C. J. 1991. 'Applied linguistics in higher education: riding the storm'. *BAAL Newsletter* 38: 45–9.

Brumfit, C. J. (ed.). 1995a. *Language Education in the National Curriculum*. Oxford: Blackwell.

Brumfit, C. J. 1995b. *People's Choice and Language Rights: EFL in Language Policy*. Plenary Lecture to IATEFL Conference, University of York, April 1995.

Brumfit, C. J. 1995c. 'Teacher professionalism and research' in G. Cook and B. Seidlhofer (eds.). 1995: 27–41.

Brumfit, C. J. 1996. 'Educational linguistics, applied linguistics and the study of language practices' in G. Blue and R. F. Mitchell (eds.). 1996: 1–15.

Brumfit, C. J. 1999. 'Applied linguistics and language policy for "English": the British case'. Paper presented to BAAL Annual Meeting, Edinburgh, September 1999.

Brumfit, C. J. 2000. 'Modern languages within a policy for language in education', in S. Green (ed.). 2000.

Brumfit, C. J. , R. Ellis, and J. Levine. (eds.). 1985. *English as a Second Language in the United Kingdom*. Oxford: Pergamon Press.

Brumfit, C. J. and R. F. Mitchell. (eds.). 1990. *Research in the Language Classroom*. Basingstoke: Macmillan.

Brumfit, C. J., R. F. Mitchell, and J. V. Hooper. 1996. '"Grammar", "language", and classroom practice', in M. Hughes (ed.). 1996.

Bruner, J. S. 1985. 'Vygotsky: a historical and conceptual perspective' in J. V. Wertsch. 1985: 21–34.

Bruner, J. S. 1986. *Actual Minds, Possible Worlds*. Cambridge, Mass.: Harvard University Press.

Buckingham, T. and D. Eskey. 1980. 'Towards a definition of applied linguistics' in R. Kaplan (ed.). 1980: 1–3.

Byram, M. 1990. 'Foreign language teaching and young people's perceptions of other cultures' in B. Harrison (ed.). 1989: 76–87.

Byram, M., C. Morgan, *et al.* 1994. *Teaching-and-Learning Language-and-Culture*. Clevedon: Multilingual Matters.

Calderhead, J. 1988. *Teachers' Professional Learning*. London: Falmer Press.

Cameron, D., E. Frazer, P. Harvey, M. B. H. Rampton, and K Richardson. 1992. *Researching Language: Issues of Power and Method*. London: Routledge.

Canale, M. 1983. 'From communicative competence to communicative language pedagogy' in J. C. Richards and R. Schmidt (eds.). 1983: 2–27.

Canale, M. and M. Swain. 1980. 'Theoretical bases of communicative approaches to second-language teaching and testing'. *Applied Linguistics* 1/1: 1–47.

Candlin, C. N. 1971. 'Sociolinguistics and communicative language teaching', paper delivered to IATEFL Conference, London, mimeo.

Carter, R. A. 1990a. 'Introduction' in R. A. Carter (ed.). 1990: 1–20.

Carter, R. A. (ed.). 1990b. *Knowledge about Language and the Curriculum: the LINC Reader*. London: Hodder and Stoughton.

Charvet, J. 1994. 'Contractarianism and international political theory' in D. Boucher and P. Kelly (eds.). 1994: 175–90.

Chaudron, C. 1988. *Second Language Classrooms*. Cambridge: Cambridge University Press.

Cheshire, J. 1996. 'Language policy and language practice in education' in G. Blue and R. F. Mitchell (eds.). 1996: 41–51.

Chomsky, N. 1957. *Syntactic Structures*. The Hague: Mouton.

Chomsky, N. 1965. *Aspects of the Theory of Syntax*. Cambridge, Mass.: MIT Press.

Christie, F. 1989. *Language Education*. Oxford: Oxford University Press.

Cohen, L. and L. Manion. 1994. *Research Methods in Education* (4th ed. first published 1980). London: Routledge.

Cole, P. and J. Morgan. (eds.). 1975. *Syntax and Semantics, Vol. 3, Speech Acts*. New York: Academic Press.

Cook, G. 2000. *Language Play, Language Learning*. Oxford: Oxford University Press.

Cook, G. and B. Seidlhofer. (eds.). 1995. *Principle and Practice in Applied Linguistics*. Oxford: Oxford University Press.

Cook, V. J. 1990. 'The I-language approach and classroom observation' in C. J. Brumfit and R. F. Mitchell (eds.). 1990: 71–7.

Cooper, R. L. 1968. 'An elaborated language testing model'. *Language Learning Special Issue No.3*: 57–72.

Corder, S. P. 1973. *Introducing Applied Linguistics*. Harmondsworth: Penguin.

Corder, S. P. 1981. *Error Analysis and Interlanguage*. Oxford: Oxford University Press.

Coulmas, F. 1992. *Language and Economy*. Oxford: Blackwell.

Crowley, T. 1989. *The Politics of Discourse*. Basingstoke: Macmillan.

Crowley, T. 1991. *Proper English? Readings in Language, History and Cultural Identity*. London: Routledge.

Crystal, D. 1980. *First Dictionary of Linguistics and Phonetics*. London: Andre Deutsch.

Crystal, D. 1981. *Directions in Applied Linguistics*. London: Academic Press.

Crystal, D. 1985. 'How many millions? The statistics of English today'. *English Today* 1: 7–9.

Crystal, D. 1987. *The Cambridge Encyclopaedia of Language*. Cambridge: Cambridge University Press.

Daniel, S. 1950. *Poems and A Defence of Rime*. (1599), ed. A. C. Sprague. London: Routledge and Kegan Paul.

Davies, A. 1991. *The Native Speaker in Applied Linguistics*. Edinburgh: Edinburgh University Press.

Davies, A., C. Criper, and A. P. R. Howatt. (eds.). 1984. *Interlanguage*. Edinburgh: Edinburgh University Press.

Day, R. R. 1982. 'Children's attitudes towards language', in E. B. Ryan and H. Giles (eds.). 1982: 116–31.

DES. 1975. *A Language for Life* (Bullock Report). London: HMSO.

DES. 1985. *Education for All: The Report on the Committee of Inquiry into the Education of Children from Ethnic Minority Groups* (Swann Report). London: HMSO.

DES. 1988. *Report of the Committee of Inquiry into the Teaching of English Language* (Kingman Report). London: HMSO.

DES. 1989. *English for Ages 5–16* (Cox Report). London: Department of Education and Science.

DES. 1990. *National Curriculum Modern Foreign Languages Working Group: Initial Advice* (Harris Report). Darlington: Department of Education and Science.

Dore, J. 1974. 'A pragmatic description of early language development'. *Journal of Psycholinguistic Research* 3/4: 343–50.

Doughty, P., J. Pearce, and G. Thornton. 1971. *Language in Use*. London: Edward Arnold.

Doyle, B. 1989. *English and Englishness*. London: Routledge.

Dudley-Evans, T. and W. Henderson. (eds.). 1990. *The Language of Economics: the Analysis of Economics Discourse*. Basingstoke: Macmillan.

Dunn, J. 1979. *Western Political Theory in the Face of the Future*. Cambridge: Cambridge University Press.

Dunn, T. 1994. 'The "British" in British Studies', *British Studies* 4: 11.

Eagleton, T. 1983. *Literary Theory*. Oxford: Blackwell.

Edwards, D. and N. Mercer. 1987. *Common Knowledge*. London: Methuen.

Ellis, R. 1984. *Classroom Second Language Development*. Oxford: Pergamon Press.

Ellis, R. 1997. *SLA Research and Language Teaching*. Oxford: Oxford University Press.

Esarte-Sarries, V. and M. Byram. 1989. 'The perception of French people by English students: findings from Durham Cultural Studies Project'. *Language, Culture and Curriculum* 2/3: 153–65.

Evans, C. 1988. *Language People: the Experience of Teaching and Learning Modern Languages in British Universities*. Milton Keynes: The Open University Press.

Evans, C. 1993. *English People: the Experience of Teaching and Learning English in British Universities*. Milton Keynes: The Open University Press.

Evensen, L. S. 1995. *General and Applied Linguistics Compared*. Mimeo.

Fagles, R. 1990. *The Iliad of Homer*. New York: Viking Press.

Fairclough, N. 1989. *Language and Power*. Harlow: Longman.

Fairclough, N. 1995. *Critical Discourse Analysis: the Critical Study of Language*. Harlow: Longman.

Featherstone, M. 1991. *Consumer Culture and Postmodernism*. London: Sage Publications.

Feiman-Nemser, S. and R. E. Floden. 1986. 'The cultures of teaching' in M. C. Wittrock (ed.). 1986: 505–26.

Ferguson, C. A. 1977. 'Baby talk as a simplified register' in C. E. Snow and C. A. Ferguson (eds.). 1977: 219–35.

Fillmore, C., D. Kempler, and W. S-Y. Wang. (eds.). 1979. *Individual Differences in Language Ability and Language Behaviour*. New York: Academic Press.

Fillmore, L. W. 1979. 'Individual differences in second language acquisition' in C. Fillmore, D. Kempler, and W. S-Y. Wang (eds.). 1979: 203–28.

Finocchiaro, M. and C. J. Brumfit. 1983. *The Functional–Notional Approach: from Theory to Practice*. New York: Oxford University Press.

FIPLV. 1992. *FIPLV World News*, 58, January.

FIPLV. 1993. *FIPLV World News*, 61, January.

Foucault, M. 1979. *Discipline and Punish: the Birth of the Prison*. Harmondsworth: Penguin.

Fowler, A. 1982. *Kinds of Literature*. Oxford: Oxford University Press.

Fröhlich, M., N. Spada, and J. P. B. Allen. 1985. 'Differences in the communicative orientation of L2 classrooms'. *TESOL Quarterly* 19/1: 27–57.

Gardiner, R. 1966. *A World of Peoples*. London: Longman.

Gardner, R. C. and W. E. Lambert. 1972. *Attitudes and Motivation in Second Language Learning*. Rowley, Mass.: Newbury House.

Geach, J. (ed.). 1989. *Coherence in Diversity*. London: CILT.

Gee, J. P. 1990. *Social Linguistics and Literacies: Ideology in Discourses*. Lewes: Falmer.

Gibbon, G. 1989. *Explanation in Archaeology*. Oxford: Blackwell.

Giles, H. (ed.). 1977. *Language, Ethnicity, and Intergroup Relations*. London: Academic Press.

Golby, M. 1989. 'Curriculum traditions', in B. Moon, P. Murphy, and R. Raynor (eds.). 1989: 29–42.

Gorky, M. 1911. *The Life of Matvei Kozhemyakin* (cited from translation by M. Wettlin. 1960. Moscow: Progress Publishers).

Gowers, E. 1954. *The Complete Plain Words*. London: HMSO.

Green, S. (ed.). 2000. *A New Prescription for Languages*. Clevedon: Multilingual Matters.

Greenall, G. M. and J. E. Price. (eds.). 1980. *Study Modes and Academic Development of Overseas Students. ELT Documents* 109. London: The British Council.

Gregersen, F. 1991. 'Relationships between linguistics and applied linguistics: some Danish examples' in R. Phillipson, E. Kellerman, L. Selinker, M. Sharwood Smith, and M. Swain (eds.). 1991: 11–28.

Grenfell, M. J. 1993. *The Initial Training of Modern Language Teachers: a Social Theoretical Approach*. Unpublished PhD thesis, University of Southampton.

Grenfell, M. J. 1998. *Training Teachers in Practice*. Clevedon: Multilingual Matters.

Grice, H. 1975. 'Logic and conversation', in P. Cole and J. Morgan (eds.). 1975: 41–59.

Habermas, J. 1970. 'On systematically distorted communication'. *Inquiry* 13/3: 205–18.

Habermas, J. 1984 and 1987. *Theory of Communicative Action*, Vols. 1 & 2. Boston: Beacon Press.

Habermas, J. 1994. 'Struggles for recognition in the democratic constitutional state', in C. Taylor *et al*. 1994: 107–48.

Halliday, M. A. K. 1970. 'Language structure and language functions', in J. Lyons (ed.). 1970: 140–65.

Halliday, M. A. K. 1975. *Learning How to Mean*. London: Edward Arnold.

Halliday, M. A. K. 1978. *Language as Social Semiotic*. London: Edward Arnold.

Halliday, M. A. K., A. McIntosh, and P. D. Strevens. 1964. *The Linguistic Sciences and Language Teaching*. Harlow: Longman.

Halliday, M. A. K. and R. Hasan. 1989. *Language, Context, and Text*. Oxford: Oxford University Press.

Hamilton, E. and H. Cairns. 1961. *The Collected Dialogues of Plato*. Princeton: Princeton University Press.

Hammersley, M. 1996. 'On the foundations of critical discourse analysis'. *Centre for Language in Education Occasional Papers*, 42. Centre for Language in Education, University of Southampton.

Hammersley, M. 1997. 'Educational research and teaching: a response to David Hargreaves's TTA lecture'. *British Educational Research Journal* 23/7: 141–62.

Hammersley, M. and A. Hargreaves. (eds.). 1983. *Curriculum Practice: Some Sociological Case Studies*. London: Falmer Press.

Hargreaves, D. 1996. *Teaching as a Research Based Profession*. London: Teacher Training Agency.

Harris, M. 1994. 'Evolving linguistic patterns in Europe'. *Centre for Language in Education Occasional Papers* 17. Centre for Language in Education, University of Southampton.

Harris, R. 1996. *The Language Connection: Philosophy and Linguistics*. Bristol: Thommes Press.

Harrison, B. (ed.). 1990. *Culture and the Language Classroom*. Basingstoke: Macmillan.

Hatch, E. and H. Farhady. 1982. *Research Design and Statistics for Applied Linguistics*. Rowley, Mass.: Newbury House.

Hawkes, T. 1977. *Structuralism and Semiotics*. London: Methuen.

Hawkey, R. 1982. *An Investigation of Inter-relationships between Personality, Cognitive Style and Language Learning Strategies*. Unpublished PhD thesis, University of London.

Heaton, B., P. Adams, and P. Howarth. (eds.). 1991. *Socio-cultural Issues in English for Academic Purposes*. Basingstoke: Macmillan.

Hirst, P. 1974. *Knowledge and the Curriculum*. London: Routledge and Kegan Paul.

Hirst, P. (ed.). 1983. *Educational Theory and its Foundation Disciplines*. London: Routledge and Kegan Paul.

HMI. 1984. *English 15–16*. London: HMSO.

Hobsbawm, E. J. 1962. *The Age of Revolution*. London: Sphere Books.

Holquist, M. 1990. *Dialogism: Bakhtin and his World*. London: Routledge.

Honey, J. 1998. *Language is Power*. London: Faber.

Hornby, A. S. 1995. *Oxford Advanced Learners' Dictionary*, 5th ed. Oxford: Oxford University Press.

Howatt, A. P. R. 1984. *A History of English Language Teaching*. Oxford: Oxford University Press.

Hughes, M. (ed.). 1996. *Teaching and Learning in Changing Times*. Oxford: Blackwell.

Hymes, D. 1967. 'Models of the interaction of language and social setting'. *Journal of Social Issues* 23/2: 9–28.

Hymes, D. 1972. 'On communicative competence' in J. B. Pride and J. Holmes (eds.). 1972. 269–93.

Hymes, D. 1985. 'Towards linguistic competence'. *AILA Review* 2: 9–23.

Jakobovits. L. 1970. 'Prolegomena to a theory of communicative competence' in R. C. Lugton (ed.). 1970: 1–39.

Johnson, K. 1982. *Communicative Syllabus Design and Methodology*. Oxford: Pergamon Press.

Johnson, K. and K. Morrow. (eds.). 1981. *Communication in the Classroom*. Harlow: Longman.

Joll, J. 1979. *The Anarchists*. London: Methuen.

Joseph, J. E. and T. J. Taylor. 1990. *Ideologies of Language*. London: Routledge.

Kachru, B. B. 1991. 'Liberation linguistics and the Quirk concern'. *English Today* 25: 3–13.

Kamanda, M. C. 1999. *A Basis of Language Planning for Education for Future Sierra Leone*. Unpublished PhD thesis, University of Southampton.

Kaplan, R. B. 1980a. 'On the scope of linguistics, applied and non' in R. B. Kaplan (ed.). 1980b: 57–66.

Kaplan, R. B. (ed.). 1980b. *On the Scope of Applied Linguistics*. Rowley, Mass.: Newbury House.

Kaplan, R. B. and H. G. Widdowson. 1992. 'Applied linguistics' in W. Bright (ed.). 1992: 76.

Kasper, G. (ed.). 1986. *Learning, Teaching and Communication in the Foreign Language Classroom*. Aarhus, Denmark: Aarhus University Press.

Kenner, C. 1996. *Social Scripts: Young Learners Encountering Literacy*. Unpublished PhD thesis, University of Southampton.

Kramsch, C. 1993. *Context and Culture in Language Teaching*. Oxford: Oxford University Press.

Krashen, S. 1979. 'A response to McLaughlin "The monitor model: some methodological considerations"'. *Language Learning* 29/1: 151–67.

Krashen, S. 1980. 'Towards a redefinition of applied linguistics' in R. B. Kaplan (ed.). 1980: 12–13.

Krashen, S. 1981. *Second Language Acquisition and Second Language Learning*. Oxford: Pergamon Press.

Labov, W. 1972. *Sociolinguistic Patterns*. Philadelphia: University of Pennsylvania Press.

Lacan, J. 1979. *The Four Fundamental Concepts of Psycho-Analysis*. Harmondsworth: Penguin.

Lawton, D. 1979. *The End of the Secret Garden? A Study in the Politics of the Curriculum.* Inaugural Lecture, 15 November 1978. London: University of London Institute of Education.

Leavis, F. R. 1948. *The Great Tradition*. Harmondsworth: Penguin.

Lechte, J. 1994. *Fifty Key Contemporary Thinkers: from Structuralism to Postmodernism*. London: Routledge.

Leith, R. 1983. *A Social History of English*. London: Routledge and Kegan Paul.

Littlewood, W. 1981. *Communicative Language Teaching*. Cambridge: Cambridge University Press.

Lo Bianco, J. 1987. *National Policy on Languages*. Canberra: Australian Government Publishing Service.

Lock, A. J. 1980. *The Guided Reinvention of Language*. London: Academic Press.

Long, M. 1993. 'Assessment strategies for SLA theories'. *Applied Linguistics* 14/3: 225–49.

Lugton, R. C. (ed.). 1970. *English as a Second Language: Current Issues*. Philadelphia: Center for Curriculum Development.

Lyons, J. (ed.). 1970. *New Horizons in Linguistics*. Harmondsworth: Penguin.

Lyons, J. and R. J. Wales. (eds.). 1966. *Psycholinguistics Papers*. Edinburgh: Edinburgh University Press.

Lyotard, J-F. 1984. *The Post Modern Condition*. Manchester: Manchester University Press.

Mackey, W. F. 1966. 'Applied linguistics: its meaning and use'. *English Language Teaching*, 20/1: 197–206 (cited from J. P. B. Allen and S. P. Corder (eds.). 1973: 247–55).

Marenbon, J. 1987. *English Our English*. London: Centre for Policy Studies.

Martin, J. R. 1989. *Factual Writing: Exploring and Challenging Social Reality*. Oxford: Oxford University Press.

Masny, D. 1996. 'Examining assumptions in second language research: a postmodern view'. *CLCS Occasional Paper* no. 45. Trinity College, Dublin.

McArthur, T. 1981. *Longman Lexicon of Contemporary English*. Harlow: Longman.

McNamara, T. 1996. *Measuring Second Language Performance*. Harlow: Longman.

Mead, G. H. 1934. *Mind, Self and Society*. Chicago: University of Chicago Press.

Meara, P. and A. Ryan. (eds.). 1991. *Language and Nation*. British Studies in Applied Linguistics 6. London: CILT.

Mehan, H. 1979. *Learning Lessons: Social Organisation in the Classroom*. Cambridge, Mass.: Harvard University Press.

Mercer, N. 1995. *The Guided Construction of Knowledge*. Clevedon: Multilingual Matters.

Midgley, M. 1984. Review of Sissela Bok, 'Secrets', *Times Literary Supplement*, 6 April: 363.

Milroy, J. and L. Milroy. 1991. *Authority in Language*. London: Routledge.

Milroy, J. and L. Milroy. (eds.). 1993. *Real English*. Harlow: Longman.

Mitchell, R. F. 1985. 'Process research in second language classrooms'. *Language Teaching* 18: 330–52.

Mitchell, R. F. 1988. *Communicative Language Teaching in Practice*. London: CILT.

Mitchell, R. F. 1991. 'Multilingualism in British schools: future policy directions' in P. Meara and A. Ryan. 1991: 107–16.

Mitchell, R. F. and C. J. Brumfit. 1997. 'The national curriculum experience of bilingual learners'. *Educational Review* 49/2: 159–80.

Mitchell, R. F. and R. Johnstone. 1986. 'The routinization of communicative methodology'. in C. J. Brumfit (ed.). 1986: 123–43.

Mitchell, R. F. and F. Myles. 1998. *Second Language Learning Theories*. London: Edward Arnold.

Mitchell, R. F., B. Parkinson, and R. Johnstone. 1981. *The Foreign Language Classroom: an Observational Study*. Stirling: University of Stirling.

Montgomery, M. 1993. 'Institutions and discourse'. *British Studies*, July: 2–3.

Moon, B., P. Murphy, and J. Raynor. (eds.). 1989. *Policies for the Curriculum*. London: Hodder and Stoughton.

Moss, G. and D. Attar. 1999. 'Boys and literacy: gendering the reading curriculum' in J. Prosser (ed.). 1999: 133–44.

Mühlhäusler, P. 1996. *Linguistic Ecology*. London: Routledge.

Myles, F . J., J. V. Hooper, and R. F. Mitchell. 1998. 'Rote or rule? Exploring the role of formulaic language in classroom foreign language learning'. *Language Learning* 48/3: 323–63.

Munby, J. L. 1978. *Communicative Syllabus Design*. Cambridge: Cambridge University Press.

Naiman, N., M. Fröhlich, H. H. Stern, and A. Todesco. 1978. *The Good Language Learner*. Toronto: OISE (reprinted 1996, Clevedon: Multilingual Matters).

NEPI. 1992. *Language: Report of the NEPI Language Research Group*. Cape Town: Oxford University Press.

Ngugi wa Thiong'o. 1981. *Writers in Politics*. London: Heinemann.

Oller, J. 1969. 'Language communication and second language learning' in P. Pimsleur and T. Quinn (eds.). 1971: 171–90.

Omodiaogbe, S. A. 1992. '150 years on: English in the Nigerian school system—past, present and future'. *ELT Journal* 46/1: 19–28.

Orwell, G. 1970. *Collected Journalism and Letters*, Vol. 2. Harmondsworth: Penguin.

Painter, C. 1985. *Learning the Mother Tongue*. Oxford: Oxford University Press.

Palmer, J. D. 1980. 'Linguistics in medias res' in R. B. Kaplan (ed.). 1980: 21–7.

Parkinson, B. and C. Howell-Richardson. 1990. 'Learner diaries' in C. J. Brumfit and R. F. Mitchell (eds.). 1990: 128–40.

Peck, A. 1988. *Language Teachers at Work*. Hemel Hempstead: Prentice-Hall.

Pennycook A. 1994. *The Cultural Politics of English as an International Language*. Harlow: Longman.

Peters, R . S. (ed.). 1973. *The Philosophy of Education*. Oxford: Oxford University Press.

Phillipson, R. 1992. *Linguistic Imperialism*. Oxford: Oxford University Press.

Phillipson, R., E. Kellerman, L. Selinker, M. Sharwood Smith, and M. Swain. (eds.). 1991. *Foreign/Second Language Pedagogy Research*. Clevedon: Multilingual Matters.

Pimsleur, P. and T. Quinn. (eds.). 1971. *The Psychology of Second Language Learning*. Cambridge. Cambridge: Cambridge University Press.

Plato. c.400 BC. 'Philebus' in E. Hamilton and H. Cairns (eds.). 1961: 1086–1150.

Politzer, R. L. 1972. *Linguistics and Applied Linguistics: Aims and Methods*. Concord, Mass.: Heinle and Heinle.

Popper, K. R. 1994a. *The Myth of the Framework*. London: Routledge.

Popper, K. R. 1994b. *Knowledge and the Body-Mind Problem*. London: Routledge.

Prabhu, N. S. 1987. *Second Language Pedagogy*. Oxford: Oxford University Press.

Pride, J. B. and J. Holmes. (eds.). 1972. *Sociolinguistics*. Harmondsworth: Penguin.

Prosser, J. (ed.). 1999. *School Cultures*. London: Paul Chapman.

Protherough, R. 1989. *Students of English*. London: Routledge.

Purvis, J. 1992. 'The historiography of British education' in A. Rattansi and D. Reeder (eds.). 1992: 249–66.

Quirk, R. 1982. *Style and Communication in the English Language*. London: Edward Arnold.

Quirk, R. 1990. 'Language varieties and standard language'. *English Today* 21.

Rampton, M. B. H. 1990. 'Displacing the "native speaker": expertise, affiliation, and inheritance'. *ELT Journal* 44/2: 97–101.

Rampton, M. B. H. 1995a. 'Politics and change in research in applied linguistics'. *Applied Linguistics* 16/2: 233–56.

Rampton, M. B. H. 1995b. *Crossing*. Harlow: Longman.

Rampton, M. B. H. 1997. 'Retuning in applied linguistics'. *International Review of Applied Linguistics* 7/1: 3–25.

Rattansi, A. and D. Reeder. (eds.). 1992. *Rethinking Radical Education*. London: Lawrence and Wishart.

Rawls, J. 1972. *A Theory of Justice*. Oxford: Oxford University Press.

Reid, E. 1978. 'Social and stylistic variation in the speech of children: some evidence from Edinburgh' in P. Trudgill (ed.). 1978: 158–75.

Richards, J. C., J. Platt, and H. Platt. 1985. *Longman Dictionary of Applied Linguistics*. Harlow: Longman. (2nd ed. 1992 as Longman Dictionary of Language Teaching and Applied Linguistics).

Richards, J. C. and T. S. Rodgers. 1986. *Approaches and Methods in Language Teaching*. Cambridge: Cambridge University Press.

Richards, J. C. and R. W. Schmidt. (eds.). 1983. *Language and Communication*. Harlow: Longman.

Rivers, W. 1972. *Speaking with Many Tongues*. Rowley, Mass.: Newbury House.

Roberts, C., M. Byram, A. Barro, S. Jordan, and B. Street. 2000. *Language Learners as Ethnographers*. Clevedon: Multilingual Matters.

Roberts, C., E. Davies, and T. Jupp. 1992. *Language and Discrimination*. London: Longman.

Robins, R. H. 1967. *A Short History of Linguistics*. Harlow: Longman.

Romaine, S. 1984. *The Language of Children and Adolescents*. Oxford: Basil Blackwell.

Ryan, E. B. and H. Giles. (eds.). 1982. *Attitudes towards Language Variation: Social and Applied Contexts*. London: Edward Arnold.

Sanderson, D. 1983. *Modern Language Teachers in Action*. York: University of York.

Sapir, E. 1921. *Language*. New York: Harcourt Brace.

Sassoon, D. 1996. *A Hundred Years of Socialism: the Western European Left in the Twentieth Century*. London: I. B. Tauris.

Saussure, F. de. 1916. *Course in General Linguistics* (trans. R. Harris. 1983 London: Duckworth).

Savignon, S. 1972. *Communicative Competence: an Experiment in Foreign Language Teaching*. Philadelphia, Center for Curriculum Development.

Savignon, S. 1983. *Communicative Competence: Theory and Classroom Practice.* Reading, Mass.: Addison-Wesley.

Schreiner, O. 1883. *The Story of an African Farm.* London: Chapman and Hall.

Skilbeck, M. 1976. *Culture, Ideology and Knowledge.* Open University Course E203, Unit 3. Milton Keynes: The Open University Press.

Skutnabb-Kangas, T. and **R. Phillipson.** 1989. *Wanted! Linguistics Human Rights.* Rolig papir 44. Roskilde: Roskilde Universits-center.

Snow, C. E. and **C. A. Ferguson.** 1977. *Talking to Children.* Cambridge: Cambridge University Press.

Spolsky, B. 1978. *Educational Linguistics.* Rowley, Mass.: Newbury House.

Stark, F. 1951. *Beyond Euphrates, Autobiography 1928–1933.* London: Century.

Statham, E. 1994. *Scattered in the Mainstream: Educational Provision for Isolated Bilingual Learners.* Unpublished PhD thesis, University of Southampton.

Steedman, C. 1982. *The Tidy House.* London: Virago.

Stephen, L. (ed.). 1885. *Dictionary of National Biography*, Vol.1. London: Smith Elder.

Stern, H. H. 1983. *Fundamental Concepts of Language Teaching.* Oxford: Oxford University Press.

Stevick, E. W. 1976. *Memory, Meaning and Method.* Rowley, Mass.: Newbury House.

Street, B. 1993. *Cross-cultural Approaches to Literacy.* Cambridge: Cambridge University Press.

Strevens, P. 1980. 'Statement for AILA' in R. B. Kaplan (ed.). 1980: 17–20.

Stubbs, M. W. 1986. *Educational Linguistics.* Oxford: Basil Blackwell.

Swales, J. M. 1985. *Episodes in ESP.* Hemel Hempstead: Prentice-Hall.

Swales, J. M. 1990. *Genre Analysis.* Cambridge: Cambridge University Press.

Swarbrick, A. (ed.). 1994. *Teaching Modern Languages.* London: Routledge in association with The Open University.

Tannen, D. 1989. *Talking Voices: Repetition, Dialogue and Imagery in Conversational Discourse.* Cambridge: Cambridge University Press.

Taylor, C. 1994. 'The politics of recognition' in C. Taylor and A.Gutman. 1994: 25–74.

Taylor, C. and **A. Gutman.** 1994. *Multiculturalism.* Princeton, N.J.: Princeton University Press.

Taylor, T. J. and **D. Cameron.** 1987. *Analysing Conversation.* Oxford: Pergamon Press.

Thomas, G. 1991. *Linguistic Purism.* Harlow: Longman.

Tibble, J. W. (ed.). 1966. *The Study of Education.* London: Routledge and Kegan Paul.

Tickoo, M. L. (ed.). 1993. *Simplification: Theory and Application.* Singapore: SEAMEO Regional Language Centre.

Tollefson, J. W. 1991. *Planning Language Planning Inequality: Language Policy in the Community.* Harlow: Longman.

Trilling, L. 1969. *Sincerity and Authenticity.* New York: Norton.

Trim, J. L. M. 1988. *Consolidated Report of the Programme of International Workshops for Trainers of Teachers of Modern Languages 1984–1987.* Strasbourg: Council of Europe.

Trudgill, P. (ed.). 1978. *Sociolinguistic Patterns in British English.* London: Edward Arnold.

Tucker, G. R., E. Hamayan, and **F. H. Genesee.** 1976. 'Affective, cognitive and social factors in second language acquisition'. *Canadian Modern Language Review* 32/3: 214–26.

UKCOSA. 1979. *Suffering for Success.* London: United Kingdom Council for Overseas Student Affairs.

Usher, R. and R. Edwards. 1994. *Postmodernism and Education*. London: Routledge.
van Lier, L. 1988. *The Classroom and the Language Learner*. Harlow: Longman.
Vygotsky, L. 1962. *Thought and Language*. Cambridge, Mass.: MIT Press.
Wales, R. J. and J. C. Marshall. 1966. 'The organisation of linguistic performance'. in J. Lyons and R. J. Wales (eds.). 1966: 29–80.
Walkerdine, V. 1988. *The Mastery of Reason*. London: Routledge.
Wardhaugh, R. 1974. *Topics in Applied Linguistics*. Rowley, Mass.: Newbury House.
Welford, A. T. 1968. *Fundamentals of Skill*. London, Methuen.
Wells, G. 1981. *Learning through Interaction*. Cambridge: Cambridge University Press.
Wertsch, J. V. (ed.). 1985. *Culture, Communication and Cognition: Vygotskian Perspectives*. New York: Cambridge University Press.
West, M. 1953. *A General Service List of English Words*. London: Longman.
Widdowson, H. G. 1972. 'The teaching of English as communication'. *English Language Teaching* 28/1: 15–19.
Widdowson, H. G. 1978. *Teaching Language as Communication*. Oxford: Oxford University Press.
Widdowson, H. G. 1979. *Explorations in Applied Linguistics*. Oxford: Oxford University Press.
Widdowson, H. G. 1980. 'Models and fictions'. *Applied Linguistics* 1/2: 165–70.
Widdowson, H. G. 1983. *Learning Purpose and Language Use*. Oxford: Oxford University Press.
Widdowson, H. G. 1995. 'Discourse analysis: a critical view'. *Language and Literature* 4/3: 157–72.
Wittrock, M. C. (ed.). 1986. *Handbook of Research on Teaching*, third edition. New York: Macmillan.
Wilkins, D. A. 1976. *Notional Syllabuses*. Oxford: Oxford University Press.
Willes, M. 1988. 'Courses in the study of language at the West Midlands College of Education 1968–1975: a Record and Some Reflections' in C. J. Brumfit (ed.). 1988: 71–91.
Woodcock, G. 1962. *Anarchism*. Harmondsworth: Penguin.
Wragg, E. C. (ed.). 1984. *Classroom Teaching Skills*. London: Croom Helm.
Wuthnow, R., J. D. Hunter, A. Bergesen, and E. Kurzweil. 1984. *Cultural Analysis*. London: Routledge.
Young, M. F. D. (ed.). 1971. *Knowledge and Control*. London: Routledge and Kegan Paul.
Zotou, V. 1994. *Effective Foreign Language Teaching: a Greek Case Study*. Unpublished PhD thesis, University of Southampton.

Index